Public Speaking
AND CIVIC ENGAGEMENT

Linda D. Manning
Christopher Newport University

Kendall Hunt
publishing company

Cover image © Shutterstock, Inc.

www.kendallhunt.com
Send all inquiries to:
4050 Westmark Drive
Dubuque, IA 52004-1840

Published in the United States of America

Contents

Acknowledgements

I would like to thank my colleagues in the Department of Communication for helping me develop the vision for this textbook. In particular, I thank Mary D. Best, Sean Connable, Jeanne Hubbard, Joe Sery, Scott Smith, and Mark Steiner for their suggestions, feedback, and support. As with all my projects, I thank my husband, David Gosser, for his wit, wisdom, encouragement, and insight, all of which helped me see this project to fruition. Finally, I thank my son, Mark Gosser, who helped with proofreading transcripts and brings joy to my life every day.

Letter from the Chair of the Department of Communication

Dear COMM 201 Students:

I am so pleased you have decided to take COMM 201: Public Speaking and Civic Engagement. The COMM faculty has created this course to show you how public speaking is central to civic engagement, which is fundamental to the creation and perpetuation of a healthy and vibrant democratic society.

As Dr. Joe Sery so eloquently explains:

Given the prominent role that public speaking has played in shaping and reshaping American society, this course cultivates an appreciation for the spoken word and hones students' rhetorical skills so that they can be active, engaged members of a robust democratic society. Rather than positioning public speaking as solely the province of politicians or those with power, students are encouraged to view themselves and their fellow citizens as active players in the ongoing issues that define our culture. Public speaking functions as an important channel through which individuals interact with any democratic or civic institution. At the end of the day, the course celebrates the importance of citizens finding and utilizing their voices and stresses the necessity of an active, articulate public body working toward a healthy democratic society.*

In order to demonstrate the importance of public speaking, most chapters begin with a speech of significance from U.S. history. I hope you will read the transcripts of the speeches to understand how great orators have engaged principles of public speaking. Many of these principles will be relevant as you craft your own speeches. I am thankful that technological innovations, like GoReact, allow you to review your own public speaking efforts.

I am confident that the COMM faculty will provide an excellent learning environment. I encourage you to engage in the intellectual discussion, wrestle with the content of this

---

* Contributed by Jose Sery. © Kendall Hunt Publishing Company

course, and challenge yourself to move beyond your comfort zone. I hope that through your participation in this course you will better understand how the passions of the past resonate in our 21st century world.

Warmly,

Linda D. Manning, Ph.D.
Chair and Associate Professor
Department of Communication
Christopher Newport University

Chapter 1

Communication and Community Engagement

Autumn Edwards

Communication can alone create a great community.
— John Dewey (1927, *The Public and Its Problems*)

SPEECH: Patrick Henry — Liberty or Death

The winter of 1774–1775 was a tense period. The country was divided in the belief that America could remain peacefully within the British Empire. Many held out hope that King George would respond favorably to the colonists' petition before the Continental Congress met again in May 1775; many believed that he would not. Patrick Henry (1736–1799), a lawyer from the newly settled western part of Virginia, was one person who believed that war was the course of action that the colonists needed to take. His audience in the Virginia legislature (officially the House of Burgesses, although the body called itself the Virginia Convention) was ambivalent. While many shared his long-standing opposition to British policies, many also perceived him as too militant. Patrick Henry delivered this speech on March 23, 1775 at Henrico Parrish on Church Street in Richmond Virginia at the Second Virginia Convention. William Wirt, Patrick Henry's biographer, reconstructed the following speech. Wirt interviewed people who had heard the speech over 25 years earlier. Thus, the transcript that follows is likely a mix of what people recalled Henry saying and what Wirt hoped he had said.

Source: Reid, R. F. (1995). *American Rhetorical Discourse* (2nd ed.). Prospect Heights, IL: Waveland Press, pp. 113–114.

Give Me Liberty Or Give Me Death
Patrick Henry, March 23, 1775.

No man thinks more highly than I do of the patriotism, as well as abilities, of the very worthy gentlemen who have just addressed the House. But different men often see the same subject in different lights; and, therefore, I hope it will not be thought disrespectful to those gentlemen if, entertaining as I do opinions of a character very opposite to theirs, I shall speak forth my sentiments freely and without reserve. This is no time for ceremony. The question before the House is one of awful moment to this country. For my own part, I consider it as nothing less than a question of freedom or slavery; and in proportion to the magnitude of the subject ought to be the freedom of the debate. It is only in this way that we can hope to arrive at truth, and fulfill the great responsibility which we hold to God and our country. Should I keep back my opinions at such a time, through fear of giving offense, I should consider myself as guilty of treason towards my country, and of an act of disloyalty toward the Majesty of Heaven, which I revere above all earthly kings.

Mr. President, it is natural to man to indulge in the illusions of hope. We are apt to shut our eyes against a painful truth, and listen to the song of that siren till she transforms us into beasts. Is this the part of wise men, engaged in a great and arduous struggle for liberty? Are we disposed to be of the number of those who, having eyes, see not, and, having ears, hear not, the things which so nearly concern their temporal salvation? For my part, whatever anguish of spirit it may cost, I am willing to know the whole truth; to know the worst, and to provide for it.

I have but one lamp by which my feet are guided, and that is the lamp of experience. I know of no way of judging of the future but by the past. And judging by the past, I wish to know what there has been in the conduct of the British ministry for the last ten years to justify those hopes with which gentlemen have been pleased to solace themselves and the House. Is it that insidious smile with which our petition has been lately received? Trust it not, sir; it will prove a snare to your feet. Suffer not yourselves to be betrayed with a kiss. Ask yourselves how this gracious reception of our petition comports with those warlike preparations which cover our waters and darken our land. Are fleets and armies necessary to a work of love and reconciliation? Have we shown ourselves so unwilling to be reconciled that force must be called in to win back our love? Let us not deceive ourselves, sir. These are the implements of war and subjugation; the last arguments to which kings resort. I ask gentlemen, sir, what means this martial array, if its purpose be not to force us to submission? Can gentlemen assign any other possible motive for it? Has Great Britain any enemy, in this quarter of the world, to call for all this accumulation of navies and armies? No, sir, she has none. They are meant for us: they can be meant for no other. They are sent over to bind and rivet upon us those chains which the British ministry have been so long forging. And what have we to oppose to them? Shall we try argument? Sir, we have been trying that for the last ten years. Have we anything new to offer upon the subject? Nothing. We have held the subject up in every light of which it is capable; but it has been all in vain. Shall we resort to entreaty and humble supplication? What terms shall we find which have not been already exhausted? Let us not, I beseech you, sir, deceive ourselves. Sir, we have done everything that could be done to avert the storm which is now coming on. We have petitioned; we have remonstrated; we have supplicated; we have prostrated ourselves before the throne, and have implored its interposition to arrest the tyrannical hands of the ministry and Parliament. Our petitions have been slighted; our remonstrances have produced additional violence and insult; our supplications have been disregarded; and we have been spurned, with contempt, from the foot of the throne! In vain, after these things, may we indulge the fond hope of peace and reconciliation. There is no longer any room for hope. If we wish to be free—if we mean to preserve inviolate those inestimable privileges for which we have been so long contending—if we mean not basely to abandon the noble struggle in which we have been so long engaged, and which we have pledged ourselves never to abandon until the glorious object of our contest shall be obtained—we must fight! I repeat it, sir, we must fight! An appeal to arms and to the God of hosts is all that is left us!

They tell us, sir, that we are weak; unable to cope with so formidable an adversary. But when shall we be stronger? Will it be the next week, or the next year? Will it be when we are totally disarmed, and when a British guard shall be stationed in every house? Shall we gather strength by irresolution and inaction? Shall we acquire the means of effectual resistance by lying supinely on our backs and hugging the delusive phantom of hope, until our enemies shall have bound us hand and foot? Sir, we are not weak if we make a proper use of those means which the God of nature hath placed in our power. The millions of people, armed in the holy cause of liberty, and in such a country as that which we possess, are invincible by any force which our enemy can send against us. Besides, sir, we shall not fight our battles alone. There is a just God who presides over the destinies of nations, and who will raise up friends to fight our battles for us. The battle, sir, is not to the strong alone; it is to the vigilant, the active, the brave. Besides, sir, we have no election. If we were base enough to desire it, it is now too late to retire from the contest. There is no retreat but in submission and slavery! Our chains are forged! Their clanking may be heard on the plains of Boston! The war is inevitable—and let it come! I repeat it, sir, let it come.

It is in vain, sir, to extenuate the matter. Gentlemen may cry, Peace, Peace—but there is no peace. The war is actually begun! The next gale that sweeps from the north will bring to our ears the clash of resounding arms! Our brethren are already in the field! Why stand we here idle? What is it that gentlemen wish? What would they have? Is life so dear, or peace so sweet, as to be purchased at the price of chains and slavery? Forbid it, Almighty God! I know not what course others may take; but as for me, give me liberty or give me death!

http://avalon.law.yale.edu/18th_century/patrick.asp

Almost every aspect of American life involves concerns for community, or the balancing of individual freedoms with social responsibility (Shepherd & Rothenbuhler, 2001, p. ix). In friendships, families, neighborhoods, and workplaces, through face-to-face and mediated behaviors, we work to balance the need to come together with the need to be apart; the need to be part of something larger with the need to maintain our individuality.

Over the past few decades, politicians, scholars, journalists, and everyday citizens have expressed a common worry that our sense of community is weakening. In his best-selling book *Bowling Alone* (2000), Harvard University professor Robert Putnam documented the recent decline in "social capital" (which refers to the resources available to individuals that arise from their connections to others) and related deteriorating sense of community in the United States. Putnam demonstrated that civic participation (especially membership in large voluntary associations like social clubs, charities, and political parties) and trust in others have been decreasing for several decades. In fact, a great many of the problems of contemporary life (including political disengagement, loneliness, broken families, heartless corporations, unsteady jobs, faceless technologies, and a general loss of neighborliness and civility) are problems associated with a loss of community (Shepherd & Rothenbuhler, 2001, p. ix).

Frequently, when we talk about the problems of community, we end up talking about communication, and the role it plays in strengthening or weakening our collective ties. At times, certain communication practices are blamed for the destruction of community (e.g., violent video games, explicit lyrics, desensitizing movies, and disempowering news coverage). More often, communication is held up as the best hope for restoring and enriching community. Both academic scholarship and popular outlets (e.g., talk shows) prescribe more communication (and more openness, honesty, and care in our current communication) as the cure for many of life's social troubles. And, it is the crucial link between communication and community that is the driving force behind COMM 201, and, of course, behind the current chapter. Thus, the purpose of this chapter is to (a) define communication, (b) define community, and (c) discuss the important relationship between communication and community engagement.

👉 Communication

The debate about how best to define communication goes back to Aristotle's time and has persisted ever since. Defining communication is a difficult business because definitions are tools, and different tools are good for different purposes. We will rely on a definition developed by communication theorist Gregory J. Shepherd (2006). This definition was chosen because it is particularly well suited to the study and practice of communication in the context of community engagement.

Communication is *the simultaneous experience of self and other* (Shepherd, 2006, p. 22). Let us briefly consider the key terms in this definition. The term *experience* refers to the totality of your lived personal participation in an event or series of events. Communication is the experience of a particular type of event—one that happens when you experience both yourself and someone else. Importantly, your sense of *self* is not something with which you were born. According to George Herbert Mead (1934), the self arises from interactions with others. Thus, we become who we are through our social relationships. And because we are continuously moving in and out of various relationships and conversations, we are continuously becoming who we are. In this way, our selves are "always becoming" through communication. Just as communication allows you the opportunity to make and expand your sense of self, so it does for the *other*. In communication, we experience one another as you become you and I become me, and we develop a sense of sharedness and being together by engaging with one another. That this happens *simultaneously* means that you experience your own presence and someone else's at once: that is the essence of communication.

Shepherd points out that the definition of communication as *the simultaneous experience of self and other* goes back to communication's Latin root word *munia*, meaning gifts and services. When combined with the prefix *co-*, meaning with or together, communication translates as mutual giving and servicing. And the gift that is given (and received) in communication is the gift of self. In Shepherd's words, "communication is mutual giving of selves, which serves others" (2006, p. 25).

👉 Community

A longing for community characterizes our present moment in history, but also stretches far back in time. The questions of what community is and how best to achieve it trace through ancient Greece all the way to the present. This historical yearning for community is understandable because of the enormous importance of community for human development. Members of stronger communities experience lower levels of mental and physical illness, psychological distress, and mortality when compared to members of weaker communities (Putnam, 2000). Furthermore, the social capital that arises from vibrant communities is associated with higher incomes, lower levels of violent crime, more collective action at the community level, and the maintenance of democratic forms of life. If all that was not enough, community is also what allows us to experience life as something larger than a solitary individual: to be part of something that transcends the boundaries of our single selves to enrich us all.

In our conversations, we often refer to communities as places. However, communities (whether face-to-face or virtual) are more aptly described as processes. After all, features of social interaction are what lend each community its unique character and determine its quality. And, as we all know, a collection of people in the same place is not necessarily a community. Following the American Progressive John Dewey (1916/1966), community is defined as *a socially accomplished mode of associated living*. Community is a form of shared life, or relatedness, made possible by social interaction.

According to Dewey (1916/1966), good communities share two important characteristics. The first is that there is a broad and deep level of common interests between people. Imagine a community in which the only thing members have in common is that they are enrolled at the same university. Consider how much more satisfying life in this community would be if the students also shared interests in music, entertainment, and sports, held commitments to similar social causes, and shared some of the same values. Most high school seniors who are looking at universities would say that the latter community sounds much more appealing!

The second characteristic of good communities is that their members have high levels of participation in various other forms of association. In other words, the borders of good communities are permeable; members are able to move in and out of them and to be part of multiple communities. Good communities do not restrict their members from participating with the outside world. They encourage it, with the recognition that meaningful participation in a wider circle of social life educates and enlarges experience. In fact, Dewey's second characteristic of good communities is crucial to an ethical and humane approach to community. This is because communities inevitably entail boundaries. In our attempts to create community, we draw a circle of inclusion around a group of people. But, by doing so, we have also drawn a circle of exclusion. In order to say that everyone inside the circle is "one of us," we have inadvertently said that everyone outside the circle is "not one of us." American philosopher Richard Rorty (1989) suggests the goal of drawing an ever-widening circle of human inclusiveness to "extend our sense of 'we' to people whom we have previously thought of as 'they'" (p. 192).

☞ Communication and Community Engagement

It is no mere coincidence that the term community shares both a prefix and a root word with the term communication. As we will see, the two concepts are strongly connected. The basic idea that communities are welded together by communication traces back as far as Aristotle's *Politics*. Aristotle says that community (koinonia) "makes something one and common (koinon)" out of separate things (Aristotle, *History of Animals* 1.1448a8). It is speech (logos) that binds separate people to form a household community, separate household communities to form a national community, and so on. Although Aristotle's ideas form the basis of how we think about the relationship between communication and community today, communication theorists have modified his ideas to reflect our current understandings of the nature of the individual, or self.

In other words, the separate people that Aristotle spoke of are now recognized as themselves being products of communication. Thus, communication creates individual identity. But, in communication, something else is created, as well. According to Shepherd (2001), "when communication occurs, something communal is made. It is something of self and other, but not self and other. It is something synergistic. It is community" (p. 32). In other words, when we communicate, or experience our self and another at once, the byproduct is community, or a socially accomplished mode of associated living. It is communication that creates and sustains community.

This leads to an unorthodox, but empowering understanding of community engagement. The call to "get more engaged in the community" brings to mind activities like attending meetings, signing petitions, organizing rallies, and donating time or money. All of these are valuable community building endeavors, but community engagement can be much simpler. Community engagement involves a minor transformation in perspective that has massive implications. "What is key here is seeing others, whether in our homes, on the street, on the other end of a modem connection, or on the screen, not as performers to be observed, but rather as partners to be engaged" (Shepherd, 2001, p. 33). Community engagement means opening yourself to communication; freely giving your gift of self and accepting the gift of (an)other's self. As Shepherd (2006) acknowledges, this sense of communication implies a responsibility:

> Without your gift of self, the possibilities of communication cannot be realized. Without your gift of self, others will miss the opportunity to expand their senses of self. Without your gift of self, the potential sense of community that lies waiting to be accomplished will always be limited. Without your gift of self, the need for relationship that all of us have will be to some degree unmet. Without your gift of self, we will all be smaller, less than we could have been. (p. 27)

References

Dewey, J. (1916/1966). *Democracy and education*. New York: The Free Press.

Mead, G. H. (1934). *Mind, self, & society*. Chicago: The University of Chicago Press.

Putnam, R. D. (2000). *Bowling alone: The collapse and revival of American community*. New York: Simon and Schuster.

Rorty, R. (1989). *Contingency, irony, and solidarity*. Cambridge: Cambridge University Press.

Shepherd, G. J. (2001). Community as the interpersonal accomplishment of communication. In G. J. Shepherd & E. W. Rothenbuhler (Eds.), *Communication and Community* (pp. 25–35). Mahwah, NJ: Lawrence Erlbaum.

Shepherd, G. J. (2006). Communication and transcendence. In G. J. Shepherd, J. St. John, & T. Striphas (Eds.), *Communication as...Perspectives on theory* (pp. 22–30). Thousand Oaks, CA: Sage.

Shepherd, G. J. & Rothenbuhler, E. W. (2001). Preface. In G. J. Shepherd & E. W. Rothenbuhler (Eds.), *Communication and Community* (pp. ix–xv). Mahwah, NJ: Lawrence Erlbaum.

Chapter 2

Is Citizen Engagement a Moral Responsibility?

Sandra L. Borden

Never doubt that a small group of thoughtful, committed citizens can change the world; indeed, it's the only thing that ever has.

Margaret Mead

After the levees in New Orleans gave way to the fury of Hurricane Katrina in 2005, professor Michael Ignatieff suggested in a *New York Times* column that the government had violated its "contract" with citizens. By failing to guard Gulf Coast residents against the worst-imaginable disaster—and by subsequently failing to provide for their safe evacuation—public officials reneged on their obligation to us all: "Citizenship ties are not humanitarian, abstract or discretionary. They are not ties of charity. In America, a citizen has a claim of right on the resources of her government when she cannot— simply cannot—help herself" (p. 15).

Ignatieff (2005) belongs to a long tradition of thinkers who have conceived of civic bonds in terms of a social contract. A contract, of course, is a mutually binding promise for all the parties who agree to it. The state has obligations to us, but we also have obligations to the state. At a minimum, we must obey the law. In a democratic state, many people think citizens also should vote. Perhaps you think our civic responsibilities extend even further. This chapter will introduce you to different models of citizenship, discuss the relationship between communication and civic engagement, and introduce you to several theories for understanding our civic responsibilities.

Models of Citizenship

In colonial days, being a good citizen meant deferring to local leaders from your community and trusting that they deserved your vote. Later on, political parties, unions and other institutions

---

mediated the interests of citizens; citizens then voted as a matter of loyalty to these social groups. In both these periods, voting was seen as a social duty. However, the Progressives at the turn of the 20th century ushered in the era of the "informed citizen," for whom civic responsibility meant making a knowledgeable personal choice (which might include a decision not to vote at all) (Schudson, 1999).

The legal rights expansions of the 1960s (Schudson, 1999) and the application of market thinking to politics (Galston, 2001) further shifted the focus of citizenship to defending personal preferences. The latest embodiment is the "self-actualizing citizen" who "see(s) her political activities and commitments in highly personal terms that contribute more to enhancing the quality of personal life, social recognition, self esteem, or friendship relations, than to understanding, support, and involvement in government" (Bennett, n.d., p. 6). In other words, citizenship has become disassociated from duty and even from politics. What does civic engagement mean in this context, and what does it have to do with communication?

Civic Engagement and Communication

Civic engagement means simply being involved in public life. Participating in politics, or *civic participation*, is one form of civic engagement. Although voting is considered to be the most basic form of civic participation, civic engagement does not necessarily mean being directly involved in politics. Civic engagement can consist of volunteer work or filing a civil rights lawsuit. However, unless community action and politics meet, the policies that affect communities are not addressed. That's why observers are concerned when certain groups, like youth, opt out of voting. "The withdrawal of a cohort of citizens from public affairs disturbs the balance of public deliberation—to the detriment of those who withdraw, but of the rest of us as well" (Galston, 2001, p. 8).

One thing's for sure: Communication is basic to civic engagement. For one thing, communication affects whether we are motivated to engage in public life. For example, political campaign tactics that appeal to our pocketbook or other narrow interests divide us up into strategic "voter blocs." That's useful for the campaigns that are trying to win an election, but not necessarily useful for us as citizens who need to work together to solve social problems. Young people, in particular, are often written off as "no shows" on Election Day. The media primarily address young people as consumers of commercial products, rather than as citizens. For instance, if you want to make a statement about what's important to you—drink Mountain Dew! Such communication practices alienate young people from public life.

Democratic theorists have suggested that the public sphere is essentially *discursive*—in other words, it is literally an ongoing conversation about how our democracy ought to address public matters, such as security, infrastructure, and health care (Wyatt, 2007). Individual citizens are part of the conversation, and so are journalists and other professional communicators. As much as the media can dissuade us from joining this conversation, they also provide the means for us to communicate with others about common concerns, to find out about important issues, and to take political action. Bennett (n.d.) proposes the following components of civic engagement:

* **Information seeking about public affairs**: This can be done by conducting community surveys, paying attention to news, and through social networking.
* **Public deliberation and collective issue construction**: This can be done through research and networking face-to-face or online.
* **Problem solving**: This can be done by conducting research, being critical media consumers, and collaborating with others in our social networks.
* **Political action**: This can include voting, protesting, political consumerism, working on political campaigns, blogging, and posting YouTube videos.

But is civic engagement really optional—just another goal we may pursue if we choose? Or do we have a moral responsibility to be engaged in public life?

Theories of Civic Responsibility

Civic Responsibility as Contractual Exchange

The social contract tradition relies on the assumption that government is necessary for us to avoid a brutish "state of nature" in which we are constantly fearful that others will violate our rights. This tradition is associated with 17th-century English philosopher Thomas Hobbes (1994/1651), who argued that we consent to restrictions on our liberties (for example, we accept the rule of law) in exchange for social order. Contemporary contractarian John Rawls (1971) suggests, however, that we would never be willing to "trade" certain fundamental rights. These rights include the right to vote, the right to free expression and the right to private property. These rights make us equals as citizens. Without this guarantee, it wouldn't be to our advantage to "sign on" to the social contract. Furthermore, we expect everyone to abide by the terms of the social contract. No fair enjoying the benefits of social cooperation as a "free rider."

Do we have any responsibilities as citizens? A social contract theorist would say yes because (1) we have tacitly consented to the trade-offs involved in living together, (2) our equality as citizens is assured, and (3) it wouldn't be fair to take advantage of others who are doing their part to ensure that we all benefit from social cooperation.

Civic Responsibility as Grateful Response

This framework can be traced to Socrates' reasoning in the famous Platonic dialogue *Crito*. Socrates justifies his refusal to escape a death sentence at the hands of Athenian authorities on the grounds that it would be wrong for him to pick and choose which laws to obey after he has enjoyed the benefits of Athenian citizenship his whole life (Plato, 1955/360 B.C.E.). Contemporary philosopher A.D.M. Walker (1999) argues that civic responsibility is grounded in a particular duty of gratitude: the duty "not to act in ways that are contrary to the state's interests" (p. 191). In Walker's view, gratitude is not just repaying the state for the benefits it provides or playing fair. It is motivated by an attitude of good will toward the state as our benefactor. To act contrary to the state's interests would be incompatible with this attitude. Walker acknowledges that civic responsibility based on gratitude may "vary with the nature and extent of the benefits a citizen receives" (p. 195).

Do we have any responsibilities as citizens? A gratitude theorist would say yes because (1) we generally receive important benefits from the state, (2) these benefits rightly generate an attitude of good will, and (3) this duty of gratitude requires, at minimum, that we refrain from actions that go against the state's interests.

Civic Responsibility as Socially Useful

Utilitarian ethical theory claims that we are obligated to act in ways that maximize benefits and minimize harms to all those affected by our actions. This theory is usually credited to English philosopher Jeremy Bentham, who proposed the Principle of Utility (1948/1789). It's not that we are obligated, in the abstract, to obey legitimate authority or are bound in some mystical sense to our fellow citizens. Rather, as a general rule, it would seem that choosing to obey the law, to vote, and so on, tends to promote the overall good. In other words, most of us are better off if people do these things, although occasionally we might be better off if someone did not. What transforms these actions into civic responsibilities, then, are their tendency to promote more good than harm.

Do we have any responsibilities as citizens? A utilitarian would say yes, because performing certain civic actions tends to produce more utility than if we did not.

Civic Responsibility as Mutual Commitment

According to communitarianism, communities and individuals are not in an adversary relationship, but a mutual one. This tradition can be traced to the virtue theory of Confucius in Ancient China and Aristotle in Ancient Greece, as well as the classic republicanism of 18th-century French philosopher Jean-Jacques Rousseau (1959/1762). Confucius and Aristotle thought "self-cultivation," or human virtue, required the performance of social roles and that our very selves were inherently social. Rousseau thought we could not be truly free or fulfilled without joining others in the pursuit of what communitarians call the *common good*. Contemporary communitarian Michael Sandel (1982) notes that this is not the same as the overall good in utilitarianism, which consists of "adding up" what individuals find necessary and desirable. Rather, the common good refers to what is good for the "whole" in addition to what is good for the individual "parts." In this conception of community, people are motivated by a sense of solidarity.

Do we have any responsibilities as citizens? A communitarian would say yes because (1) we cannot be truly human without community membership, (2) we are bound to others by solidarity, and (3) we are all responsible for promoting the common good.

🖝 Summary

As you can see, reasonable people can disagree about civic engagement being a moral responsibility. For example, if we think of citizenship in terms of a social contract, we may conclude that civic engagement should be an option, but not a moral requirement. Further, the point of engagement would be to protect the exercise of our rights.

Even if we accept stronger grounds for civic responsibility, we may place conditions on our engagement. If we're utilitarians, we may limit our involvement to what we consider most useful. If we're taking a gratitude approach, we may base our involvement on what the government has done for us lately (think, for example, of the perspective of Katrina victims).

Of all the frameworks we have reviewed, communitarianism holds the highest expectations. Since neither individuals nor communities can flourish without engaged members, communitarians think citizens should participate generously in public life. Further, they should aim at a specific goal: promoting the common good.

What do *you* think?

🖝 References

Bennett, W. L. (n.d.) *Civic learning in changing democracies: Challenges for citizenship and civic education.* Report posted on the website of the Center for Communication and Civic Engagement. Retrieved September 21, 2008, from www.engagedcitizen.org

Bentham, J. (1948). *Introduction to the principles of morals and legislation.* New York: Hafner. (Original work published 1789).

Galston, W.A. (2001, November 16). Can patriotism be turned into civic engagement? *The Chronicle of Higher Education: The Chronicle Review.* Retrieved September 21, 2008, from http://chronicle.com

Hobbes, T. (1994). *Leviathan* (E. Curley, Ed.). Hackett: Indianapolis. (Original work published 1651).

Ignatieff, M. (2005, September 25). "The way we live now: The broken contract," *The New York Times Magazine,* p. 15.

Plato (1955). Crito. In R. Demos (Ed.), *Plato selections* (pp. 34–50). New York: Charles Scribner's Sons. (Original work published 360 B.C.E.).

Rawls, J. (1971). *A theory of justice.* Cambridge, MA: Harvard University Press.

Rousseau, J.J. (1959). *The social contract and discourses* (G.D.H. Cole, Trans.). New York: Dutton. (Original work published 1762).

Sandel, M.J. (1982). *Liberalism and the limits of justice.* Cambridge, UK: Cambridge University Press.

Schudson, M. (1999). *Good citizens & bad history: Today's political ideals in historical perspective.* Murfreesboro, TN: John Seigenthaler Chair of Excellence in First Amendment Studies.

Walker, A.D.M. (1999). Political obligation and the argument from gratitude. In G. Sher & B.A. Brody (Eds.), *Social and political philosophy: Contemporary readings* (pp. 181–196). Fort Worth, TX: Hartcourt Brace.

Wyatt, W. (2007). *Critical conversations: A theory of press criticism.* Cresskill, NJ: Hampton Press.

Chapter 3

Ethics in Public Speaking

"I do not agree with a word you say, but I will defend to the death your right to say it."

Voltaire

SPEECH: Richard M. Nixon—Checkers

In 1952, Richard M. Nixo (1913–1994), then a U.S. Senator from California, was running for Vice President on the Republican ticket with Dwight D. Eisenhower. Press reports accused Nixon of misusing a campaign fund for personal gain and of showing political favoritism to campaign contributors. The following speech was aired on national television and drew an audience of 60 million people—then a record for the largest number of broadcast viewers. Public response was generally positive and Eisenhower kept Nixon on the ticket. Nixon served two terms as Vice President.

Source: https://www.commonlit.org/texts/senator-nixon-s-checkers-speech

Text of Senator Richard Nixon's Checkers speech

My Fellow Americans:

I come before you tonight as a candidate for the Vice Presidency and as a man whose honesty and integrity have been questioned.

The usual political thing to do when charges are made against you is to either ignore them or to deny them without giving details.

I believe we've had enough of that in the United States, particularly with the present Administration in Washington, D.C. To me the office of the Vice Presidency of the United States is a great office and I feel that the people have got to have confidence in the integrity of the men who run for that office and who might obtain it.

From *Public Speaking: Choices for Effective Results*, Sixth Edition, by Gail E. Mason, Mark J. Butland, and John J. Makay. Copyright © 2012 by Kendall Hunt Publishing Company. Reprinted by permission.

13

I have a theory, too, that the best and only answer to a smear or to an honest misunderstanding of the facts is to tell the truth. And that's why I'm here tonight. I want to tell you my side of the case.

I am sure that you have read the charge and you've heard that I, Senator Nixon, took $18,000 from a group of my supporters.

Now, was that wrong? And let me say that it was wrong—I'm saying, incidentally, that it was wrong and not just illegal. Because it isn't a question of whether it was legal or illegal, that isn't enough. The question is, was it morally wrong?

I say that it was morally wrong if any of that $18,000 went to Senator Nixon for my personal use. I say that it was morally wrong if it was secretly given and secretly handled. And I say that it was morally wrong if any of the contributors got special favors for the contributions that they made.

And now to answer those questions let me say this:

Not one cent of the $18,000 or any other money of that type ever went to me for my personal use. Every penny of it was used to pay for political expenses that I did not think should be charged to the taxpayers of the United States.

It was not a secret fund. As a matter of fact, when I was on "Meet the Press," some of you may have seen it last Sunday—Peter Edson came up to me after the program and he said, "Dick, what about this fund we hear about?" And I said, "Well, there's no secret about it. Go out and see Dana Smith, who was the administrator of the fund."

And I gave him his address, and I said that you will find that the purpose of the fund simply was to defray political expenses that I did not feel should be charged to the Government.

And third, let me point out, and I want to make this particularly clear, that no contributor to this fund, no contributor to any of my campaign, has ever received any consideration that he would not have received as an ordinary constituent.

I just don't believe in that and I can say that never, while I have been in the Senate of the United States, as far as the people that contributed to this fund are concerned, have I made a telephone call for them to an agency, or have I gone down to an agency in their behalf. And the records will show that, the records which are in the hands of the Administration.

But then some of you will say and rightly, "Well, what did you use the fund for, Senator? Why did you have to have it?"

Let me tell you in just a word how a Senate office operates. First of all, a Senator gets $15,000 a year in salary. He gets enough money to pay for one trip a year, a round trip that is, for himself and his family between his home and Washington, D.C.

And then he gets an allowance to handle the people that work in his office, to handle his mail. And the allowance for my State of California is enough to hire thirteen people.

And let me say, incidentally, that that allowance is not paid to the Senator—it's paid directly to the individuals that the Senator puts on his payroll, but all of these people and all of these allowances are for strictly official business. Business, for example, when a constituent writes in and wants you to go down to the Veterans Administration and get some information about his GI policy. Items of that type for example.

But there are other expenses which are not covered by the Government. And I think I can best discuss those expenses by asking you some questions.

Do you think that when I or any other Senator makes a political speech, has it printed, should charge the printing of that speech and the mailing of that speech to the taxpayers? Do you think, for example, when I or any other Senator makes a trip to his home state to make a purely political speech that the cost of that trip should be charged to the taxpayers? Do you think when a Senator makes political broadcasts or political television broadcasts, radio or television, that the expense of those broadcasts should be charged to the taxpayers?

Well, I know what your answer is. It is the same answer that audiences give me whenever I discuss this particular problem. The answer is, "no." The taxpayers shouldn't be required to finance items which are not official business but which are primarily political business.

But then the question arises, you say, "Well, how do you pay for these and how can you do it legally?" And there are several ways that it can be done, incidentally, and that it is done legally in the United States Senate and in the Congress.

The first way is to be a rich man. I don't happen to be a rich man so I couldn't use that one.

Another way that is used is to put your wife on the payroll. Let me say, incidentally, my opponent, my opposite number for the Vice Presidency on the Democratic ticket, does have his wife on the payroll. And has had her on his payroll for the ten years—the past ten years.

Now just let me say this. That's his business and I'm not critical of him for doing that. You will have to pass judgment on that particular point. But I have never done that for this reason. I have found that there are so many deserving stenographers and secretaries in Washington that needed the work that I just didn't feel it was right to put my wife on the payroll.

My wife's sitting over here. She's a wonderful stenographer. She used to teach stenography and she used to teach shorthand in high school. That was when I met her. And I can tell you folks that she's worked many hours at night and many hours on Saturdays and Sundays in my office and she's done a fine job. And I'm proud to say tonight that in the six years I've been in the House and the Senate of the United States, Pat Nixon has never been on the Government payroll.

There are other ways that these finances can be taken care of. Some who are lawyers, and I happen to be a lawyer, continue to practice law. But I haven't been able to do that. I'm so far away from California that I've been so busy with my Senatorial work that I have not engaged in any legal practice.

And also as far as law practice is concerned, it seemed to me that the relationship between an attorney and the client was so personal that you couldn't possibly represent a man as an attorney and then have an unbiased view when he presented his case to you in the event that he had one before the Government.

And so I felt that the best way to handle these necessary political expenses of getting my message to the American people and the speeches I made, the speeches that I had printed, for the most part, concerned this one message—of exposing this Administration, the communism in it, the corruption in it—the only way that I could do that was to accept the aid which people in my home state of California who contributed to my campaign and who continued to make these contributions after I was elected were glad to make.

And let me say I am proud of the fact that not one of them has ever asked me for a special favor. I'm proud of the fact that not one of them has ever asked me to vote on a bill other than as my own conscience would dictate. And I am proud of the fact that the taxpayers by subterfuge or otherwise have never paid one dime for expenses which I thought were political and shouldn't be charged to the taxpayers.

Let me say, incidentally, that some of you may say, "Well, that's all right, Senator; that's your explanation, but have you got any proof?"

And I'd like to tell you this evening that just about an hour ago we received an independent audit of this entire fund. I suggested to Gov. Sherman Adams, who is the chief of staff of the Dwight Eisenhower campaign, that an independent audit and legal report be obtained. And I have that audit here in my hand.

It's an audit made by the Price, Waterhouse & Co. firm, and the legal opinion by Gibson, Dunn & Crutcher, lawyers in Los Angeles, the biggest law firm and incidentally one of the best ones in Los Angeles.

I'm proud to be able to report to you tonight that this audit and this legal opinion is being forwarded to General Eisenhower. And I'd like to read to you the opinion that was prepared by Gibson, Dunn & Crutcher and based on all the pertinent laws and statutes, together with the audit report prepared by the certified public accountants.

"It is our conclusion that Senator Nixon did not obtain any financial gain from the collection and disbursement of the fund by Dana Smith; that Senator Nixon did not violate any Federal or state law by reason of the operation of the fund, and that neither the portion of the fund paid by Dana Smith directly to third persons nor the portion paid to Senator Nixon to reimburse him for designated office expenses constituted income to the Senator which was either reportable or taxable as income under applicable tax laws. (signed) Gibson, Dunn & Crutcher by Alma H. Conway."

Now that, my friends, is not Nixon speaking, but that's an independent audit which was requested because I want the American people to know all the facts and I'm not afraid of having independent people go in and check the facts, and that is exactly what they did.

But then I realize that there are still some who may say, and rightly so, and let me say that I recognize that some will continue to smear regardless of what the truth may be, but that there has been understandably some honest misunderstanding on this matter, and there's some that will say:

"Well, maybe you were able, Senator, to fake this thing. How can we believe what you say? After all, is there a possibility that maybe you got some sums in cash? Is there a possibility that you may have feathered your own nest?" And so now what I am going to do-and incidentally this is unprecedented in the history of American politics-I am going at this time to give this television and radio audience a complete financial history; everything I've earned; everything I've spent; everything I owe. And I want you to know the facts. I'll have to start early.

I was born in 1913. Our family was one of modest circumstances and most of my early life was spent in a store out in East Whittier. It was a grocery store — one of those family enterprises. The only reason we were able to make it go was because my mother and dad had five boys and we all worked in the store.

I worked my way through college and to a great extent through law school. And then, in 1940, probably the best thing that ever happened to me happened, I married Pat — who is sitting over here. We had a rather difficult time after we were married, like so many of the young couples who may be listening to us. I practiced law; she continued to teach school. Then in 1942 I went into the service.

Let me say that my service record was not a particularly unusual one. I went to the South Pacific. I guess I'm entitled to a couple of battle stars. I got a couple of letters of commendation but I was just there when the bombs were falling and then I returned. I returned to the United States and in 1946 I ran for the Congress.

When we came out of the war, Pat and I — Pat during the war had worked as a stenographer and in a bank and as an economist for Government agency — and when we came out the total of our saving from both my law practice, her teaching and all the time that I as in the war — the total for that entire period was just a little less than $10,000. Every cent of that, incidentally, was in Government bonds.

Well, that's where we start when I go into politics. Now what I've I earned since I went into politics? Well, here it is — I jotted it down, let me read the notes. First of all I've had my salary as a Congressman and as a Senator. Second, I have received a total in this past six years of $1600 from estates which were in my law firm the time that I severed my connection with it.

And, incidentally, as I said before, I have not engaged in any legal practice and have not accepted any fees from business that came to the firm after I went into politics. I have made an average of approximately $1500 a year from nonpolitical speaking engagements and lectures. And then, fortunately, we've inherited a little money. Pat sold her interest in her father's estate for $3,000 and I inherited $1,500 from my grandfather.

We live rather modestly. For four years we lived in an apartment in Park Fairfax, in Alexandria, Va. The rent was $80 a month. And we saved for the time that we could buy a house.

Now, that was what we took in. What did we do with this money? What do we have today to show for it? This will surprise you, Because it is so little, I suppose, as standards generally go, of people in public life. First of all, we've got a house in Washington which cost $41,000 and on which we owe $20,000. We have a house in Whittier, California, which cost $13,000 and on which we owe $3,000. * My folks are living there at the present time.

I have just $4,000 in life insurance, plus my G.I. policy which I've never been able to convert and which will run out in two years. I have no insurance whatever on Pat. I have no life insurance on our our youngsters, Patricia and Julie. I own a 1950 Oldsmobile car. We have our furniture. We have no stocks and bonds of any type. We have no interest of any kind, direct or indirect, in any business.

Now, that's what we have. What do we owe? Well, in addition to the mortgage, the $20,000 mortgage on the house in Washington, the $10,000 one on the house in Whittier, I owe $4,500 to the Riggs Bank in Washington, D.C. with interest 4 1/2 per cent.

I owe $3,500 to my parents and the interest on that loan which I pay regularly, because it's the part of the savings they made through the years they were working so hard, I pay regularly 4 per cent interest. And then I have a $500 loan which I have on my life insurance.

Well, that's about it. That's what we have and that's what we owe. It isn't very much but Pat and I have the satisfaction that every dime that we've got is honestly ours. I should say this — that Pat doesn't have a mink coat. But she does have a respectable Republican cloth coat. And I always tell her that she'd look good in anything.

One other thing I probably should tell you because if we don't they'll probably be saying this about me too, we did get something-a gift-after the election. A man down in Texas heard Pat on the radio mention the fact that our two youngsters would like to have a dog. And, believe it or not, the day before we left on this campaign trip we got a message from Union Station in Baltimore saying they had a package for us. We went down to get it. You know what it was.

It was a little cocker spaniel dog in a crate that he'd sent all the way from Texas. Black and white spotted. And our little girl-Tricia, the 6-year old-named it Checkers. And you know, the kids, like all kids, love the dog and I just want to say this right now, that regardless of what they say about it, we're gonna keep it.

It isn't easy to come before a nation-wide audience and air your life as I've done. But I want to say some things before I conclude that I think most of you will agree on. Mr. Mitchell, the chairman of the Democratic National Committee, made the statement that if a man couldn't afford to be in the United States Senate he shouldn't run for the Senate.

And I just want to make my position clear. I don't agree with Mr. Mitchell when he says that only a rich man should serve his Government in the United States Senate or in the Congress. I don't believe that represents the thinking of the Democratic Party, and I know that it doesn't represent the thinking of the Republican Party.

I believe that it's fine that a man like Governor Stevenson who inherited a fortune from his father can run for President. But I also feel that it's essential in this country of ours that a man of modest means can also run for President. Because, you know, remember Abraham Lincoln, you remember what he said: "God must have loved the common people — he made so many of them."

And now I'm going to suggest some courses of conduct. First of all, you have read in the papers about other funds now. Mr. Stevenson, apparently, had a couple. One of them in which a group of business people paid and helped to supplement the salaries of state employees. Here is where the money went directly into their pockets.

And I think that what Mr. Stevenson should do is come before the American people as I have, give the names of the people that have contributed to that fund; give the names of the people who put this money into their pockets at the same time that they were receiving money from their state government, and see what favors, if any, they gave out for that.

I don't condemn Mr. Stevenson for what he did. But until the facts are in there is a doubt that will be raised.

And as far as Mr. Sparkman is concerned, I would suggest the same thing. He's had his wife on the payroll. I don't condemn him for that. But I think that he should come before the American people and indicate what outside sources of income he has had.

I would suggest that under the circumstances both Mr. Sparkman and Mr. Stevenson should come before the American people as I have and make a complete financial statement as to their financial history. And if they don't, it will be an admission that they have something to hide. And I think that you will agree with me.

Because, folks, remember, a man that's to be President of the United States, a man that's to be Vice President of the United States must have the confidence of all the people. And that's why I'm doing what I'm doing, and that's why I suggest that Mr. Stevenson and Mr. Sparkman since they are under attack should do what I am doing.

Now, let me say this: I know that this is not the last of the smears. In spite of my explanation tonight other smears will be made; others have been made in the past. And the purpose of the smears, I know, is this—to silence me, to make me let up.

Well, they just don't know who they're dealing with. I'm going I tell you this: I remember in the dark days of the Hiss case some of the same columnists, some of the same radio commentators who are attacking me now and misrepresenting my position were violently opposing me at the time I was after Alger Hiss.

But I continued the fight because I knew I was right. And I an say to this great television and radio audience that I have no apologies to the American people for my part in putting Alger Hiss where he is today.

And as far as this is concerned, I intend to continue the fight.

Why do I feel so deeply? Why do I feel that in spite of the smears, the misunderstandings, the necessity for a man to come up here and bare his soul as I have? Why is it necessary for me to continue this fight?

And I want to tell you why. Because, you see, I love my country. And I think my country is in danger. And I think that the only man that can save America at this time is the man that's running for President on my ticket—Dwight Eisenhower.

You say, "Why do I think it's in danger?" and I say look at the record. Seven years of the Truman-Acheson Administration and that's happened? Six hundred million people lost to the Communists, and a war in Korea in which we have lost 117,000 American casualties.

And I say to all of you that a policy that results in a loss of six hundred million people to the Communists and a war which costs us 117,000 American casualties isn't good enough for America.

And I say that those in the State Department that made the mistakes which caused that war and which resulted in those losses should be kicked out of the State Department just as fast as we can get 'em out of there.

And let me say that I know Mr. Stevenson won't do that. Because he defends the Truman policy and I know that Dwight Eisenhower will do that, and that he will give America the leadership that it needs.

Take the problem of corruption. You've read about the mess in Washington. Mr. Stevenson can't clean it up because he was picked by the man, Truman, under whose Administration the mess was made. You wouldn't trust a man who made the mess to clean it up—that's Truman. And by the same token you can't trust the man who was picked by the man that made the mess to clean it up—and that's Stevenson.

And so I say, Eisenhower, who owes nothing to Truman, nothing to the big city bosses, he is the man that can clean up the mess in Washington.

Take Communism. I say that as far as that subject is concerned, the danger is great to America. In the Hiss case they got the secrets which enabled them to break the American secret State Department code. They got secrets in the atomic bomb case which enabled them to get the secret of the atomic bomb, five years before they would have gotten it by their own devices.

And I say that any man who called the Alger Hiss case a "red herring" isn't fit to be President of the United States. I say that a man who like Mr. Stevenson has pooh-poohed and ridiculed the Communist threat in the United States — he said that they are phantoms among ourselves; he's accused us that have attempted to expose the Communists of looking for Communists in the Bureau of Fisheries and Wildlife — I say that a man who says that isn't qualified to be President of the United States.

And I say that the only man who can lead us in this fight to rid the Government of both those who are Communists and those who have corrupted this Government is Eisenhower, because Eisenhower, you can be sure, recognizes the problem and he knows how to deal with it.

Now let me say that, finally, this evening I want to read to you just briefly excerpts from a letter which I received, a letter which, after all this is over, no one can take away from us. It reads as follows:

Dear Senator Nixon:

Since I'm only 19 years of age I can't vote in this Presidential election but believe me if I could you and General Eisenhower would certainly get my vote. My husband is in the Fleet Marines in Korea. He's a corpsman on the front lines and we have a two-month-old son he's never seen. And I feel confident that with great Americans like you and General Eisenhower in the White House, lonely Americans like myself will be united with their loved ones now in Korea.

I only pray to God that you won't be too late. Enclosed is a small check to help you in your campaign. Living on $85 a month it is all I can afford at present. But let me know what else I can do.

Folks, it's a check for $10, and it's one that I will never cash.

And just let me say this. We hear a lot about prosperity these days but I say, why can't we have prosperity built on peace rather than prosperity built on war? Why can't we have prosperity and an honest government in Washington, D.C., at the same time. Believe me, we can. And Eisenhower is the man that can lead this crusade to bring us that kind of prosperity.

And, now, finally, I know that you wonder whether or not I am going to stay on the Republican ticket or resign.

Let me say this: I don't believe that I ought to quit because I'm not a quitter. And, incidentally, Pat's not a quitter. After all, her name was Patricia Ryan and she was born on St. Patrick's Day, and you know the Irish never quit.

But the decision, my friends, is not mine. I would do nothing that would harm the possibilities of Dwight Eisenhower to become President of the United States. And for that reason I am submitting to the Republican National Committee tonight through this television broadcast the decision which it is theirs to make.

Let them decide whether my position on the ticket will help or hurt. And I am going to ask you to help them decide. Wire and write the Republican National Committee whether you think I should stay on or whether I should get off. And whatever their decision is, I will abide by it.

But just let me say this last word. Regardless of what happens I'm going to continue this fight. I'm going to campaign up and down America until we drive the crooks and the Communists and those that defend them out of Washington. And remember, folks, Eisenhower is a great man. Believe me. He's a great man. And a vote for Eisenhower is a vote for what's good for America.

* Nixon meant to say $10,000.

http://watergate.info/1952/09/23/nixon-checkersspeech.html

As citizens and consumers, we are bombarded by messages each day through print and electronic media. Intense competition exists among these outlets as they strive to be the most watched, read, tweeted, blogged, etc. As media outlets look for bottom-line profits, ethical standards are occasionally bent. Such was the case in 1993 when *Dateline NBC* alleged that some General Motors pickup trucks had a tendency to explode during collisions. It was later revealed that those trucks had been rigged with incendiary devices to assure footage of an explosion. General Motors threatened litigation, which resulted in the on-air admission by journalist Stone Phillips that NBC used the devices without informing the viewers.

Ethical violations are not limited to those in the media. Politics, with its mix of power, potential profit, and public service often fosters ethical breaches by officials in powerful positions. Can we modify this sentence to say: In 2005 the news reported a scandal that provided details of unethical and unlawful activities by public officials. Ohio has proven to be a vital state in national elections and Tom Noe, a key Republican fundraiser convicted of violating federal campaign law, was the initial subject in a series of stories that reported questionable investments of state funds, the loss of millions of dollars, and a web of cover-up activities. Ultimately, even the governor of Ohio pleaded no contest to charges that he failed to report gifts he received while in office. After hearing and reading about the charges, countercharges, admitted mistakes, and denials, the general public was left with disappointment and cynicism because of these ethical violations.

Unfortunately, scandalous behavior is neither new nor limited to political leaders. Power, status, and money have led to unethical behavior and deceptive speeches throughout history, and public speaking is often a preferred instrument when this sort of abuse occurs. The media plays an important role in investigating unethical behavior and limiting future breaches. For example, during local, state, and national campaigns, the media provides the public with details of sexual misconduct, bribery, poor parenting, and unimpressive military service. No candidate is immune, which leaves the public faced with the dilemma over who is really telling the truth. Ethical violations seem commonplace in media reports, and this suggests that ethics are more important now than ever.

☞   Ethics

Ethics refers to the rules we use to determine good and evil, right and wrong. These rules may be grounded in religious principles, democratic values, codes of conduct, and a variety of other sources. Without an ethical roadmap based on socially accepted values to guide you, you could disregard your audience's need for truth and engage in self-serving deceit, ambiguity, intellectual sloppiness, and emotional manipulation. If you do, your credibility as a speaker is lost as your listeners turn elsewhere for a message—and a speaker—they can trust. Public speaking is a reciprocal process, and audience mistrust can stand in the way of communication. Therefore, an important aspect of being audience-centered is being ethical.

Every time you speak, you risk your reputation. Listeners will forgive many things—stumbling over words, awkward gestures, lack of examples—but if you lie or mislead them, they may never trust you again. For some, maintaining strong ethical standards is second nature. For others, more deliberation is needed. Some speakers rationalize their unethical behaviors so they can continue to misguide their audiences.

Our Freedom of Speech

Since the First Amendment to the U.S. Constitution was passed in 1791, American citizens have had a constitutional guarantee of freedom of speech. As a student, you are allowed to interact with your teachers, and you have opportunities to speak before your class about issues of concern. You have the right to support publicly the political party of your choice and you can engage in activities that reflect your social values. As a community resident, you have the right to speak before the city council or the local school board to express agreement or disagreement with their policies. You can write letters to the editor of your local newspaper that support or oppose the president of our nation. With the Internet, you have numerous and highly varied means of communication.

While we live with wide boundaries for speaking, periodically attempts are made to censor both our public and private lives. And as First Amendment lawyer Robert Corn-Revere (2007) notes, the "seemingly simple command" of the First Amendment becomes "exceedingly complex" when applied to electronic media. The difficulty of monitoring the use/abuse of free speech is especially true in this age of blogging, where every second a "citizen journalist" creates a new blog site, adding to the already 37 million existing sites, according to David Sifri (2006), founder of the Technorati weblog data set and link tracker/search engine. Ultimately, limitations to our freedom of speech are decided by the U.S. Supreme Court.

Freedom of expression comes with responsibility. In class, each speaker has the ethical responsibility to communicate accurately with sound reasoning and to decide what is said and best not said. This responsibility requires a speaker to be truthful without hesitation. As listeners, we are also given a responsibility: to respect the opinions of others, even those different from ours.

Freedom of expression is balanced by freedom of choice. In most situations, listeners have the ultimate power to listen or to focus elsewhere. It is the freedom to pursue our individual interests that keeps the freedom of speech of others in check. Yet this is not always a perfect system. There are times when the audience is captive and has no real choice, such as your classroom, when an attendance policy may require students to be there. It becomes the ethical responsibility of the speaker and host (your instructor) to monitor more carefully and on occasion censure inappropriate material on behalf of the captive audience.

We want to emphasize the importance of meeting your ethical responsibilities in any speech you give, whether it is informative, persuasive, or entertaining. We begin by discussing the connection between ethics and public speaking, and then turn to guidelines for incorporating ethical standards in your speeches.

The Ethics and Values Link

Inherent to a discussion about ethics in public speaking is the concept of values and how they ground us. **Values** are socially shared ideas about what is good, right, and desirable. They propel us to speak and act. They determine what we consider important and what we ignore, how we regard our listeners, and how we research and develop a speech. Values are communicated through what speakers say—and fail to say—through delivery, and through responsiveness to audience feedback.

You can speak out against anti-Semitism or remain silent. You can support, through public discourse, the university's right to displace poor families from their university-owned apartments to build another office tower or you can plead for a more humane solution. In a public speaking class, you have a forum to talk about those things you feel are right or wrong, desirable or undesirable. Though you might hesitate to speak out, you may be surprised by how many others agree with you.

Ethos and Speaker Credibility

Ethics receives attention in academic courses but is also a prominent concern in the media, government, and business. It may surprise you to learn that ethics has been systematically studied for over 2,000 years. In his text *Rhetoric*, Aristotle discussed the term **ethos**, meaning "ethical appeal." In a translation by Lane Cooper (1960), we find that **Aristotle** defined ethos in terms of the intelligence, character, and goodwill a speaker communicates during a speech:

> Speakers are untrustworthy in what they say or advise from one or more of the following causes. Either through want of intelligence they form wrong opinions; or, while they form correct opinions, their rascality leads them to say what they do not think; or, while intelligent and honest enough, they are not well disposed [to the hearer, audience], and so perchance will fail to advise the best course, though they see it.

Aristotle believed speakers can abuse their ethical relationship with their listeners when they misinterpret information or fail to collect all the information needed to give a complete and fair presentation, and when self-interest leads them to dishonesty and lack of goodwill. For example, a developer comes into a community in the hopes of building a large superstore and, in a public forum, explains how many jobs and how much revenue will be brought to the community. The developer's self-interest in this project may result in her leaving out information, such as the negative impact the superstore will have on employees and owners of the community's smaller businesses, less-than-savory environmental impacts, and potential traffic bottlenecks. As this information becomes available to the audience, the developer may lose much of her credibility.

Notice that Aristotle was also concerned with how well disposed, or liked, the speaker is by the audience. For Aristotle, even if our hypothetical building developer mentioned above had told the whole truth, included the unsavory realities, and then attempted to overcome them, but did so in a demeaning, condescending tone, she would not be successful in maximizing her speaker ethos. Your likability is an important feature and deserves attention along with your speech content.

Since Aristotle's time, scholars have made the distinction between intrinsic ethos and extrinsic ethos. Whereas **intrinsic ethos** is the ethical appeal found in the actual speech, including such aspects as supporting material, argument flow, and source citation, **extrinsic ethos** is a speaker's image in the mind of the audience. Extrinsic aspects include how knowledgeable, trustworthy, and dynamic the speaker is perceived to be. Both intrinsic and extrinsic ethos contribute to a speaker's credibility. Communication theorists McCroskey and Young (1981) tie credibility to the audience's perception of the speaker as an expert, as a person to trust, and as a person with positive and honest intent. If you are too casual, unprepared, or do not provide support for your claims, your credibility may work against you.

Plagiarism and Source Citations

An ethical speaker takes credit for his or her own ideas and, through oral source citation, credits others for their ideas. If you were to find a compelling example that would help you make a point, but that example came from a journal article, you are ethically bound to give oral credit when you use the example. This is achieved by simply saying, "According to [name of author and date of publication] in [name of journal] an excellent example of this is …" and then paraphrase the example. Oral citations are brief but effective in enhancing your credibility by showing you have conducted research and you are honorable enough to give others credit for their work. As public speakers, we orally credit others when we use their ideas, facts, statistics, organizational patterns, testimonies and quotations, stories, examples. When in doubt, give credit. An ethical speaker does not mislead audiences.

Engage in Dialogue with the Audience

Beyond citing sources orally, there are other signs that the speaker may be unethical. Monologic versus dialogic communication tendencies is one clear indicator of ethical responsibility. The least sensitive speakers engage in **monologic communication** (Johannesen, 1974). From this perspective, the audience is viewed as an object to be manipulated and, in the process, the speaker displays such qualities as deception, superiority, exploitation, dogmatism, domination, insincerity, pretense, coercion, distrust, and defensiveness—all qualities considered unethical.

In contrast, **dialogic communication** entails an honest concern for listeners' interests. This kind of speech "communicates trust, mutual respect and acceptance, open-mindedness, equality, empathy, directness, lack of pretense, and nonmanipulative intent. Although the speaker in dialogue may offer advice or express disagreement, he or she does not aim to psychologically coerce an audience into accepting his/her view. The speaker's aim is one of assisting the audience in making independent, self-determined decisions" (Johannesen, 1974). Whereas monologic speakers attempt to force an issue, dialogic speakers are interested in creating a fair, honest dialogue with their audience. The dialogic speaker does have a goal toward which he/she is attempting to move the audience but is concerned with doing so ethically.

Promoting Ethical Speaking

Dialogic styled speakers use an audience-centered approach, and all decisions made in the development process take the audience into consideration. As you recognize the importance of speaker credibility and project firm ethical standards, we encourage you to reflect on the following four principles of the ethical speaker (Wallace, 1955).

Search

In the context of public speaking and ethics, search refers to putting forth an effort to learn enough about your topic so you are able to speak knowledgeably and confidently. As you speak before your class, realize that, at that moment, you are the primary source of information about your chosen topic. You are responsible for presenting a message that reflects thorough knowledge of the subject, sensitivity to relevant issues and implications, and awareness that many issues are multifaceted. If your search is half-hearted or incomplete, you may not get it right in your speech. In the worst cases, you might mislead others with your words in such ways as to cause harm.

Justice

Justice reminds us to select and present facts and opinions openly and fairly. Instead of attempts to distort or conceal evidence, just speakers offer the audience the opportunity to make fair judgments. The Food and Drug Administration requires the pharmaceutical industry to disclose side-effects of medications in advertising. Daily we hear messages such as "side-effects may include nausea, vomiting, dizziness, rectal leakage, stroke or heart attack, and should not be taken by children under 12, women who are pregnant, or people who have heart problems, liver problems, kidney disease, or diabetes." As a result, the consumer has the opportunity to make a judgment based on known information. Similarly, if someone is considering cosmetic surgery, potential risks are disclosed in addition to the benefits.

Public Motivation

A student may be motivated to give an informative speech on the warning signs of methamphetamine (meth) abuse because of the rise in the number of meth users and meth-related deaths in her community. This is public motivation. Assuming she has reliable information on meth use and meth-related deaths, her motive is to illuminate a public problem. In contrast to public motivation is private motivation. If an instructor tries to convince students to sign up for internships in his department, not because it is a beneficial academic experience, but because as internship coordinator, he gets paid per student, his motivation is private. Keeping such **hidden agendas** is unethical behavior.

As a speaker, consider whether your motives are personal or reach beyond individual concerns. Ethical speakers reveal personal motives as well as the sources of their information and opinion. Such full disclosure and transparency assists the audience in weighing any special bias, prejudices, and self-centered motivations in a message. Avoid concealing information about your source materials and your own motives because the effectiveness of your message is weakened if they are suspect.

Respect for Dissent

Voltaire (1694–1778), a French writer, historian, and philosopher, is quoted on the first page of this chapter. He writes, "I do not agree with a word you say, but I will defend to the death your right to say it." This quote illustrates the respect for dissent. Respect for dissent allows for and encourages diversity of argument and opinion. It involves seeing a different point of view as a challenge rather than a threat.

The respect for dissent means being open to accepting views different from one's own. This does not mean we have to give in. We can still advocate our position while acknowledging that others may be as firm in their opposition to it. Ideally, in a free marketplace of competing ideas, a healthy debate ensures that truth and wisdom are exposed.

☞ Developing Ethical Speaking Habits

To ensure the above four principles are incorporated into your presentation, consider the following three guidelines and five pitfalls.

Ethical Guidelines

1. Recognize the Power of the Podium

Have you ever watched a commercial and decided you had to have that product? Have you been in church when a minister tells about a needy homeless shelter, and you were compelled to donate at that moment? Have you heard a message about environmental hazards created by plastic bottles and tossed your next empty bottle of water in the recycle bin? These examples illustrate that speaking is an influential activity.

Speakers travel to campuses across the country to address a wide range of issues related to race, ethnicity, poverty, public health, alcoholism, immigration, and national security, to name a few. Some speakers are recruited by organizations on campus; others advertise their expertise in the hopes of being allowed to speak. These people understand the power of the podium. They know they can inform audiences, they can move them emotionally, or they can move them to act.

Some speakers may have national forums through the media or through their positions, such as members of Congress, the military, or even celebrities. Some abuse that power. As speakers, we strive to be aware that we have the power to persuade and the power to pass on information to others—powers that must be used for the common good.

2. Speak Truthfully

Whenever you speak before an audience, be certain of your facts. When your listeners realize your facts are wrong, they will trust you less. For example, if you give a speech on campus thefts and you blame students for the majority of crimes, when, in fact, most thefts are committed by city residents, you will lose credibility with listeners who know the facts.

3. Become Information Literate

When collecting supporting material for a speech, determine whether you are reviewing materials from a credible professional or someone who is simply writing a story, creating a web-based commerce site, or ranting in a blog.

Certain sources have more credibility than others. If you are researching the need for college students to update vaccinations with booster shots, an article in *The New England Journal of Medicine* or *Science* would be preferable to an article in *Newsweek* or *Time*. Although the latter publications are generally reliable, scientific journals are the better choice for this specific type of information. Wikipedia may be informative, but is generally not considered a reliable source on its own, and your instructor may not approve using it as a source.

Information literacy implies consuming information wisely and appropriately. A handy way to ensure your information literacy is found in the acronym PARTS.

Point of view. Recognize whether there is a point of view or bias. Is the information making every attempt at being objective or is it likely biased to serve a special interest? Even if a source claims to be "fair and balanced," you may not be getting an unbiased view from any one reporter of that organization. Complicating matters more, media personalities play at different times the role of reporter in one instance and commentator in another. Discerning the point of view is critical to consuming information intelligently.

Authority. Consider the credentials of both the author and publisher. Are they recognized as experts and/or leaders in the field? Does the author hold a terminal degree such as Ph.D. or M.D.? Is the publisher a scholarly or reputable news source? The issue of authority is challenging online. The person who is responsible for content on some Web pages and blogs is not always clear. In these cases, it is best to look for independent confirmation in other locations to ensure accuracy.

Reliability. Even if the point of view seems unbiased and the source checks out, consider whether you can believe in the accuracy and treatment of the information. Reliability is related to the credibility, or believability, of the source. For example, recent research has shown that there are health benefits to eating chocolate and drinking a glass of red wine each day. Now, if the wine or cocoa industries commissioned those studies, one might question the reliability of the findings. If the science community came to these conclusions after independent tests, the information has greater credibility. An ethical speaker will look for the most recent, authentic, and unbiased information.

Timeliness. Timeliness refers to how current or up-to-date your information is. In some cases, information as recent as last year may be outdated. Depending on the topic, some information is still timely hundreds of years later. Evaluate how important recent information is to your topic as you gather information.

Consider this: If your specific purpose is to inform your class on the latest technology for diabetes management, a simple search may lead you to the insulin pump. However, by probing a little further and finding more recent information, you should find articles about the insulin inhaler, which has more recently hit the market.

Scope. Scope refers to the extent of your research. Check to see that your research has both depth and breadth. Does the information create an overview or develop a narrow portion of your topic? Determine who the information is intended for, and whether information is too technical and clinical, or too basic. Is it appropriate for a college audience?

Our world is changing rapidly. Old facts are often wrong facts, especially in such volatile areas as public safety, science, and even our civil liberties. As you prepare your speech, take into consideration the need for currency in matters and issues that are relevant now. If you find credible evidence that appears to undermine your position, be honest enough to evaluate it fairly and change your position if warranted. Throughout this process, keep in mind your ethical obligation to present accurate information to your listeners. Here are a few common pitfalls to keep in mind:

Ethical Pitfalls

1. Avoid Purposeful Ambiguity

When we leave out specific detail, we can paint a misleading picture. Choose words carefully to communicate your point. Realize, for example, that references to "hazing abuses" may conjure images of death and bodily injury to some, while others may think of harmless fraternity pranks. Similarly, choose your supporting materials carefully. Ambiguities often stem from inadequate or sloppy research.

2. Avoid Rumors and Innuendos

It is unethical to base your speeches on rumors. Rumors are unproven charges, usually about an individual. By using them as facts, you can tarnish—or ruin—a reputation and convey misleading information to your audience.

Pop culture is rife with rumors. Weekly entertainment magazines are filled with stories about the lives of Hollywood celebrities, many of which are based on rumors. We find out that stars are battling drug and alcohol abuse, or that they are gaining or losing weight. We read that Jen is dating Michael. Oh, no, they just broke up. Wait … they are back together. Now they are married. Oops, they are divorced. She is pregnant. Is it his? Or does it belong to old boyfriend? Every aspect of their lives is reported, frequently without any reliance on facts.

It is also ethically unacceptable to use innuendo to support a point. **Innuendos** are veiled lies, hints, or remarks that something is what it is not. Innuendo frequently surfaces in the heat of a strongly contested political race. The exaggerated rhetoric of opponents results in observations ranging from misstatements about events to hints about improprieties in the alleged behavior of the political opponent. An ethical speaker avoids any use of rumor or innuendo when preparing a speech.

3. Uphold Unpopular Ideas

Speaking in support of the public good implies a willingness to air a diversity of opinions, even when these opinions are unpopular. According to Roderick Hart (1985), professor of communication, we must "accept boat rocking, protests, and free speech as a necessary and desirable part of [our] tradition" (p. 162). Your goal as a speaker can be to encourage the "ideal of the best ideas rising to the surface of debate" (p. 46). Despite the tradition of free speech in Western society, taking an unpopular stand at the podium is not easy, especially when the speaker faces the threat of repercussions.

4. Avoid Hidden Agendas

Consider Joyce, a real estate agent with a home for sale in a suburban community that is suffering from the real estate recession. Many homes are for sale but the market contains too few buyers. Joyce is one among dozens of agents who will find it difficult to make a satisfactory living unless conditions improve. To attract potential homebuyers, Joyce gives a series of speeches in a nearby city, extolling the virtues of suburban life. Although much of what she says is true, Joyce bends some facts to make her real estate seem the most attractive and affordable. For example, she tells her listeners that jobs are available, when in fact, the job market is weak (the rosy employment figures she used are a decade old). Joyce also mentioned that the community schools are among the top in the state, when, in fact, only one in five is ranked above the state average. With her goal of restoring that community to its former economic health, Joyce feels justified in this manipulation.

Do the ends justify the means? While Joyce's intentions were good, her ethics were slimy. As a speaker, you have only one ethical choice: to present the strongest possible legitimate argument, thus allowing each listener to evaluate the argument on its merits.

5. Avoid Excessive and Inappropriate Emotional Appeals

As listeners, we expect speakers to make assertions that are supported by sound reasoning. We expect the speech to flow logically, and to include relevant supporting material. However, some speakers prey on our fears or ignorance and rely heavily on the use of excessive and inappropriate appeals to emotion. To be ethical, emotional appeals must be built on a firm foundation of good reasoning and should never be used to take advantage of susceptible listeners. In our chapter on persuasive speaking, we examine further the nature of emotional appeals. However, following are four circumstances that create ethical concern.

Deception. Your speech creates a need in your audience through deception and requires an action that will primarily benefit you. For example, it is manipulative and unethical to try to convince a group of parents that the *only way* their children will succeed in school is to purchase an educational program that is comprehensive in detail, according to the company you represent.

Manipulation. This emotional appeal is aimed at taking advantage of those particularly susceptible to manipulation. A bit of channel surfing late at night will bring the viewer to quite a number of infomercials full of emotional appeals to persuade the viewer to purchase expensive programs that are supposed to lead them to considerable wealth, health, or both.

Confusion. Emotional appeals are part of a sustained plan to confuse an audience and make them feel insecure and helpless. If, as a community leader, you oppose the effort to establish group homes for the developmentally challenged children by referring repeatedly to the threat these residents pose to the neighborhood children, you leave your listeners feeling vulnerable and frightened. Fear can become so intense that homeowners may dismiss facts and expert opinions that demonstrate developmentally challenged persons are neither violent nor emotionally unstable.

Fallacies. If a speaker realizes his/her logic will not hold up under scrutiny, he/she may appeal to audience emotions to disguise the deficit. Instead of relying on facts to convince listeners, the speaker appeals to the audience's emotional needs. Unethical speakers disguise messages and deceive listeners to achieve their goal, including the following **fallacies**: name calling, glittering generalities, testimonials, plainfolks, and bandwagoning.

Name calling involves linking a person or group with a negative symbol. In a persuasive speech, if your purpose is to convince your audience that abortion is morally wrong, you would be engaging in name calling if you referred to individuals who support a woman's right to choose as "murderers" and "baby-killers." You may believe these labels are truthful, but they are emotionally charged names that will arouse emotions in your audience, and many listeners may tune you out.

Glittering generalities rely on the audience's emotional responses to values such as home, country, and freedom. Suppose the real issues of a campaign are problems associated with the growing budget deficit, illegal immigration, and dependence on foreign oil. If a candidate avoids these issues and argues for keeping the Ten Commandments in front of courthouses, reciting the pledge of allegiance more often, and amending the Constitution to prevent flag-burning, that particular candidate is likely relying considerably on glittering generalities. Although it is acceptable to talk about these latter concerns, manipulating the audience's response so that critical judgments about major issues are clouded in other areas is unethical.

Testimonials can be both helpful and destructive. People who have had their cholesterol levels improve because of a particular prescription medicine may lead others to success. People who love their hybrid cars may help others make the decision to buy one. However, we are bombarded by celebrities touting countless products including shampoo, sports drinks, and phone service because they are paid to do so, not because they have expert knowledge of those products. In most cases no damage is done.

Years ago, however, Suzanne Somers, an actress who sells health, beauty, and fitness products, created an uproar in the scientific community when she promoted her own diet plan. In addition to the fact that she lacked professional qualifications, her diet plan de-emphasized exercise and she suggested a daily caloric threshold that was dangerous. Since it is well known that any diet or new exercise regimen should be discussed with a medical professional, her testimonial could be damaging.

Plain folks is an effort to identify with the audience. Be cautious when a speaker tells an audience, "Believe me, because I'm just like you." Speakers who present themselves as "plain folks" may be building an identification with their audience appropriately (something speakers often want to do), or they may be manipulating their listeners. An incident where an investment adviser conducting a seminar for senior citizens told his audience:

One main reason I chose this career path is because my own parents, not unlike you gathered here tonight, did not have the opportunities I am offering you. I discovered that they are struggling in their retirement years to make ends meet on a monthly basis. Like you, they worked hard throughout their careers. However, what was available to them to live on when they left their work was modest.

This speaker appeared believable, but in fact, his parents retired with considerable funds acquired from owning a successful business for 30 years. The emotional tactic of using plain folks as an emotional appeal was simply to gain sales.

Bandwagoning is another unethical method of deception. Often listeners are uncomfortable taking a position no one else supports. Realizing this reluctance, unethical speakers may convince their listeners to support their point of view by telling them that "everyone else" is already involved. For example, you may live in a residence hall on a campus where your school's mascot is being threatened with extinction. A rally will be held, and someone on your floor is going door-to-door telling all the residents that "everybody" on campus will be at the rally to support the mascot. Chances are, this is an exaggeration.

As a speaker, try to convince others of the weight of your evidence—not the popularity of your opinion. In the case above, the resident should not be asking everyone to jump on the bandwagon, but should be explaining to people why keeping the mascot is a positive thing.

☞ Avoiding Unethical Practices

After making the commitment to maintain ethical standards as a speaker, you should ensure that your research and speech delivery reflect your commitment. The following questions will help you avoid unethical practices (Johannesen, 1990).

Research
* Have I used false, fabricated, misrepresented, distorted, or irrelevant evidence to support my arguments or claims?
* Have I intentionally used unsupported, misleading, or illogical reasoning?
* Have I oversimplified complex situations into simplistic either–or, bipolar views or choices?

Delivery
* Will I represent myself as informed or as being an "expert" on a subject when I am not?
* Will I deceive my audience by concealing my real purpose, self-interest, the group I represent, or my position as an advocate of a viewpoint?
* Will I distort, hide, or misrepresent the number, scope, intensity, or undesirable aspects, consequences, or effects?
* Will I use emotional appeals that lack a supporting basis of evidence or reasoning or that would not be accepted if the audience had time to examine the subject themselves?
* Will I pretend certainty where tentativeness and degrees of probability would be more accurate?
* Will I advocate something in which I do not believe myself? (p. 254)

☞　Summary

Because of the many ethical abuses that have taken place in recent years, many have become skeptical about the ethics of public speakers. The U.S. Bill of Rights guarantees freedom of speech. This does not mean that all speech is acceptable, appropriate, or ethical. Ethics is a central part of freedom of speech and ties closely to our personal value systems.

An ethical speaker cites sources when the words spoken are not his/her own, thus avoiding plagiarizing, or using someone else's words. Ethical public speaking is anchored in the values of the speaker, his or her audience, and the larger society. Ethical speakers engage in a "dialogue" with their audience, communicating qualities such as trust and directness, while unethical speakers engage in a monologue as they manipulate their audience for their own profit. Promoting ethical speaking is accomplished by developing the habits of search, justice, public motivation, and respect for dissent. This means that speakers will research their topic, present ideas fairly, make private motives known, and allow for opinions that may conflict with their own.

Ethics is part of every step of speech development. Remember these guidelines: Understand the power of the podium, speak truthfully, and become information literate—know your facts, use credible sources, use current and reliable information, avoid ethical pitfalls, including purposeful ambiguity, rumors, and innuendo, avoiding unpopular ideas, hidden agendas, and using excessive and inappropriate emotional appeals. Unethical speakers disguise messages and deceive listeners to achieve their goal. This is accomplished using a variety of fallacies. Avoid common fallacies, including name calling, glittering generalities, testimonials, plainfolks, and bandwagoning. After committing to being an ethical speaker, you may want to check your research and delivery by asking yourself specific questions that we provide.

☞　References

Bruner, B., & Haney, E. (n.d.). *Civil Rights Timeline: Milestones in the Civil Rights Movement.* Info Please. Retrieved August 4, 2011 from www.infoplease.com/spot/civilrightstimeline1.html

Cooper, L. (1960). *The Rhetoric of Aristotle.* Upper Saddle River, NJ: Prentice Hall.

Corn-Revere, R. (2006). *Internet and the First Amendment.* Retrieved from www.firstamendementcenter.org.

Hart, R. (1985). The Politics of Communication Studies: An Address to Undergraduates. *Communication Education, 34,* 162.

Johannesen, Richard L. (1971). The Emerging Concept of Communication as Dialogue. *Quarterly Journal of Speech, 57,* 373382.

Johannesen, R. L. (1990). *Ethics in Communication.* Prospect Heights, IL: Waveland Press.

McCroskey, J. C., & Young, T. J. (1981). Ethos and Credibility: The Construct and Its Measurement After Three Decades. *The Central States Speech Journal, 22,* 24–34.

Pilkington, E. (2009, January 29). Barack Obama Inauguration Speech. *The Guardian.* Retrieved August 4, 2011 from www.guardian.co.uk/world/2009/jan/20/barack-obama-inauguration-us-speech.

The Y, Share the News. (2010, July 12). A Brand New Day: The YMCA Unveils New Brand Strategy to Further Community Impact. Washington, DC. Retrieved August 4, 2011 from www.ymca.net/news-releases/20100712-brand-new-day.html.

Sifri, D. (2006). *Chinese Bloggers Top 17 Million.* Retrieved May 26, 2006 from www.vnunet.com.

Wallace, K. 1987. An Ethical Basis of Communication. *The Speech Teacher, 4,* 1–9.

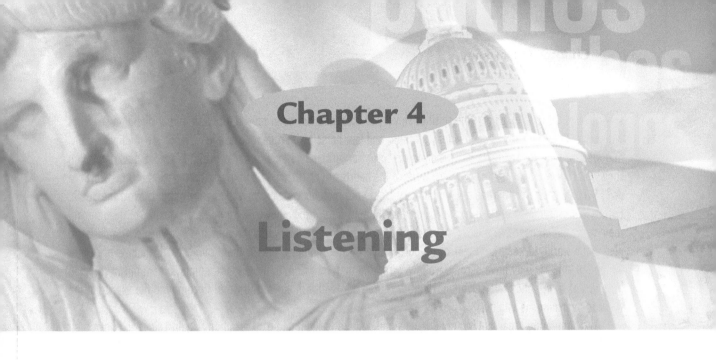

Chapter 4

Listening

"We have two ears and only one tongue in order that we may hear more and speak less."
—Diogenes Laërtius

SPEECH: Angelina Grimké Weld—Pennsylvania Hall Speech

Pennsylvania Hall was built in Philadelphia to provide a space for abolitionists to speak out against the evils of slavery. Monday, May 14, 1838 marked the official opening of the building. On Tuesday, the Anti-Slavery Convention of American Women met in the hall. Outside, an increasingly unruly mob was assembling. Angelina Grimké Weld (1805–1879), a strong advocate against slavery, spoke to the audience of over 3,000 reformers for over an hour. At the end of her speech, amid verbal and physical threats from the protesters, the assembled abolitionists linked arms and left the hall. The angry mob returned the next day and burned the building to the ground.

Source: http://www.pbs.org/wgbh/aia/part4/4p2938.html

Angelina Grimké Weld's speech at Pennsylvania Hall on May 15, 1838

Men, brethren and fathers—mothers, daughters and sisters, what came ye out for to see? A reed shaken with the wind? Is it curiosity merely, or a deep sympathy with the perishing slave, that has brought this large audience together? [A yell from the mob without the building.] Those voices without ought to awaken and call out our warmest sympathies. Deluded beings! "they know not what they do." They know not that they are undermining their own rights and their own happiness, temporal and eternal. Do you ask, "what has the North to do with slavery?" Hear it—hear it.

Those voices without tell us that the spirit of slavery is *here*, and has been roused to wrath by our abolition speeches and conventions: for surely liberty would not foam and tear herself with rage, because her friends are multiplied daily, and meetings are held in quick succession to set forth her virtues and extend her peaceful kingdom. This opposition shows that slavery has done its deadliest work in the hearts of our citizens. Do you ask, then, "what has the North to do?" I answer, cast out first the spirit of slavery from your own hearts, and then lend your aid to convert the South. Each one present has a work to do, be his or her situation what it may, however limited their means, or insignificant their supposed influence. The great men of this country will not do this work; the church will never do it. A desire to please the world, to keep the favor of all parties and of all conditions, makes them dumb on this and every other unpopular subject. They have become worldly-wise, and therefore God, in his wisdom, employs them not to carry on his plans of reformation and salvation. He hath chosen the foolish things of the world to confound the wise, and the weak to overcome the mighty.

As a Southerner I feel that it is my duty to stand up here to-night and bear testimony against slavery. I have seen it—I have seen it. I know it has horrors that can never be described. I was brought up under its wing: I witnessed for many years its demoralizing influences, and its destructiveness to human happiness. It is admitted by some that the slave is not happy under the *worst* forms of slavery. But I have *never* seen a happy slave. I have seen him dance in his chains, it is true; but he was not happy. There is a wide difference between happiness and mirth. Man cannot enjoy the former while his manhood is destroyed, and that part of the being which is necessary to the making, and to the enjoyment of happiness, is completely blotted out. The slaves, however, may be, and sometimes are, mirthful. When hope is extinguished, they say, "let us eat and drink, for tomorrow we die." [Just then stones were thrown at the windows,—a great noise without, and commotion within.] What is a mob? What would the breaking of every window be? What would the leveling of this Hall be? Any evidence that we are wrong, or that slavery is a good and wholesome institution? What if the mob should now burst in upon us, break up our meeting and commit violence upon our persons—would this be any thing compared with what the slaves endure? No, no: and we do not remember them "as bound with them," if we shrink in the time of peril, or feel unwilling to sacrifice ourselves, if need be, for their sake. [Great noise.] I thank the Lord that there is yet life left enough to feel the truth, even though it rages at it—that conscience is not so completely seared as to be unmoved by the truth of the living God.

Many persons go to the South for a season, and are hospitably entertained in the parlor and at the table of the slave-holder. They never enter the huts of the slaves; they know nothing of the dark side of the picture, and they return home with praises on their lips of the generous character of those with whom they had tarried. Or if they have witnessed the cruelties of slavery, by remaining silent spectators they have naturally become callous—an insensibility has ensued which prepares them to apologize even for barbarity. Nothing but the corrupting influence of slavery on the hearts of the Northern people can induce them to apologize for it; and much will have been done for the destruction of Southern slavery when we have so reformed the North that no one here will be willing to risk his reputation by advocating or even excusing the holding of men as property. The South know it, and acknowledge that as fast as our principles prevail, the hold of the master must be relaxed. [Another outbreak of mobocratic spirit, and some confusion in the house.]

How wonderfully constituted is the human mind! How it resists, as long as it can, all efforts made to reclaim from error! I feel that all this disturbance is but an evidence that our efforts are the best that could have been adopted, or else the friends of slavery would not care for what we say and do. The South know what we do. I am thankful that they are reached by our efforts. Many times have I wept in the land of my birth, over the system of slavery. I knew of none who sympathized in my feelings—I was unaware that any efforts were made to deliver the oppressed—no voice in the wilderness was heard calling on the people to repent and do works meet for repentance—and my heart sickened within me. Oh, how should I have rejoiced to know that such efforts as these were being made. I only wonder that I had such feelings. I wonder when I reflect under what influence I was brought up that my heart is not harder than the nether millstone. But in the midst of temptation I was preserved, and my sympathy grew warmer, and my hatred of slavery more inveterate, until at last I have exiled myself from my native land because I could no longer endure to hear the wailing of the slave. I fled to the land of Penn; for here, thought I, sympathy for the slave will surely be found. But I found it not. The people were kind and hospitable, but the slave had no place in their thoughts. Whenever questions were put to me as to his condition, I felt that they were dictated by an idle curiosity, rather than by that deep feeling which would lead to effort for his rescue. I therefore shut up my grief in my own heart. I remembered that I was a Carolinian, from a state which framed this iniquity by law. I knew that throughout her territory was continual suffering, on the one part, and continual brutality and sin on the other. Every Southern breeze wafted to me the discordant tones of weeping and wailing, shrieks and groans, mingled with prayers and blasphemous curses. I thought there was no hope; that the wicked would go on in his wickedness, until he had destroyed both himself and his country. My heart sunk within me at the abominations in the midst of which I had been born and educated. What will it avail, cried I in bitterness of spirit, to expose to the gaze of strangers the horrors and pollutions of slavery, when there is no ear to hear nor heart to feel and pray for the slave. The language of my soul was, "Oh tell it not in Gath, publish it not in the streets of Askelon." But how different do I feel now! Animated with hope, nay, with an assurance of the triumph of liberty and good will to man, I will lift up my voice like a trumpet, and show this people their transgression, their sins of omission towards the slave, and what they can do towards affecting Southern mind, and overthrowing Southern oppression.

We may talk of occupying neutral ground, but on this subject, in its present attitude, there is no such thing as neutral ground. He that is not for us is against us, and he that gathereth not with us, scattereth abroad. If you are on what you suppose to be neutral ground, the South look upon you as on the side of the oppressor. And is there one who loves his country willing to give his influence, even indirectly, in favor of slavery—that curse of nations? God swept Egypt with the besom of destruction, and punished Judea also with a sore punishment, because of slavery. And have we any reason to believe that he is less just now?—or that he will be more favorable to us than to his own "peculiar people?" [Shoutings, stones thrown against the windows, etc.]

There is nothing to be feared from those who would stop our mouths, but they themselves should fear and tremble. The current is even now setting fast against them. If the arm of the North had not caused the Bastille of slavery to totter to its foundation, you would not hear those cries. A few years ago, and the South felt secure, and with a contemptuous sneer asked, "Who are the abolitionists? The abolitionists are nothing?"—Ay, in one sense they were nothing, and they are nothing still. But in this we rejoice, that "God has chosen things that are not to bring to nought things that are." [Mob again disturbed the meeting.]

We often hear the question asked, "What shall we do?" Here is an opportunity for doing something now. Every man and every woman present may do something by showing that we fear not a mob, and, in the midst of threatenings and revilings, by opening our mouths for the dumb and pleading the cause of those who are ready to perish.

To work as we should in this cause, we must know what Slavery is. Let me urge you then to buy the books which have been written on this subject and read them, and then lend them to your neighbors. Give your money no longer for things which pander to pride and lust, but aid in scattering "the living coals of truth" upon the naked heart of this nation,—in circulating appeals to the sympathies of Christians in behalf of the outraged and suffering slave. But, it is said by some, our "books and papers do not speak the truth." Why, then, do they not contradict what we say? They cannot. Moreover the South has entreated, nay commanded us to be silent; and what greater evidence of the truth of our publications could be desired?

Women of Philadelphia! allow me as a Southern woman, with much attachment to the land of my birth, to entreat you to come up to this work. Especially let me urge you to petition. *Men* may settle this and other questions at the ballot-box, but you have no such right; it is only through petitions that you can reach the Legislature. It is therefore peculiarly *your* duty to petition. Do you say, "It does no good?" The South already turns pale at the number sent. They have read the reports of the proceedings of Congress, and there have seen that among other petitions were very many from the women of the North on the subject of slavery. This fact has called the attention of the South to the subject. How could we expect to have done more as yet? Men who hold the rod over slaves, rule in the councils of the nation: and they deny our right to petition and to remonstrate against abuses of our sex and of our kind. We have these rights, however, from our God. Only let us exercise them: and though often turned away unanswered, let us remember the influence of importunity upon the unjust judge, and act accordingly. The fact that the South look with jealousy upon our measures shows that they are effectual. There is, therefore, no cause for doubting or despair, but rather for rejoicing.

It was remarked in England that women did much to abolish Slavery in her colonies. Nor are they now idle. Numerous petitions from them have recently been presented to the Queen, to abolish the apprenticeship with its cruelties nearly equal to those of the system whose place it supplies. One petition two miles and a quarter long has been presented. And do you think these labors will be in vain? Let the history of the past answer. When the women of these States send up to Congress such a petition, our legislators will arise as did those of England, and say, "When all the maids and matrons of the land are knocking at our doors we must legislate." Let the zeal and love, the faith and works of our English sisters quicken ours—that while the slaves continue to suffer, and when they shout deliverance, we may feel the satisfaction of *having done what we could.*

Credit: History of Pennsylvania Hall which was Destroyed by a Mob on the 17th of May, 1838
Negro Universities Press, A Division of Greenwood Publishing Corp,
New York, 1969

http://www.pbs.org/wgbh/aia/part4/4h2939t.html

Listening is often considered THE most important communication skill. Without it, messages frequently go unheard or are misunderstood. Without skillful listening (often referred to as "active listening"), positive situations can deteriorate into negative situations, and negative situations can disintegrate into chaos, hostility, even warfare.

Consider the following scenario. In the midst of a heated disagreement, your partner blurts out: "That's the problem with our relationship—you never listen to me!" Frustrated, you reply, "Oh, yeah? Well, you never listen to *me*!" Then you both go to separate rooms and slam the door. Animosity builds. You think, "Why can't I find anyone who's a good listener?"

All of us witness or experience situations like these daily. They annoy us, they cause pain, they cost money. Yet they continue. Why? The answer lies in our failure to value and consciously try to improve our listening skills. This chapter provides a guided tour through the listening process. First, we explore what listening is, discovering that our careless definitions of listening may be one reason why we listen so poorly. Next, we examine why we usually do not learn to listen well and the costs incurred by poor listening. Then our tour takes us to the stages of the listening process, where we learn about how to improve each stage of listening. We then deal with barriers to effective listening and how to overcome them. Our final destination offers ways to apply our listening skills in specific contexts such as classes, relationships, and oral presentations.

👉   What Is Listening?

Too often we tend to take listening for granted. After all, I listen to everything anyone says—don't you? Of course not! We often have mistaken notions about listening, then the costs of poor listening become apparent only after our listening has failed. So, what does listening involve?

To understand what listening is, we first should recognize what it is not. **Hearing** is the physical process of receiving sound. If someone has difficulty hearing, the challenge may lie in physical barriers such as a distracting communication environment or damage to the person's auditory abilities (for example, nerve damage). Hearing also can be unintentional. While waiting outside a professor's door, we may accidentally catch part of a private conversation. In a classroom, you might notice a classmate's stomach growling. At other times, we might strain to hear, making a conscious effort to catch every word. Many medical devices are available to assist with various types of hearing reduction or loss. For example, hearing aids can amplify sound volume and reduce distortions. Yet there are no prospects for any sort of technology that can serve as a listening aid. Why not?

Listening does include hearing, but it goes far beyond the physical process of receiving sounds (Rane, 2011). Figure 4.1 summarizes these differences between hearing and listening. The International Listening Association (1996) defines **listening** as "the process of receiving, constructing meaning from, and responding to spoken and/or nonverbal messages." Let's examine the main ingredients of our definition.

In the definition, *process* indicates that listening is a complex series of activities and events that are ever changing, ongoing, and irreversible—just as communication itself is a process. In your past you have failed to listen to messages that you later wished that you had listened to, and you have listened to messages that you wished you had ignored. The process begins with an event in time with many available sensations such as sights, sounds, aromas, etc. The listener chooses to hear a spoken verbal message and the accompanying nonverbal elements such as voice inflection, rate, and tone. The listener then interprets the words and phrases and makes the association with his or her mental concepts (such as recognizing a voice as belonging to a friend). The listener then makes inferences, generalizes, abstracts, and/or concludes from the mental associations and responds verbally and/or nonverbally and activates degrees of memory. So we find that listening requires effort and decoding or interpreting sounds once they are heard.

Receiving refers to the initial step in the listening process in which the verbal message is taken in or perceived through the sense of hearing and the nonverbal messages perceived through sight,

Hearing	**Listening**
Can be accidental or purposeful	Intentional
Automatic	Requires effort and training
Physiological process	Interpretive process
Receive sounds	Decode messages

Figure 4.1   Hearing Versus Listening

hearing, and sometimes touch. You as the listener choose or select whether you attend to the spoken verbal message among a multitude of stimuli within a particular situation or environment.

It is very difficult to listen to someone speaking while you are reading or hearing a different verbal message and expect to comprehend both. CNN Headline News, MSNBC, and Fox News (and many other news networks) give you the opportunity to prove it for yourself. Try reading the text of other news stories scrolling across the bottom of the screen at the same instant you are listening to the commentator. You may tune in and out but cannot fully perceive both at the same time. Similarly, we find it very difficult to process verbal and visual messages that conflict. Try to say aloud the *color* of the words printed below (not the words, but the color of the type) in the order they appear:

ORANGE RED GREEN
PURPLE BLUE **BROWN**
WHITE

Why was that apparently straightforward task so difficult? You were receiving inconsistent messages. Your visual perception told you the color of the type, but your verbal perception cued you to say the word. The lesson: When we send mixed or competing signals, reception suffers.

Constructing meaning is the association of words and phrases with references or concepts previously experienced and established in one's mind. Meanings have to be negotiated between communicators. Listeners decide what words mean and how much importance they have. The meanings of the words "freedom" and "democracy" are very abstract and rely on each listener to create verbal meaning. The same point holds for collections of words. Anthologies of "great speeches" emerge from audiences reacting to those presentations over time, not by the speakers deciding how they should be interpreted. More broadly, listeners ultimately have the power to decide whether someone's communication is understood, laughed at, respected, preserved, or ignored.

Responding to spoken verbal and accompanying nonverbal messages is a reaction to what speakers say and the way they say it. The listener's verbal response may be in the form of questions, paraphrased messages, or repeating what the speaker said. The nonverbal, visual responses may be change in eye behavior, nod of the head, shrug of the shoulders, turning away, smiling, altering body posture, or hand gestures.

Why Care about Listening?

Listening is one of the four fundamental language skills along with reading, writing, and speaking. Listening is the first language skill we use, yet ironically the skill that we least study and develop. It is the skill that employers respect most in an employee, and the skill that lovers admire most in loved ones. Throughout formal schooling, the average student spends at least half of the time listening (Atwater, 1992). The typical manager spends about 60 percent of each day listening (HighGain.com, 2004). As much as 80 percent of an ordinary person's time awake is spent doing some sort of listening (Pearce, Johnson, & Barker, 1995).

Amazingly, although we use listening more than any other communication skill, we tend to spend the least time learning how to do it. How many years did you spend learning to write? If you are taking a course in writing, you are still learning! You probably recall entire classes throughout elementary school devoted to teaching you how to read. Speaking usually gets far less attention, but formal practice in speaking is widespread at colleges and universities. Many high schools offer speech courses or formal speech activities such as competitive debate.

What about listening? Chances are that until this course relatively few of your classmates received specific instruction in listening. Curricular studies confirm this experience. On the average, "students get 12 years of formal training in writing, 6–8 years in reading, 1–2 years in speaking, and from 0–1/2 year in listening" (Hyslop & Tone, 1988). An estimated 5 percent of the population has any formal training in listening (Lindahl, 2003), and businesses are scrambling to address this lack of listening background because it could reduce employee performance (Cooper, 1997; Shepherd, Castleberry, & Ridnour, 1997).

Although "listening in business is a basic competency," the sad fact is that many "graduates are considered, by both themselves and their employers, to lack adequate listening skills" (Stone, Lightbody, & Whait, 2013, p. 169).

Why haven't we learned how to listen? Traditionally, the study of communication has focused on the speaker or the message source. For centuries, texts on public speaking never mentioned listening. Instead the authors preferred the more visible communication skill of presenting speeches. We also may be self-centered as communicators. In the competitive worlds of academics and business, people prefer to promote their own viewpoints instead of allowing time for others to express theirs (Hayakawa, 1955).

Somebody definitely *should* teach us listening. Measurements of listening performance show abysmal results. Since we tend to take listening for granted, we assume that listening is easy and natural. We often develop false confidence that we listen well, claiming that we are good listeners (Halone et al., 1998). Yet the average listener, including students and employees, understands and remembers only about 50 percent of a conversation, and within two days it drops to only 25 percent. Imagine studying for a test and remembering only one-quarter of the material 48 hours later! Overall listening accuracy hovers around 25 percent (Alessandra, 1995; Atwater, 1992; Pearce, Johnson, & Barker, 1995).

We need to learn how to listen because the stakes are high. Poor listening incurs tremendous costs. First, consider the financial costs. Listening specialist Don Stacks estimated that poor listening causes businesses to lose $1 billion per day (Arthur W. Page Society, 2004). "Listening is a critical skill for success. The impact of ineffective listening can be significant. If poor listening habits caused every worker in the United States to make just one $5 mistake a year, the total cost would be more than half a billion dollars!" (McKeone, 2004). Within professional organizations, the ability to listen accurately proves to be a key factor in how far and how fast an employee will advance (Atwater, 1992). Listening to customers has been rated the top factor in successful selling and the number one reason for poor sales performance (Shepherd, Castleberry, & Ridnour, 1997). Supervisors also rate listening to employees as the most vital tool in evaluating and directing them (Hunsaker & Alessandra, 1986). If you want to be considered an effective communicator on the job, you had better learn to listen. Co-workers associate good job performance with good listening (Johnson, Pearce, Tuten, & Sinclair, 2003).

Next, think about the emotional toll. Marital and familial ties weaken under pressure of poor listening. "Ineffective listening is also acknowledged to be one of the primary contributors to divorce and to the inability of a parent and child to openly communicate" (Alessandra, 1995). We know how frustrating and insulting it can be to interact with someone who seems not to listen. People commonly list "good listener" as one of the most desirable characteristics in a friend or mate.

Finally, listening has academic consequences. Improving your listening skills has immediate and long-term benefits. Considering that the average student retains only one out of every four words uttered in the classroom, the better listener will have a more accurate record of class discussions. Your notes should become more precise and more helpful as a study guide. In the long term, as you become a better listener you will get more involved in your classes. You will be more likely to ask questions and engage in discussion, so you will deepen your understanding of the subject. Faculty agree. Surveys indicate that faculty consider effective listening highly important for the academic success of students—especially those who speak English as a second language (Johns, 1981).

The Listening Process

Although we may have developed the bad habit of listening haphazardly, listening is a structured process. Listening consists of five stages: receiving, understanding, evaluating, recalling, and responding. This section explains each stage of listening, identifies challenges associated with each stage, and offers ways to improve that component of listening. Before delving into those stages, let's consider what we listen to in the first place and how we process it.

Listening Filters

With the number of messages coming toward us in the communication environment, it is impossible to process everything. The challenge is to get and process the important, relevant messages while ignoring or de-emphasizing the distractions and distortions. **Listening filters** help sort the confused mass of incoming messages into sensible, manageable information. When our listening filters work well, we receive and deal with only the information we need. An effective filter keeps useful material while screening out everything else. Problems arise, however, when our filters interfere with the listening process.

Initially, **selective attention** determines which incoming messages we process at all. Selective attention leads us to seek out and concentrate on communication that we find acceptable. We hear what we want to hear. A rally of Republicans will tend to attract a Republican audience, for example. Selective attention does help listeners sort through the mass of messages competing for attention. The problem is that selective attention also can restrict our exposure to new and possibly beneficial information because we never leave our comfort zone. You might see a college dining hall filled with tables of students who seem racially or culturally segregated, with everyone sitting at a table alongside people of similar identity. Selective attention contributes to this self-segregation. Since listeners tend to prioritize familiar, agreeable messages, they may avoid a novelty such as a different culture. We need to expand our selective attention when we seek to widen our knowledge and understanding.

Selective interpretation can lead us to alter message content to conform with our beliefs. We can protect ourselves against possibly distorting messages through selective interpretation. We can take a cue from scientists, who recognize that our conclusions should be shaped by our experiences instead of force-fitting our experiences to conform to pre-existing beliefs. Scientists recognize that we often must modify our beliefs to accommodate new experiences. Another precaution would be to check our interpretations by comparing them to those of other listeners. How do you know your class notes are accurate and do not reflect only your own perspective on the course material? Don't wait until the next test to find out. Compare your notes with the notes of several other students to improve accuracy and escape from the biases of your own worldview.

Step One: Receiving

At the **receiving** stage, listening is equivalent to hearing. Reception involves the ways that we obtain sounds. This step must come first in the listening process. With all of the sounds we encounter, we must strategically select what we will receive. If sounds are inaudible, garbled, or otherwise distorted, we should not proceed with listening until we can clarify what was heard. If we receive only part of a message, trying to listen is like trying to read a book with random pages missing.

Challenges to Receiving

Information Overload. Reception becomes a bigger problem year after year because of **information overload**: The number of incoming messages exceeds our ability to process them. I distinctly recall the days prior to cable television when "good" reception meant three or four channels. Now a cable or satellite package with fewer than 150 channels seems meager. The Internet allows us to access most major news sources in every country throughout the world. Bloggers (people who post online diaries/commentaries) track events throughout the world as they happen. Electronic gadgets beg for our attention as we can check text messages, play video games, take photos, and browse the Internet all through our cell phone that might ring at any moment. The problem is that while the sources of information expand exponentially, we still process the information at about the same speed as our grandparents and great-grandparents did. We might get 500 channels on TV, but a 30-minute program still takes 30 minutes to watch. We can bookmark 50 sites on our Web browser, but we still have to read them one screen at a time. A 10-minute speech still takes 10 minutes to listen to. With all this data coming to us so fast, it's no wonder we miss a lot.

Aside from the sheer number of messages heading toward us, we may not prioritize messages well. Often we find ourselves preoccupied by irrelevant stimuli that lure us away from the speaker's message. If you have many incoming messages, try to focus only on the most important ones (the ones most relevant to your task or to your relationship) and defer or ignore the other messages.

Examples: Poor Prioritization

1. Your mother is having a serious conversation with you about finances. You answer a call on your cell phone. Mom's conclusion: "My child doesn't value me." Better choice: You can return the call, so delay responding to it until after the conversation.
2. (True story) A professor returns a call from a student. After a minute of conversation, the student places the professor on hold to talk with a friend. What would you do in this situation if you were the student? If you were the professor?

Consider what you want to accomplish in the communication situation. If you receive messages from other sources (a friend enters the room, etc.), decide whether the new message can improve the communication you are in already. Ideally, you might connect competing stimuli. For example, suppose you notice a rare, expensive sports car pull up next to the window while a speaker is giving a presentation on air pollution. Instead of ignoring the speech and admiring the sports car, connect the new stimulus (the fancy sports car) to the speaker's message. You might consider, "I wonder how much pollution that car emits," or "The speaker just mentioned the Clean Air Act reducing factory smokestack emissions. Would the Clean Air Act apply to cars like that as well?" Instead of distracting you, the new experience (the car's arrival) has urged you to expand your understanding and application of the speaker's topic.

Speed of Speaking and Listening. Another challenge to reception is the **speaking-listening gap**: We can listen much more rapidly than most people speak. Generally, a rate of about 150 to a bit more than 200 words per minute sounds "normal" in a conversation or lecture. Yet we can listen at a rate of 400 to 800 words per minute with minimal loss of comprehension (Atwater, 1992; Alessandra, 1995). Since we process speech at two to four times the rate most speakers are talking, we have a lot of time for our minds to wander. How do you occupy this "spare time"? Chances are that you, like most of us, start thinking of all sort of irrelevant things. Try to occupy your listening time with activities that can enhance your listening experience: take notes, think about questions, or try repeating to yourself the speaker's most recent point.

Self-Centered Listening. Focusing only on yourself—what you want from the message rather than what the speaker has to offer—distorts messages by not considering the speaker's motives. Self-centered listeners tend to listen only long enough to reach a hasty judgment, usually one that confirms a pre-existing opinion. Show respect for speakers by taking their views seriously and giving them a hearing even if you disagree (Smith, 2004). To maximize your listening ability, focus on the speaker's rationale for sharing the information. Instead of listening only for what pleases you or confirms your own beliefs, allow the other person a chance to have his or her say. Wait to speak until there is a natural lapse in conversation or an appropriate time for questions.

Making Time to Listen. Finally, you might discover that you simply cannot devote adequate time and effort to the listening situation. If you find this happening, you should try to defer the communication until a time when you can devote more energy to it. For example, I am amazed at the students who will attend class while they are dreadfully ill, semi-conscious, and clearly cannot attend to what is happening in the classroom. They would benefit more by informing the instructor of the situation and then reviewing the class notes or discussing the class when they can process the information fully. In group situations, you should recognize when you cannot take the time or have the mental focus to listen properly. Listening does take time and effort, so choose to listen only when you can invest in the endeavor.

How to Improve Receiving

Reduce Distractions. Anything that competes with the communicator's message qualifies as a distraction. Students claim that some of the most distracting elements in classrooms are the noises and behaviors of the students sitting near them. Other distractions include room temperature, the student's own preoccupations and tiredness, and lack of interest. When studying in an online environment, the distractions multiply. Do you work on your online course units while keeping several unrelated windows open on your screen—maybe your e-mail, a social networking site, and research for a project in another course, or all of the above? How many times has your online coursework been interrupted by a text message or a Facebook chat request?

All of these distractions can be alleviated by the student listener *and* by the design/ delivery of the message received. The most common excuse for not attending or receiving the instructor's message is that either the professor or the material is "boring." This excuse puts all of the responsibility on the speaker or message source when in reality at least half of the responsibility is with the listener.

Distractions fall into two categories: external distractions and internal distractions. *External distractions* consist of everything in your environment that could draw your attention away from the communicator's message. For example, my students have identified the following sorts of things that could become external distractions for them: harsh lighting in the room, noisy air conditioners, crowded seating, cell phones ringing, unusual clothing worn by the presenter or audience members. *Internal distractions* are physical or psychological aspects of the listener that reduce focus on the communication. For example, my students have admitted to the following items as some of their internal distractions: hunger, fatigue, uncomfortable clothing, focusing on a test in another class, planning for an event later in the evening, and even a hangover.

Reducing distractions requires identifying them as early as possible (preferably before they arise) and taking proactive measures to prevent them or reduce their impact. It is never enough simply to know what your distractions are; you must gain control over them. When you complete your inventory of distractions, you may be surprised to find that you can eliminate most of them by taking specific—sometimes simple—actions.

You can control the communication situation not only to help you as a listener, but to aid the presenter. Avoiding interruptions is also a way of granting the speaker a sense of importance. In an office you could close the door, hold calls, not read materials on your desk, and not write except to make notes related to what you and the person are talking about. If you are in a classroom, clear your desk of anything unrelated to the class. Turn off your cell phone if you brought it. Just turning off the ringer isn't enough, since you still might be tempted to check text messages.

Maintain Eye Contact. Another excellent way to improve your ability to receive communication is to establish **direct eye contact** with the presenter. When your parents shouted, "Look at me when I'm talking to you!" they did so for a reason. In most American cultures direct eye contact with another communicator signals involvement and interest. As a listener, you benefit from direct eye contact because you can pay attention to all the nonverbal messages a communicator sends. Some researchers estimate that more than half of message content comes from gestures, facial expressions, and other body language that we must watch to comprehend (Burley-Allen, 1982). Studies by Mehrabian (1981) show that people decide whether they like a speaker's message based mostly on the speaker's facial qualities (accounting for 55 percent of liking) and vocal qualities (38 percent), with only 7 percent of liking or disliking derived from the words themselves.

So *listen with your eyes* by maintaining eye contact with the person speaking to you. Not only will you gain a better understanding of the message by being receptive to visual stimuli, but you will signify that you care about what the speaker has to say. Direct eye contact also has payoffs in the classroom. If the speaker is your instructor, you will find you get more direct attention and interest—and probably better conversations—when you look at him or her during class. That sort of direct interaction enhances relationships and can't hurt grades!

Step Two: Understanding

The second stage of listening is **understanding**. In listening that term has special significance. To listen effectively, we must comprehend communication *in the presenter's own terms*. We must temporarily set aside what we as listeners want or believe and try to remain as open as possible—at least during this stage—to the speaker's viewpoint (Nichols, 1995). Understanding comes only after reception. If the message we receive is incomplete or distorted, we cannot get an accurate idea of what was communicated.

Challenges to Understanding

It seems so simple. All we need to do as listeners is figure out what the other person is saying. But we know better. Understanding can be quite elusive.

Mutually Assumed Understanding. A common error at the second stage of listening is **mutually assumed understanding:** We believe our messages are clear and rarely doubt the perfection of our listening skills; therefore, we always assume we have the correct information. Each of us thinks everybody else interprets things exactly the way we do. But how can we be sure? The problem is that 10 different people have at least 10 different ways of understanding the world, and all 10 think their way is the right way for everybody else. To prevent this problem, Wendell Johnson (1956) recommended that we should assume misunderstanding until we get positive proof that others share our interpretations. Tell other people when we don't understand something they say. Don't rely on puzzled looks or frowns—people interpret the signals differently. Say the magic words: "I don't understand" or "Could you clarify that?" The next time someone gives you important instructions, for example, check for misunderstanding. Paraphrase the message. Say something like, "If I get your point, you were asking me to do *x*."

Confusing Understanding with Agreement. Understanding has nothing to do with agreement. I might understand how to make a taco, but that does not imply that tacos are my favorite food. So far we have not reached the stage of listening that involves judging communication in any way. Ultimately, the test of understanding would be whether we could state the communication's cognitive and emotional content and the presenter would respond, "Yes, that's exactly what I was trying to get across." As listeners, we should not respond to communication until we get some indication that we have understood the message first. If nothing else, confirming understanding can clarify where you and the other communicator disagree.

How to Improve Understanding

Suspend Judgment. Probably the biggest threat to effective understanding is the rush to judge. We must resist that urge for now and recognize that understanding precedes judgment. It is especially tempting to react quickly to people different from ourselves, jumping to conclusions about someone's motives, intelligence, or ability. I sometimes encounter people who assume that anyone with a southern accent must lack intelligence. People who communicate in sign language may find that they are judged as mentally deficient because they do not communicate verbally. These inaccurate perceptions result from placing judgment as the first step in communicating with others. Unfortunately, hasty judgments suffer from inaccuracy and they may prevent us from gaining knowledge and enjoyment from communication that was dismissed as unimportant.

Paraphrase. An excellent way to check understanding is to **paraphrase** a presenter's message, restating content in your own words. A paraphrase goes beyond parroting back a speaker's words. A parent might say to a child, "Take out the trash now. Do you understand me?" The child replies, "Yeah. Sure. Take out the trash now," and does nothing. That is a parrot, not a paraphrase. A paraphrase shows that you recognize not only the words someone says, but the emotional and cognitive substance of the message. Skill at paraphrasing also will help you in your research. If you can capture the gist of what someone says or writes, you can refer to that information without the legal and academic risk of copying someone else's words.

Ask Questions—Even if Only to Yourself. In any class where you believe you are not an effective listener, along with your regular note taking behavior, write at least one question every five minutes about the specific information being presented at the time. You don't even have to have your questions answered, but it would help if you asked for answers from the lecturer or someone else who had experienced the same class session. Personally, as a speaker or lecturer, I am very pleased to have questions by listeners because I know one has to listen to ask questions.

Receiving Versus Perceiving. When you attempt to understand, carefully distinguish the messages you receive from your opinions of the messages. Contrary to reception, which involves physically getting messages, **perception** refers to how we view ourselves and the world. Earlier in this chapter, we recognized that we tend to fall prey to selective interpretation, understanding what we experience in ways that distort message content. These distortions systematically tend to protect ourselves and put us in the best possible light. Selective interpretation can strongly influence understanding.

We engage in **self-serving bias** by accepting responsibility for whatever is good and blaming others for problems. Avid American sports fans who watch the same football game, for example, will claim to "see" the opposing team play miserably, deserve far more penalties, and commit more unfair plays, even when both teams play almost identically (Snibbe, Kitayama, Markus, & Suzuki, 2003). Of course, the fans thought any penalties against their favorite team supposedly resulted from poor officiating.

We often listen to *confirm pre-existing beliefs.* Why? Because we attend to what we need, are interested in, or what we expect. It is more comfortable to reinforce what we already think and feel, so we may skew information to avoid challenging assumptions. To avoid this trap, do not try to rationalize or guess the motives behind a message. Instead, remain faithful to the original message content.

Step Three: Evaluation

Only after we have received all relevant information can we reach the evaluation stage. In **evaluation**, we judge the merits of messages. Evaluation includes several layers of judgments.

* Should listening continue? We must decide whether the message is important enough to remember and whether it deserves a response. When we check our voice mail, we first decide whether to erase the message or make a note of it. Then we also consider whether to return the call. The same judgments apply to e-mail. Should we keep the message or delete? Should we hit the reply key or archive the message?
* How important is the communication? Is the matter urgent? Should we interrupt other communication to shift attention to this interaction?
* What are the strengths and weaknesses of the message? At this point we engage in **critical listening** by considering the pros and cons of what the speaker has said. How reliable is the information? What are the advantages and disadvantages of the position the speaker takes? What has the speaker left out?

Challenges to Evaluation

Polarized Judgments. The greatest challenge to careful evaluation is the temptation to make sweeping overall judgments that oversimplify the value of the message. A common trap is falling into the tendency to evaluate only in all-or-nothing terms such as good/bad, right/wrong, or yes/no. While you may want to reach an overall judgment of this type, there usually are other alternatives. Remain open to the possibility that a message may be partially accurate and not just 100 percent true or 100 percent false. For example, how often have you watched a movie and adored every scene? Usually, you will find some parts of the movie appeal to you and others turn you off. The movie critics who give a film a simple "thumbs up" or "thumbs down" have oversimplified evaluation.

Evaluating People Instead of Performance. If you ever watched the television show *American Idol*, you know how the judges sometimes crush the dreams of the contestants, ridiculing them mercilessly when they sing badly. This behavior exemplifies poor evaluation. Just because someone sings poorly in an audition does not mean he has no talent whatsoever.

Many of your classes, including this one, may require you to evaluate presentations by other students. To help the presenter, you should always focus your comments on specific behaviors that can be improved. Whenever you find something that the presenter does not do well, identify what should change. If you concentrate on evaluating what someone *does* instead of who someone *is*, the presenter will recognize the criticism as constructive and not become defensive (Blanchard & Johnson, 1982).

Be careful how you phrase evaluations, since that can make the difference between insulting a presenter and improving the presenter's performance. Consider the following evaluations. Which would you rather hear from a listener? Which would help you become a better communicator?

<u>Examples</u>: Evaluations

1. "You did a terrible interview. What was wrong with you?"
2. "Your questions in the interview were vague and difficult to follow."
3. "Your questions in the interview could be more specific. Try listing categories of information you want, then write individual questions that could generate that information."

The third evaluation identifies a specific area needing improvement and offers a suggestion. The first two evaluations sound more like accusations and provide no foundation for improving communication.

How to Improve Evaluation

Evaluate Along Many Dimensions. An excellent way to become a better evaluator is to consider the various types of values that might affect your judgment. Using the basic judgment of quality, begin with the most general overall value of good/bad. To reach a more precise evaluation, break down the good/bad quality into several categories and expand your range of judgment.

To help you expand the range of your evaluations, here are several categories of values that you might consider applying to the ideas a speaker presents.

* Aesthetic
* Moral
* Practical (time, cost, resources, etc.)
* Health
* Emotional (frightening, humorous, sad, etc.)

A quick visit to the contents of a good thesaurus (such as *Roget's International Thesaurus*) will give you long lists of qualities that can guide your evaluations.

Use "I" Statements. To respect other people's feelings, evaluations should not sound like accusations. Take ownership of your evaluations. State what you experience, observe, or feel instead of claiming you already know what the other person means, feels, or believes. Notice the different impact each of the statements has in Figure 4.2. The "I" statements claim responsibility for feelings instead of seeming to blame the other person. If you begin your evaluations with "I" statements, you can express your feelings without getting into attack and defense (Burns, 1999).

Compare the examples of "you" statements with the examples of "I" statements. Which would you rather hear and why?	
"You" Statements	**"I" Statements**
1. "You're wrong."	1. "I disagree with you."
2. "You speak unclearly."	2. "I could not understand what you said."
3. "You make me so angry when you say _____."	3. "I feel angry when I hear you say _____."

Figure 4.2   "You" Statements and "I" Statements

Step Four: Recalling

After you decide that information is valuable enough to keep, **recalling** encompasses remembering and using the information. Recall can be long-term or short-term. We may need to retain information only long enough to write an answer on an exam and then forget it. Other information, such as how to ride a bicycle or a favorite recipe for lamb kidneys, might stick with us for a lifetime. Effective recall extends past regurgitating individual facts. Recall allows us to relate new information to what we already know, so we recognize when to use what we learn. Since almost all academic tests place high value on recall, improving our recall skills can lead to handsome payoffs in academic performance. Remembering important occasions such as birthdays and anniversaries can improve relationships. Even more important: Listen to input from your relational partners. If your father expressed dissatisfaction about getting a necktie for his birthday, listen to that reaction and remember to select a different gift next year.

Challenges to Recalling

The main barrier to effective recall lies in the information glut discussed earlier in this chapter. Too many messages, too little time. But if we can't reduce the sheer amount of incoming information, maybe we can improve the way we sort messages and file them away in our memory. If you surf the Web for a few minutes, you will find all sorts of memory improvement courses and techniques. Every truly effective memory enhancement program shares the same trick: patterning information in systematic ways. These techniques of patterning information in ways that make it easier to remember are known as **mnemonics**. The reason we seem plagued by poor memory is that we fail to notice relationships among the isolated items that we encounter. Suppose you meet 50 people at a party. Unless you have some ways to organize these names and faces, they will remain an anonymous blur afterwards.

How to Improve Recalling

Connect the Unknown with the Known. Unfamiliar information often presents problems because we don't know how it fits with our current knowledge. How can we file something in our memory if we don't know where it belongs? The best way to cope with new information is to relate it to something you already know. For example, you meet an important client for the first time and you want to remember her name. She introduces herself as Julia, so you could make a connection with the actress Julia Roberts. If you prefer visual associations, try connecting new information with colors or objects. Perhaps you would write each of the five stages of listening in a different color so you remember, for example, that recall is green. Finding or creating associations between new and known information makes the task of recall far less threatening. Sometimes vivid visual associations help us remember names and terms. You might not remember General Norman Schwarzkopf by name, but your recall might get a boost if you recognize that his name means "black head" in German (it's true). Now you have a clearer visual image that could help you recall the name.

Show as Well as Say. Effective listening involves more than mere repetition. An effective listener is able to act appropriately. An effective listener never simply claims to understand. The effective listener demonstrates understanding. One of my students was a supervisor at a turkey processing plant. Part of his job included training new employees how to use the meat slicers. These machines were huge assemblies of razor-sharp, rotating blades. He showed a group of newcomers how to use the equipment. As usual, he concluded by asking for questions. Naturally, there were none. After all, what new employee would want to look foolish or seem not to understand? A few weeks later, one of the trainees was slicing turkey, and along with slicing the turkey, she sliced off a good portion of her finger. This was the first serious accident one of this supervisor's trainees had. He was distraught and desperately asked, "What should I have done to prevent this accident?"

The answer lies in listening. He could redesign the training so that every trainee had to demonstrate proper cutting technique (with the blades turned off so that mistakes could serve as education, not amputation). Instead of relying on the claim to recall the training, the trainees would have to *prove* they could put the information into practice. This example shows how recall goes beyond just knowing information and includes knowing how to put information into practice.

As a speaker, you can verify accurate recall. If you ask "Do you understand?" or "Is that clear?" who will say no? Nobody wants to admit publicly to being a poor listener. This reluctance explains why when teachers ask such questions in the classroom, they usually encounter silence. The teacher then proceeds to the next topic, unaware that students may remain confused.

Use Grouping and Patterns. When trying to remember large volumes of information, break up the material into smaller chunks. How small? The number of items people tend to remember in a cluster of information is between five and nine, often referred to as the "magic seven" (Miller, 1956). Check the groupings of numbers that you remember easily, and they follow this pattern. American ZIP codes consist of five digits followed by a group of four. American telephone numbers are sequences of three digits followed by four. So if you need to recall a lot of information, divide it into groups of about seven items apiece.

Your recall also will improve if you develop patterns that connect different bits of information. We tend to remember better when we organize material in some systematic manner. For example, how might you remember the stages in the listening process? The five stages of listening are: receiving, understanding, evaluating, recalling, and responding. Since these stages occur in a particular order, you need to preserve the sequence. So you could begin by remembering the first letter of each step—RUERR. If you look at the terms, you find that all end in –ing, so you might order the steps by creating a short version of the steps that you can recite as a reminder: -ving, u-ding, -ting, -ling, r-ding. You can continue to find patterns in any group of information. These patterns give structure to information that otherwise might be an indistinguishable mass. Methods of structuring information for recall include

* Rhyming: Search for rhyming words or construct a short poem or song to help you recite the rhyming items.
* Drawing: Write key terms, names, or numbers in a pattern than illustrates the concept. For example, write the word "circle" by arranging the letters in a circle.
* Acronyms: Selected letters in key words might spell something that will stimulate recall.

These suggestions might seem silly now, but they can dramatically increase the amount and duration of recall. Listeners tend to discover which tricks work best for them. Try some of these recall methods the next time you need to study for a test and you will see their value.

Step Five: Responding

The final step in listening, **responding**, is equivalent to feedback: offering explicit verbal or nonverbal reactions to communication. The reactions we give are crucial in maintaining positive relationships with others: To avoid causing the people you care about to feel ignored, unimportant, or rejected, do not react to their communications with silence, an immediate change of subject, or interrupting with your own personal stories. Take the time to acknowledge what was said and even allow for expansion on it.

Example:

Elvis: "I got an 'A' on my roadkill recipe project."
Priscilla: "Oh, I bet you feel good about that. What do you think was the best part of the project?"

Challenges to Responding

False Feedback. To give the impression that they are listening carefully, some listeners will aim to please the speaker by giving visible signs of positive reaction regardless of their genuine feelings about the communication. In their eagerness to appear attentive, listeners may offer misleading responses such as direct eye contact and nodding even when they disagree with or fail to understand the presenter. For example, someone might address you in an unfamiliar language, yet you smile and say, "Oh, really?" although you have no idea what the person is saying. False feedback confuses speakers by sending the wrong message. Since speakers respond to the reactions of their listeners, nonverbal signals of understanding signal the speaker to move on and assume the listeners are following. In the classroom, show your confusion or puzzlement if you don't follow what the instructor is saying. Skilled teachers quickly recognize when a student does not grasp an idea. If you find your instructor tends not to explain concepts well, it might be because the student reactions are saying "We understand" when their facial expressions and questions should indicate "Slow down and help us."

Conflicting Responses. Communicators sometimes face a challenge reacting because the communicator offers mixed signals. If a presenter's words conflict with the nonverbal behavior, listeners may not know whether to believe their ears or their eyes. For example, I have interviewed many candidates for jobs who say they are confident and outgoing, yet they mumble their answers and avoid direct eye contact with me during the interview. Most listeners tend to respond more to what a person does than to what they say. In the interview example, the interviewer probably would get a negative impression because the applicant's actions speak louder than words. To determine how you should react, look for cases where the presenter's words and behaviors reinforce each other. In those cases, you can be more confident that the presenter is sending a clear message. When the verbals and nonverbals conflict, indicate your puzzlement by asking questions or showing facial expressions of confusion. In the interview, I might respond to the interviewees by asking how confident they feel right now speaking with me. If they admit some nervousness, I recognize the reasons for their behavior. But if these interviewees continue to claim confidence while displaying signs of fear, I begin to doubt their sincerity.

How to Improve Responding

Offer Explicit Reactions. Reactions keep a conversation going and keep a presenter tuned in to the audience, ready to adapt to their feedback. Don't expect others magically to guess what you are thinking and feeling, even in intimate relationships. Often we mistakenly think that our close friends should know our reactions even when we offer no visible indication of our emotions. Those people you identify as your best listeners probably show they are listening by visible signs such as their eye contact. Eye contact here means short durations of perhaps 5 seconds at a time and not a stare. Experiment for yourself by looking someone directly in the eyes. How long did it take before you became uncomfortable? If the listener stares into space or never changes expression, you can bet that the person is not listening.

Facial expressions and body attitude offer important nonverbal visual responses. Do you let other communicators know how you feel about the subject or their behavior by your expressions? Or do you expect others magically to guess how you feel? With our eyes, facial expression and body attitude, we communicate our feelings and whether we agree, disagree, or are indifferent.

Choose Questions that Build Dialogue. We already discussed the value of questions to improve understanding. Here we examine how you can use questions to generate the mutual openness of **dialogue**, a conversation where all communicators can participate fully and openly express themselves. Even if you think of yourself as a skilled conversationalist, you can do your part by identifying your own and the other person's feelings and asking clarifying or open-ended questions.

Good questions show your attentiveness and encourage reactions in return. "What?" questions can perform this function. "How?" "When?" and "Where?" questions also can be useful invitations to dialogue. "What did you like about the movie?" stimulates a more informative response than simply "Did you like the movie?" The "what" question encourages a fuller reaction. The yes/no question invites only a single syllable or a grunt in response. Questions that can be answered only with yes or no are poor choices for dialogue because they do little to keep a conversation going.

Poor questions, especially in relationships, tend to be "why?" questions that place others on the defensive. Although "why?" questions can be useful, beware of "why?" questions that sound like accusations.

Examples of poor "why?" questions:

1. "Why would you say such a thing?"
2. "Why didn't you look at me when you said that?"

These questions immediately place the other communicator in the position of justifying a claim or behavior. If you rephrase your questions, they sound less accusatory.

Examples of better questions:

1. "What did you mean when you said _____?"
2. "What were you thinking about when you looked away from me?"

The revised questions ask the other communicator to discuss ideas and feelings without having to justify them.

Listening Roadblocks and Remedies

We now turn to factors that affect whether the entire listening process succeeds. The five stages of listening can work properly only when we cultivate good listening habits. These good listening habits include the techniques of active listening and recognizing the obligations communicators assume in listening.

Active Listening

Effective listeners do not simply sit passively and absorb information like a sponge absorbs water. Healthy listening is **active listening**: being fully engaged in the speaker-listener relationship, using all the steps of the listening process, and taking deliberate actions to improve communication.

Active listening requires the ability to listen with **empathy**—the willingness to set aside our own agendas and understand reality as the other person does. When we empathize, we place ourselves in the other person's shoes and try to recognize their perspective. When we empathize, we are able to explain the content of a communicator's message *and* acknowledge the feelings that are being expressed (Burns, 1999).

Empathy differs from sympathy. Empathy enables us to imagine how someone else feels. **Sympathy** involves feeling sorry *for* someone; empathy allows us to feel *with* them. When I accidentally shut the window on my cat's tail, I sympathized with her because she obviously was in pain. But I could not empathize with her because I don't have a tail and cannot possibly imagine what it would feel like to have one.

Active listening truly involves the listener as well as the speaker. It is not merely going through the motions of listening, simply nodding your head as you think about other things or what you are going to say next. The skill of active listening requires three subsidiary skills:

1. *Attending behaviors:* Nonverbal signals that signify you are attentive. These behaviors communicate "I am interested in what you have to say," "I want to hear what you have to say," or at least, "I am willing to hear what you have to say," or "I'm not afraid of what you have to say, I can handle it." Attending behaviors include:
    - Eye contact with the other person.
    - Facing the other person.
    - Body open to the other person (arms and legs uncrossed).
    - Body inclined toward the other person.
2. *Verifying content:* Listening for the substance of the message and letting the other person know you have heard the main ideas and facts. Check the accuracy of your understanding as soon as possible, before distractions arise or the message fades. This content check allows for misunderstanding to be cleared up quickly; it also gives the speaker a sense of truly being valued.
3. *Listening for feelings* being communicated and letting the other person know you heard and accept those feelings by tentatively naming them. This identification of feelings is a wonderful way to show the other person you accept them as a whole person, someone with feelings as well as ideas.

Example:

"It sounds as if you are pretty upset with your boss because when she criticized you for being late, she had not criticized others and you think you were treated unfairly."

Listening as a Shared Responsibility

We often think of the physical and psychological aspects of listening, but listening also has an ethical side. We conveniently accuse others of poor listening and place the burden of improving listening entirely on them. My favorite examples are the contradictory complaints I hear from students and teachers. Walk into a teacher's lounge and you will hear: "Our students don't pay attention. They refuse to listen. They won't follow instructions. It's their fault if they get bad grades." Go to the student union or school cafeteria and you will hear students saying: "Our teachers don't help us out. They refuse to tell us what they want. They won't give clear instructions. It's their fault if we get bad grades." Who is correct?

Everybody is half right and half wrong. Since communication is transactional, speakers and listeners share a relationship by affecting how each experiences the interaction. Speakers and listeners share the responsibility for effective communication. This shared responsibility places obligations on all communicators, whether the context is groups, interviews, conversations, or public speeches.

Speakers need to respond to reactions from the audience. If a speaker encounters signs of impatience such as checking text messages, looking at clocks in a room, drumming fingers on desks, and tapping feet, the audience is sending a message that requires a response. In this case, the speaker needs to move on to the next point or conclude. Few things alienate an audience more than being ignored, so speakers should "read" the audience and prepare to adjust accordingly.

Listeners incur the obligation to be assertive and take action to improve the communication situation. Speak up or alter your communication environment if you are unable to listen effectively because of poor timing, distractions, or other factors. Several years ago, I was distressed to receive a comment on a course evaluation from a student in a large class who complained of never being able to see the whiteboard in our classroom and blamed me for not making the notes more visible. I wish this student had spoken to me so we could have made some arrangements to improve listening. I could have reserved a seat for the student near the front of the room or enlarged the visuals, for example. I remained ignorant of the problem and the student missed important information.

Speakers and listeners share another obligation: knowing when to keep silent. Let the other communicators have their say—that is the only way you can be sure you receive the entire message. Interrupting a speaker is not only rude, but it may deprive you of information that you need to understand and evaluate the message. Interruptions also signify that you value your own ideas and feelings more than those of others, so you may create an impression that you are self-centered and domineering.

☞ Listening in Context

Sometimes the communication context places special demands on listeners. The final stop on our tour of listening takes us to two situations beyond the classroom: listening to give advice and listening in close personal relationships.

Listening to Give Advice

One of the most important everyday situations that requires us to become active listeners is when someone turns to us for advice. Our ability to give good advice depends on our ability to listen carefully enough to diagnose what the other person needs from us. Offering advice is part of your "job description" as a parent, supervisor, or friend.

Contrary to what we might think, advice-giving is the *last* step in the process. We need a clear grasp of the individual's problem, issue, or needs before accurate advice can be given and accepted. First, the advice/help seeker needs to feel comfortable, respected as a person totally, and that his or her problem—whatever it is—counts as important and is understood. Without this security of being appreciated, all your great wisdom and knowledge will fall on deaf ears.

In fact, researchers have found that people react more positively when listeners first respond with active listening that "communicates that the listener understands and cares about the speaker's thoughts and feelings. Our findings suggest that active listening appears to accomplish this goal better than either giving unsolicited advice or offering simple verbal and nonverbal acknowledgements" (Weger, Bell, & Robinson, 2014, p. 24).

Nonverbal communication assumes paramount importance: It communicates respect and raises the comfort level of the interaction. Invite the individual into your office or another private space that you can dedicate entirely to your conversation. Do as much as you can to ensure privacy, and demonstrate respect by avoiding interruptions. Be open and nonjudgmental to the advice-seeker (open body language, no barriers such as big desks between you and her) to show respect and promote trust. Engage in all the attending behavior skills of active listening.

Verbal input is also important. Paraphrase what the speaker tells you, both the content and the feelings expressed. Active listening helps you get a clear handle on the problem of this particular individual so your advice can be more accurate and specific. Active listening also helps the advice-seeker feel or believe that you do understand his or her problem. Before giving advice inquire as to what ideas, actions, plans, or options the individual has considered. Often advice is not really what the person wants. The advice-seeker may actually want validation of what she or he has already figured out, or the individual may simply need someone to listen so the speaker can ventilate.

We need to become adept at listening to advise and to validate. Researchers such as Deborah Tannen (1990) contend that men tend to gravitate toward giving advice, feeling fulfillment from guiding others toward solutions. By contrast, women often want listeners to validate their right to have opinions and feelings, not necessarily to provide suggestions for solutions. Not all men or women listen in the same way, and the research points to different approaches rather than genetic absolutes. Given these different perspectives, Tannen cautions that we need to develop sensitivity toward the other communicator. Does the advice-seeker want the listener to play "Fix-It," or does the communicator prefer confirmation of thoughts and emotions?

Listening in Relationships

Listening in relationships requires some special considerations. We need to listen in ways that assure a safe place to share emotions so we draw closer to each other. Relational contexts place priority on revealing emotional content instead of on winning a point or establishing superiority. Relational listening employs several techniques.

1. *Tune-in time:* Take time to listen within, to be aware of and responsible for your own feelings. Do not use this time to set up your "arguments." Use the time to really listen to yourself and to consider how best to express the feelings you are becoming aware of. The word "best" is used in terms of getting your feelings across—not in the sense of how well crafted or how good they will sound.

2. *Expression of feelings:* Both partners should agree to be as open as possible, both in expressing their own feelings and in allowing the other freedom to express. If only one partner deeply shares, that partner often develops negative feelings of having to carry the relationship alone. Try to share the awareness you developed during the tune-in time. Avoid intellectualizing. Avoid generalization. Avoid labels and accusations. Stay in the first person as much as possible ("I," "me," "my"), as discussed in the evaluation stage of listening. Own your feelings and your perceptions—as perceptions, not as The Ultimate Truth.

3. *Empathic listening:* Try very hard to hear what your partner in saying, to actually feel what your partner is feeling. Try to see and feel things as your partner is seeing and feeling them. Avoid planning your "retort."

4. *Summarizing:* Before sharing one's own feelings, the listener should work on trying to indicate through summary that what the other person was trying to communicate was heard and understood. Do not use this summary as a weapon. ("See how well I know you"; "You can't fool me.") The tone of voice and manner are very important. Use this process in the most helpful way possible: demonstrate that you are truly *with* the other person.

5. *Processing:* Stop occasionally to process the interaction. Note the communication patterns. Is the communication working? Do you feel you are being heard? Do you feel you are getting enough opportunity to express your feelings and views? Do you feel your partner is being receptive? Do you feel your partner is being open? Do you feel you are being open, receptive, and specific?

Throughout your conversation, avoid accusations that place your partner on the defensive. Sometimes it is best to start with what you feel is positive so far about the exchange, especially if either you or your partner starts getting verbally aggressive or defensive. If the process is not working well, perhaps some more tune-in time is needed so you can individually clarify the emotions you want to communicate.

Our tour of listening should have provided you with several souvenirs in the form of listening habits that you can implement in your academic, personal, and professional life. Hopefully you not only read this chapter, but experimented with practicing the techniques of effective listening. A lot is at stake in listening, since remaining content with merely hearing exacts a hefty price economically, intellectually, and personally. Every stage of the listening process—receiving, understanding, evaluating, recalling, and responding—allows us to examine our own listening behaviors and find how we can become more active listeners. Communication succeeds only to the extent that people listen well.

References

Alessandra, T. (1995). The power of listening. *Speakers platform.* Retrieved from http://www.speaking.com/articles_html/ TonyAlessandra, Ph.D.,CSP,CPAE_107.html

Arthur W. Page Society. (2004, September 13). *Page Society annual conference closes with a world-view of listening.* Retrieved from http://www.awpagesociety.com/newroom/apsconf091504.asp

Atwater, E. (1992). *I hear you* (Rev. ed.). Pacific Grove, CA: Walker.

Blanchard, K., & Johnson, S. (1982). *The one minute manager.* New York: William Morrow.

Burley-Allen, M. (1982). *Listening: The forgotten skill.* New York: John Wiley.

Burns, D. D. (1999). *The feeling good handbook* (Rev. ed.). New York: Plume.

Cooper, L. (1997). Listening competency in the workplace: A model for training. *Business Communication Quarterly, 60*, 75–84.

Halone, K. K., Cuncoran, T. M., Coakley, C. G., & Wolvin, A. D. (1998). Toward the establishment of general dimensions underlying the listening process. *International Journal of Listening, 12*, 12–28.

Hayakawa, S. I. (1955, Autumn). How to attend a conference. *Et Cetera, 13*, 5–9.

HighGain.com (2004). *The business of listening*. Retrieved from http://www.highgain.com/html/the_business_of_listening.html

Hunsaker, P. L., & Alessandra, A. J. (1986). *The art of managing people*. New York: Simon & Schuster.

Hyslop, N. B., & Tone, B. (1988). *Listening: Are we teaching it, and if so, how?* (ERIC Digest No. 3). ED295132. Retrieved from http://www.ericdigests.org/pre-928/listening.htm

International Listening Association. (1996). Definition of listening. Retrieved from http://www.listen.org

Johns, A.M. (1981). Necessary English: A faculty survey. *TESOL Quarterly, 15*, 51–57.

Johnson, I. W., Pearce, C. G., Tuten, T. L., & Sinclair, L. (2003). Self-imposed silence and perceived listening effectiveness. *Business Communication Quarterly, 66*, 23–45.

Johnson, W. (1956). *Your most enchanted listener*. New York: Harper.

Lindahl, K. (2003). *Practicing the sacred art of listening*. Woodstock, VT: Skylight Paths.

McKeone, L. (2004). *The executive extra. Listen up!* Retrieved from http://www.executiveextra.com/listen_up.htm

Mehrabian, A. (1981). *Silent messages: Implicit communication of emotions and attitudes* (2nd ed.). Belmont, CA: Wadsworth.

Miller, G. A. (1956). The magical number seven, plus or minus two: Some limits on our capacity for processing information. *Psychological Review, 63*, 81–97.

Nichols, M. P. (1995). *The lost art of listening*. New York: Guilford Press.

Pearce, C., Johnson, I., & Barker, R. (1995). Enhancing the student listening skills and environment. *Business Communication Quarterly, 58*, 28–33.

Rane, D. B. (2011). Good listening skills make efficient business sense. IUP Journal of Soft Skills, 5(4), 43–51.

Shepherd, C. D., Castleberry, S. B., & Ridnour, R. E. (1997). Linking effective listening with salesperson performance: An exploratory investigation. *Journal of Business and Industrial Marketing, 12*, 315–322.

Smith, A. (2004). *The communication gap*. Institute for Youth Development. Retrieved from http://www.youthdevelopment.org/articles/fp059901.htm

Snibbe, A. C., Kitayama, S., Markus, H. R. O. S. E., & Suzuki, T. (2003). They saw a game: A Japanese and American (football) field study. Journal of Cross-Cultural Psychology, *34*, 581–595.

Stone, G., Lightbody, M., & Whait, R. (2013) Developing accounting students' listening skills: Barriers, opportunities and an integrated stakeholder approach. Accounting Education, *22*(2), 168–192.

Tannen, D. (1990). *You just don't understand: Women and men in conversation*. New York: William Morrow.

Weger, H., Bell, G., & Robinson, M. C. (2014). The relative effectiveness of active listening in initial interactions. *International Journal of Listening, 28*(1), 13–31.

Zabava Ford, W. S., Wolvin, A. D., & Chung, S. (2000). Students' self-perceived listening competencies in the basic speech communication course. *International Journal of Listening, 14*, 1–13.

Chapter 5

Organizing and Outlining Your Ideas

"Let our advance worrying become advance thinking and planning."

Winston Churchill

Have you ever had a friend tell you a story, and at some point, you interrupt to say, "Huh? What?" You express confusion over the point of the story, or you don't know the context, or maybe even the people involved? Your friend left something out.

Imagine Professor Plunkett whose unorganized, rambling lessons gallop along, often jumping from topic to topic. Listening to his lecture is like watching a pingpong ball bounce aimlessly across the table; you never know where the professor will land or what direction his comments will take next. His students—those still awake, that is—often struggle to comprehend what the professor wants them to take away from his message.

☛ The Importance of Organizing a Speech

A good speech flows smoothly and consists of a clear introduction, body, and conclusion. Your listeners should be able to identify these parts of your speech. Also, listeners expect your speech to be logical and organized. A speech that is missing a clear introduction or that has main points unrelated to the introduction will confuse, irritate, or simply turn off your listeners. It doesn't matter if you have gathered astounding facts or if you have incredible quotations to support your points if your speech is not structured logically.

Rather than just starting to write your speech, first consider how best to organize it. If you spend time outlining your ideas, you will discover where you have deficiencies in research, where you have too much information, or where you haven't made appropriate connections from one point to the next. This chapter leads you through organizing the body of a speech step-by-step. We begin with selecting and supporting main points. Next, we present several organizational patterns as well as a template for organizing your main points. You have many decisions to make when organizing, such as the pattern of organization, the number of main points needed, what relevant subpoints to include, and where to put transitions and internal previews. We conclude with a discussion of outlining as a tool to aid you in becoming an organized speaker.

👉 Organizing the Body of Your Speech

The **organization of ideas** in public speaking refers to the placement of lines of reasoning and supporting materials in a pattern that achieves your chosen general purpose and specific purpose by supporting your thesis. Following a consistent pattern of organization helps listeners pay attention to your message. An organized speech with connected main points helps you maintain a clear focus that leads listeners to a logical conclusion. An organized speech flows smoothly and clearly, from introduction through body to conclusion.

Your introduction and conclusion support the body of your speech. The **introduction** should capture your audience's attention and indicate your intent. The **conclusion** reinforces your message and brings your speech to a close. The **body** includes your main points and supporting material that bolster your specific purpose and thesis statement. The introduction and conclusion are important, but audiences expect you to spend the most time and effort amplifying your main points.

For the body of your speech to flow in an organized, logical way, reflect first on your general purpose, specific purpose, and thesis statement. Your **general purpose** is either to inform, persuade, or entertain. Since your **specific purpose** is a statement of intent and your **thesis statement** identifies the main ideas of your speech, referring to them as you determine your main points prevents misdirection. For example, consider a speech discussing how family pets help children with psychological problems. You might develop the following:

> **General Purpose:** To inform
> **Specific Purpose:** To explain to my class how pets can provide unexpected psychological benefits for children with emotional problems by helping to bolster their self-esteem
> **Thesis Statement:** A close relationship with a family pet can help children with emotional problems feel better about themselves, help therapists build rapport with difficult-to-reach patients, and encourage the development of important social skills.

Your thesis statement indicates your speech will address self-esteem, rapport with therapists, and the development of social skills. This suggests that there are many peripheral topics you will *exclude*, such as the type of pet, pet grooming tips, medical advances in the treatment of feline leukemia, how to choose a kennel when you go on vacation, and so on.

Select Your Main Points

Organizing the body of your speech involves a *four-step process: select the main points, support the main points, choose the best organizational pattern, and create unity throughout the speech.* Before organizing your speech, determine your main points. Main points are the key ideas, or most important issues you want to discuss with your audience. One way to discover your main points is through **brainstorming**. Brainstorming can occur at any stage of a process, but brainstorming for main points should happen *after* you have gathered sufficient information during topic research.

A best practice is to arrive at *no fewer than two and not more than five main points*. If you add more, you may confuse your listeners, and you may not have time to provide adequate support. All ideas must relate to your general purpose, specific purpose, and thesis statement. The audience analysis you have done previously should ensure your main points are audience-centered.

For purposes of illustration, consider the following:

General Purpose: To inform
Specific Purpose: To describe to my class the causes, symptoms, and treatment of shyness
Thesis Statement: Shyness, which is an anxiety response in social situations that limits social interactions, may respond to appropriate treatment.

Your brainstorming process for the topic of shyness might result in a list of possible main points that include, but are clearly not limited to, the following: symptoms of shyness, shyness and heredity, shyness as an anxiety response, physical and psychological indications of shyness, number of people affected by shyness, shyness and self-esteem, how to handle a job interview if you are shy, treatment for shyness, and what to do when your date is shy.

On reflection, you may realize that several of these points overlap, and others do not relate as much to your thesis statement and should be discarded. So, you make the following list of six possible important points: symptoms of shyness, causes of shyness, treatment for shyness, number of people affected by shyness, shyness as an anxiety response, and shyness and self-esteem.

With six being too many main points to develop, you decide that "shyness as an anxiety response" describes a symptom of shyness and that "shyness and self-esteem" describes a cause. You decide that a discussion of the number of people affected by shyness belongs in your introduction because it is startlingly widespread. Your final list of main points may look like this: symptoms of shyness, causes of shyness, treatment for shyness.

Through this process, you transformed a random list into a focused set of idea clusters reflecting broad areas of your speech. Your main points should be mutually exclusive; each point should be distinct. In addition, each point must relate to and support your thesis statement. We now turn our attention to supporting your points.

Support Your Main Points

After selecting your main points, use the supporting material you gathered to strengthen each main point. Fitting each piece of research into its appropriate place may seem like completing a complex jigsaw puzzle. Patterns must be matched, rational links must be formed, and common sense must prevail. Each point underneath the main point is called a subpoint (and subsubpoint, and so on). Each subpoint is an extension of the point it supports. If the connection seems forced, reconsider the match. Here, for example, is one way to develop three main points for the speech on shyness. As you sit at your computer, you can expand phrases into sentences. So for now, you can begin to think in terms of the language of your speech. Keep in mind, we are focusing on organization, not the formal outline.

I. **Main Point 1:** The symptoms of shyness fall into two categories: those that can be seen and those that are felt.
   A. Objective symptoms (symptoms that can be seen) make it apparent to others that you are suffering from shyness, including blushing, dry mouth, cold clammy hands, trembling hands and knocking knees, excessive sweating, and belligerence.
   B. According to psychologist Philip Zimbardo, many shy people never develop the social skills necessary to deal with difficult situations (symptoms that are felt).
   C. They may experience embarrassment, feelings of inferiority or inadequacy, feelings of self-consciousness, a desire to flee, and generalized anxiety. They overreact by becoming argumentative.
   D. Internal symptoms like an unsettled stomach and dizziness make the experience horrible for the sufferer.

II. **Main Point 2:** Recent research has focused on three potential causes of shyness.
   A. Heredity seems to play a large part.
   B. Psychologists at Yale and Harvard have found that 10 to 15 percent of all children are shy from birth. Dr. Jerome Kagan of Harvard found that shy children are wary and withdrawn even with people they know.
   C. Shyness is also the result of faulty learning that lowers self-esteem instead of boosting self-confidence.
      1. When parents criticize a child's ability or appearance or fail to praise the child's success, they plant the seeds of shyness by lowering self-esteem.
      2. Older siblings may destroy a child's self-image through bullying and belittlement.
   D. Shyness is also attributable to poor social skills, due to never having learned how to interact with others, which leaves shy people in an uncomfortable position.

III. **Main Point 3:** Shyness is not necessarily a life sentence; treatment is possible and so is change.
   A. In a survey of 10,000 adults, Stanford University researchers found that 40 percent said that they had been shy in the past but no longer suffered from the problem.
   B. People who are extremely shy may benefit from professional therapy offered by psychiatrists and psychologists.

As you weave together your main points and support, your speech should grow in substance and strength. It will be clear to your listeners that you have something to say and that you are saying it in an organized way.

Choose the Best Pattern for Organizing Your Main Points

The way you organize your main points depends on your general purpose, specific purpose and thesis statement, the type of material you are presenting, and the needs of your audience. As you develop your main points, consider what you want to emphasize. Assuming you have established three main points, choose how to weight your main points. Three options are possible. First, you may choose the **equality pattern**, which involves giving equal time to each point. This means that you will spend approximately the same time on each main point as you deliver the body of your speech.

Using the **strongest point pattern** is a second option. In this case, your first point would take about half of the time you devote to the body of your speech, the second point would be given about one-third, and your final point would receive the least. The advantage to this method is in getting the audience to process, retain, and recall your strongest points. When testing memory, psychologists discovered that, when presented with a list of items, individuals remembered information that was presented either at the beginning of the list *or* at the end. The strongest point pattern, which weighs the first point more heavily than the other points, reflects the phenomenon known as the **primacy effect**. Note there is danger of using this pattern. Our strongest points may also be the most complex and if discussed early in the speech may confuse or turn off the audience.

A third option is to follow a **progressive pattern**. This involves presenting your least important point first and your most important point last. The amount of time given to each is the inverse of the strongest point pattern, so that the last point receives the lion's share of time, the second point receives less, and the first point is the briefest. **Recency effect** suggests people will remember most what they have just processed. Anyone who has heard the phrase "What have you done for me lately?" understands the recency effect. A danger of this pattern is present when we lose our audience by providing weak material first, and in so doing, fail to capture interest.

The pattern for weighting your main points depends on your topic and audience. Based on these three options, keep in mind that your strongest argument does not go in the middle of your main points.

In addition to weighting your main points for emphasis, your information should fit within an overall organizational framework. Many choices exist for any given speech but based on the general purpose, specific purpose, and thesis sentence, one pattern of organization is generally more appropriate than the others. Typically, the right organizational pattern emerges organically as you work with the body of your speech, provided you know in advance what patterns to look for. The five effective patterns of organization to look for are chronological, spatial, causal, problem–solution and topical. To show how different organizational patterns affect the content and emphasis of a speech, we choose a topic, establish different purposes for speaking, and show how the presentation differs when the organizational pattern is changed.

Chronological Organization

In a chronological speech, information is focused *on relationships in time*. Events are presented in the order in which they occur. When developing your speech chronologically, you might choose to organize your ideas by starting at the beginning and moving to the present, then looking to the future, as in a story, or going step-by-step, as you would if following a recipe.

Topic: The development of the European Union
General Purpose: To inform
Specific Purpose: To inform the class about crucial events that occurred over a 40-year span that influenced the development of the European Union (EU)
Thesis Statement: Although the European Union was formed in 1993, the creation of a coal and steel community, establishment of a common market, and direct elections to the European Parliament were critical events that influenced its development.

Main Points:
 I.   West Germany, together with France, Italy, and Benelux, signed the Treaty of Paris in 1951 which created the European Coal and Steel community.
 II. In 1957 the Treaty of Rome established the European Economic Community, known as the common market to English-speaking countries.
 III. In 1979 the first direct elections to the European Parliament were held.
 IV. In 1992, with the signing of the Maastricht Treaty, the European Union was created.

Chronological order can also be used to construct a past-present-future organizational pattern. For example, in a speech addressing the development of the European Union, one could present the same topic with a slightly different specific purpose statement that would lead to a different thesis statement and different focus for the main points. Consider the following:

Topic: The development of the European Union
General Purpose: To inform
Specific Purpose: To inform the class how the European Union became a 27-member community that is poised to grow significantly
Thesis Statement: Developed after three important treaties, the 27-member European Union is poised to add another nine countries to its community.

Main Points:
 I.   Treaties of Paris, Rome, and Maastricht were crucial to the development of the European Union.
 II. Currently, the European Union is a community of 27 member states connected both politically and economically.
 III. As an indicator of future growth, at least nine countries are potential candidates for inclusion in the European Union.

Past-Present-Future

Using a past-present-future order allows a speaker to provide perspective for a topic or issue that has relevant history and future direction or potential. Notice that in the regular chronological pattern, the three treaties are the main focus of the speech. In the past-present-future pattern, the three treaties would receive much less coverage.

Step-by-Step

Chronological patterns can be used to describe the steps in a process. Here is a step-by-step description of how college texts are produced. Like the other patterns, the process shows a movement in time:

> **Step 1:** The author, having gathered permissions for use of copyrighted material, delivers a manuscript to the publisher.
> **Step 2:** The manuscript is edited, a design and cover are chosen, photos are selected, and illustrations are drawn.
> **Step 3:** The edited manuscript is sent to a compositor for typesetting and set in galley and page proof form.
> **Step 4:** The final proof stage is released to the printing plant where the book is printed and bound.

Spatial Organization

In speeches organized according to a spatial pattern, the sequence of ideas moves from one physical point to another—from London to Istanbul, from basement to attic, from end zone to end zone. To be effective, your speech must follow a consistent directional path. If you are presenting a new marketing strategy to the company sales force, you can arrange your presentation by geographic regions—first the East, then the South, then the Midwest, and finally, the West. So, in a speech on the European Union, one could use a spatial organization pattern to discuss the growth of the EU over time.

> I. Six Western European countries joined to establish the European Union.
> II. Countries bordering the Eastern Mediterranean are candidates for inclusion in the European Union.
> III. As Central and Eastern European countries emerged from dictatorship, they wanted to join the European Union to avoid falling back into the Russian sphere of influence.

Notice the differences between the main points for this speech organized spatially versus chronologically. A speech with the above three points would focus more on the countries involved with the European Union than how the EU came about.

Cause and Effect

With the cause and effect organizational pattern, the speaker can focus specifically on why something happened and what the consequences of the event or action were. The following statements could be developed into a speech that uses a cause and effect pattern:

* Difficult economic times after World War II created the necessity for European countries to work together.
* Alcoholism damages American family life.

* Too much positive feedback in primary school results in young adults being unable to cope with life's problems.
* Fast food is a significant contributor to obesity in America.
* Traveling abroad reduces prejudice.
* Smoking hurts relationships.

Note that in each case, the speaker is trying to provide that something caused something to happen. For example, the effect alcoholism has on family life is that it causes harm. The effect traveling has on people is reducing prejudice. Therefore, traveling is seen as a cause. Some topics have direct links that can be made with facts and/or statistics (Smoking causes cancer) and others have indirect links that must be proved with facts and other forms of support, such as testimony, examples, or illustrations (Smoking hurts relationships).

Problem–Solution Organization

A common strategy, especially in persuasive speeches, is to present an audience with a problem and then examine one or more likely solutions. For example, in a classroom speech, one student described a serious safety problem for women walking alone on campus after dark. He cited incidents in which women were attacked and robbed, and described unlit areas along campus walkways where the attacks had taken place. Next, he turned to a series of proposals to eliminate, or at least minimize, the problem. His proposals included a new escort service, sponsored and maintained by campus organizations, the installation of halogen lights along dark campus walks, and the trimming of bushes where muggers could hide.

Occasionally, speakers choose to present the solution before the problem. Had this student done so, he would have identified how to provide effective security before he explained why these solutions were necessary. Many audiences have trouble with this type of reversal because they find it hard to accept solutions when they are not familiar with the problems that brought them about.

Later in this chapter is an outline of a speech entitled "Revisiting Standard American English." The topic is developed using a problem–solution pattern.

> **Problem:** Requiring speakers and writers to use Standard American English only promotes racism and classism.
> **Solution:** Insist that teachers teach grammar by separating written English and spoken English and study the differences in grammar of both styles in the classroom.

Here the goal is to persuade an audience that a problem still exists and to have listeners agree about how it can be effectively handled.

Topical Organization

The most frequently used organizational system is not tied to time or space, problem or solution, or cause-and-effect, but to the unique needs of your topic. The nature and scope of your topic dictate the pattern of your approach.

If you are delivering an after-dinner humorous speech on the responses of children to their first week of preschool, you can arrange your topics according to their level of humor. For example:

1. The *school supplies* preschoolers think are necessary to survive at school
2. The *behavior of youngsters at school* when they do not get their own way
3. Children's stories of *their lives at home*
4. *The reasons children believe their parents send them to school*

These topics relate to children and their first week at school, but there is no identifiable chronological pattern, so topical order makes sense. When organizing topically, think about how to link and order topics. Transitions can help the audience understand the connections and are discussed in the following section.

☞ Creating Unity through Connections

Without connections, your main points may be difficult to follow. Your audience may wonder what you are trying to say and why you have tried to connect ideas that do not seem to have any relationship with each other. To establish the necessary connections, use transitions, internal previews, and internal summaries.

Transitions

Transitions are the verbal bridges between ideas. They are words, phrases, or sentences that tell your audience how ideas relate. Transitions are critical because they clarify the direction of your speech by giving your audience a means to follow your organization. With only one opportunity to hear your remarks, listeners depend on transitions to make sense of your ideas.

It helps to think of transitions as verbal signposts that signal the organization and structure of your speech. Here are several examples:

"The first proposal I would like to discuss ..."

This tells listeners that several more ideas will follow.

"Now that we've finished looking at the past, let's move to the future."

These words indicate a movement in time.

"Next, I'll turn from a discussion of the problems to a discussion of the solution."

This tells your listeners that you are following a problem–solution approach.

"On the other hand, many people believe ..."

Here you signal an opposing viewpoint.

The following is a list of common transitional words that reflect the speaker's purpose in using them.

Table 5.1   Suggested Transitional Words

Speaker's Purpose	
1. To define	*that is to say; according to; in other words*
2. To explain	*for example; specifically*
3. To add	*furthermore; also; in addition; likewise*
4. To change direction	*although; on the other hand; conversely*
5. To show both sides	*nevertheless; equally*
6. To contrast	*but; still; on the contrary*
7. To indicate cause	*because; for this reason; since; on account of*
8. To summarize	*recapping; finally; in retrospect; summing up*
9. To conclude	*in conclusion; therefore; and so; finally*

(Makay & Fetzger, 1984, p. 68)

Internal Previews and Summaries

Internal previews are extended transitions that tell the audience, in general terms, what you will say next. These are frequently used in the body of the speech to outline in advance the details of a main point. Here are two examples:

* I am going to discuss the orientation you can expect to receive during your first few days on the job, including a tour of the plant, a one-on-one meeting with your supervisor, and a second meeting with the personnel director, who will explain the benefits and responsibilities of working for our corporation.
* Now that I've shown you that "junk" is the appropriate word to describe junk bonds, we will turn to an analysis of three secure financial instruments: bank certificates of deposit, Treasury bonds, and high-quality corporate paper.

While the first example would be found at the end of the introduction, notice that in the second example, the speaker combines a transition linking the material previously examined with the material to come. Previews are especially helpful when your main point is long and complex. Previews give listeners a set of expectations for what they will hear next. Use them whenever it is necessary to set the stage for your ideas (Turner, 1970, pp. 24–39).

Internal summaries follow a main point and act as reminders. Summaries are especially useful if you are trying to clarify or emphasize what you have just said, as is shown in the following two examples:

* In short, the American family today is not what it was 40 years ago. As we have seen, with the majority of women working outside the home and with divorce and remarriage bringing stepchildren into the family picture, the traditional family—made up of a working father, a nonworking mother, and 2.3 kids—may be a thing of the past.
* By and large, the job market seems to be easing for health care professionals, including nurses, aides, medical technicians, physical therapists, and hospital administrators.

When summaries are combined with previews, they emphasize your previous point and make connections to the point to follow:

> Overall, it is my view that cigarette advertising should not be targeted specifically at minority communities. As we have seen, R. J. Reynolds test-marketed a cigarette for African Americans known as "Uptown," only to see it come under a barrage of criticism. What is fair advertising for cigarette makers? We will discuss that next.

Organization plays an important role in effective communication. The principles rhetoricians developed five centuries ago about the internal arrangement of ideas in public speaking have been tested by time and continue to be valid. Internal previews and summaries help the speaker create meaning with the audience by reinforcing the message and identifying what comes next. Keep in mind that audience members do not have the opportunity to replay or to stop for clarification. Using transitions, previews, and internal summaries are tools a speaker can use to facilitate understanding and reduce the potential for misunderstanding (Clarke, 1963, pp. 23–27; Daniels & Whitman, 1981, pp. 147–160).

☞ Constructing an Outline and Speaker's Notes

Presenting your ideas in an organized way requires a carefully constructed planning outline and a key-word outline to be used as speaker's notes. Both forms are critical to your success as an extemporaneous speaker who relies on notes rather than a written manuscript. Your outline is your diagram connecting the information you want to communicate in a rational, consistent way. It enables you to assemble the pieces of the information so that the puzzle makes sense to you and communicates your intended meaning to your audience. Think of outlining as a process of layering ideas on paper so that every statement supports your thesis. It is a time-consuming process, but one that pays off in a skillful, confident presentation (Sprague & Stuart, 1992, p. 92).

Be familiar with the criteria for each speech assignment. Each instructor has his/her own requirements. Some may want to see your planning outline and speaker's notes while others may not. Instead of a planning outline, your instructor may ask you to turn in a full-sentence outline that includes points, subpoints, source citations, and reference pages, but excludes statements about transitions or speech flow. The following discussion is designed to help you develop and, by extension, deliver an effective speech. Your instructor will have specific ideas about the outline and note cards.

The Planning Outline

The planning outline, also known as the full-content outline, includes most of the information you will present in your speech. It does not include every word you plan to say, but gives you the flexibility required in extemporaneous speaking. An effective outline has four main components: parallelism, coordination, subordination, and division (Tardiff & Brizee, 2011).

Parallelism. On the face of it, parallelism and consistency may sound like the same thing. However, consistency refers to the numbering of sections and points of your outline, whereas parallelism refers to how you construct your sentences. For example, if one point is, "Having a pet gives your children responsibility," another main point *should not* be stated, "When should you *not* have a pet?" Instead, that main point would be phrased something like, "Knowing when to not have a pet is important." Following are a few brief examples:

* **Point 1:** Destroyed are the great redwoods that have survived over the centuries.
* **Point 2:** Vanished is the small animal life that used to grow in the great forests of our nation.
* **Point 1:** Joining the military will provide specific job skills.
* **Point 2:** Staying in the military will provide a stable income.

Parallelism goes beyond phrasing sentences, however. True parallel structure means that your introduction and your conclusion are related. For example, let's say that in your introduction to a speech on world harmony, you paint a picture of how life would be if all people on earth lived together without war or international conflict. With parallel structure, you bring back this picture after the body of your speech, so that you can show your audience that if they did what you're asking them to do (travel, communicate with people from other countries, accept differences, or whatever you propose), this is what life would be like. Using parallel structure is an effective organizational tool and provides listeners with a sense of closure.

Coordination. Coordinate points are your main ideas. We suggested earlier that your speech be composed of three to five main points. Generally speaking, each of your coordinate points should have the same significance, even though, for purposes of an informative or persuasive speech, you may find one point to be your strongest argument or one point to be your most valuable piece of information. In a speech, each coordinate point will require supporting material. In the above example about the military, it can be argued that specific job skills and stable income are two equally significant benefits of being in the military. Finding facts and statistics about these two points is part of your research process for such a speech.

Subordination. Subordinate points support your main or coordinate points. Information in your coordinate points is more general, while information in the subordinate points is more specific. Subordinate points provide relevant supporting material, such as facts, statistics, examples, or testimony. Every speech, and therefore every outline, will have both coordinate and subordinate points. For example, if you were trying to convince college students to buy a scooter, you might include the following main, or coordinate, point with the corresponding subordinate points.

I. Buying a scooter saves money
   A. A new scooter costs less than $2,500, which is only a fraction of what a new car costs.
   B. A Scooter gets between 80 and 100 miles per gallon, thus saving hundreds of dollars each year.
   C. An on-campus parking sticker for a scooter only costs $5.

Notice that the cost of a scooter, the gas mileage, and the parking sticker costs are all facts that support the idea that buying a scooter saves money.

As you notice in the examples, coordinate and subordinate points are stated as one full sentence that represents one idea. Phrases and incomplete sentences will not state your points fluently, nor will they help you think in terms of the subtle interrelationships among ideas, transitions, and word choice. *Singularity* refers to the notion that each point and subpoint comprises one, separate, but logically connected, idea. A main point should not be "We should all volunteer, and we should require that each person partake in six months of community service before age 21." These are two separate points. A well-constructed planning outline ensures a coherent, well thought-out speech. Using full sentences defines your ideas and guides your choice of language.

Division. Division refers to the fact that points and subpoints are distinct and identifiable on your outline. Each level has at least two points. So if you have a Roman numeral "I," minimally, you will see a "II." If you have a capital "A," minimally, you will see a "B." You should never have just one point or subpoint. Technically, there is no limit to how many main points or subpoints you include on your outline. If you have a large number of points, however, you may want to see if some of them can be combined, making sure you are still developing one fluid idea.

As you develop your outline, check to see how many subpoints you have under each main point. Perhaps you are providing an information overload in one section but you lack support in another area. If you believe that there isn't more than one subpoint under a main point, then perhaps you do not have an adequate main point, and you need to rethink the general structure of your argument.

In addition to addressing the four components of an effective outline, your outline should follow a consistent pattern. In a traditional outline, roman numerals label the speech's main ideas. Subordinate points are labeled with letters and numbers.

The proper positioning of the main and subordinate points with reference to the left margin is critical, for it provides a visual picture of the way your speech is organized. Be consistent with your indentation. The main points are along the left margin, and each subpoint is indented. Each subsubpoint is indented under the subpoint. This visual image presents a hierarchy that expresses the internal logic of your ideas.

In summary, as you construct your outline, check to see that you are following the principles of outlining. Doing so identifies strengths and weaknesses in support and logic, and overall, helps you create an effective speech. The following "boilerplate" suggests the format for a speech.

Name:
Specific Purpose:
Thesis Statement:
Title of Speech:

Introduction

    I. Capture attention and focus on topic
   II. Set tone and establish credibility
  III. Preview main points

Body

I. First main point
   A. First subordinate (sub-) point to explain first main point
      1. First subpoint/supporting material for first subpoint
         a. Subpoint that provides greater details or explanations
         b. Subpoint that provides more details, examples, or explanations to clarify and explain
      2. Second subpoint/supporting material for first subpoint

B. Second subordinate (sub-) point to explain first main point
   1. First subpoint/supporting material for second subpoint
   2. Second subpoint/supporting material for second subpoint
      a. Subpoint that provides greater details or explanations
      b. Subpoint that provides more details, examples, or explanations to clarify and explain

II. Second main point
   A. First subordinate (sub-) point to explain second main point
      1. First subpoint/supporting material for first subpoint
         a. Subpoint that provides greater details or explanations
         b. Subpoint that provides more details, examples, or explanations to clarify and explain
      2. Second subpoint/supporting material for first subpoint
   B. Second subordinate (sub-) point to explain second main poin
      1. First subpoint/supporting material for second subpoint
      2. Second subpoint/supporting material for second subpoint

III. Third main point
   A. First subordinate (sub-) point to explain third main point
   B. Second subordinate point to explain third main point
      1. First subpoint/supporting material for second subpoint
      2. Second subpoint/supporting material for second subpoint

Conclusion

   1. Summary of main points
   2. Relate to audience
   3. Provide closure/final thought

References (on separate sheet)

Notice the particulars:
1. Your name, the specific purpose, thesis statement, and title of your speech are all found at the top of the page.
2. Each section (introduction, body, and conclusion) is labeled.
3. Each section begins with a Roman numeral.
4. Each point is not developed identically. In some cases, there are subpoints and subsubpoints. One point may need more development than another point.

Check with your instructor to see if you should have a regular planning outline or a full-sentence outline. A full-sentence outline requires that each point be written as one full sentence. This means no sentence fragments, and no more than one sentence per point.

Include at the end of your planning outline a reference page listing all the sources used to prepare your speech, including books, magazines, journals, newspaper articles, videos, speeches, and interviews. If you are unfamiliar with documentation requirements, check the style guide preferred by your instructor, such as the *American Psychological Association (APA) Publication*

Manual (www.apastyle.apa.org) and the *Modern Literature Association (MLA) Handbook for Writers of Research Papers* (www.mla.org). For additional help with the style sheets, check out the home page of the online writing lab at owl.english.purdue.edu.

Check with your instructor to see how detailed your source citations should be in the outline. They should include last name, credentials, type of book (or magazine, journal, Web page, etc.), year/date of publication.

Transitional sentences are valuable additions to your planning outline. They are needed when you move from the introduction to the body to the conclusion of the speech. They also link main points within the body and serve as internal previews and summaries. Put these sentences in parentheses between the points being linked and use the language you may actually speak. When appropriate, include internal summaries and previews of material yet to come.

Here is an example of a planning outline that includes transitional sentences.

Speaker's Name: Corey Schultz
Specific Purpose: To persuade my audience that Standard American English (SAE) should be considered as only one of many acceptable forms of spoken English
Thesis Statement: Since Standard American English (SAE) promotes racism and classism, and is difficult to enforce, it should be only one of many acceptable forms of spoken English.
Title of Speech: Revisiting Standard American English

Introduction

I. It is a common belief shared by almost all Americans that there is only one form of acceptable spoken English, known to linguists as Standard American English (SAE).
   A. An enforced standardization of language is a common occurrence within languages across the world, and is created out of the perception that the natural evolution of language is harmful.
   B. As a result, most grammar is taught without acknowledging a difference between spoken English and written English.

II. Recent research suggests, however, that SAE's prescriptive grammar instruction is not the most ideal form.
   A. Grammar instruction in public education almost exclusively teaches SAE, which has led to the belief that "nonstandard" forms of English like African American Vernacular English, Chicano English, or Southern dialects are somehow incorrect.
   B. This stigma encourages the marginalization of several groups.

(Transition): Because most of us have learned that there is actually one form of "correct" grammar, I see a lot of confused faces in the audience. However, the perpetuation of Standard American English only serves to marginalize racial and socioeconomic groups, and should therefore be considered as only one of many acceptable forms of spoken English.

In this speech, I will examine the problems with the standardization of spoken English, such as its promotion of racism and classism. Next, I will discuss its causes, before finally addressing its solutions.

Body

I. Initially, Standard English promotes racism and classism.
  A. According to a recent personal interview with Dr. K. Aaron Smith, author of *The Development of the English Progressive*, mandating the use of Standard English in American classrooms remains the largest, most unapologetic form of racism left in the United States.
  B. In the 2010 article "Codeswitching: Tools of Language and Culture Transform the Dialectically Diverse Classroom," authors Wheeler and Swords argue that commenting on the invalidity of a student's language indirectly makes a statement about the invalidity of that student's culture.

II. By not addressing the validity of "nonstandard" English, all students are missing out on unique, important cultural perspectives.
  A. Many people do not understand that African American Vernacular English, Chicano English, and all other dialects of the language have a structured and complex system of grammar and phonology.
    1. For example, according to the previously cited interview with Dr. Smith, "aks" is one of the most commonly corrected aspects of African American Vernacular English.
    2. Aks most likely derived from the Old English verb "acsian," meaning "to ask," was considered standard English until about 1600.
    3. As "aks" is still maintained in African American Vernacular English, Jamaican English, and many dialects of British English, it isn't wrong, it's only different.
  B. Failing to open a dialogue with students about differences in dialects and vernaculars teaches students to ignore the important history of language, and teaches students to blindly follow them assuming, that their English is the only "correct" English.

(Transition): While we now understand the problems with the enforcement of Standard American English, it is also equally as important to study its causes.

III. First, English speakers hold the belief that speech must be formal to be intelligent.
  A. In 1712, Jonathan Swift wrote *A Proposal for Correcting, Improving and Ascertaining the English Tongue*, in which, among other things, he advocated for the creation of an English Academy literally for the purpose of making the language sound fancier.
    1. The concept of the double negative, which is something that many students of English struggle with, was instated to reflect the rules of math: Two negatives make a positive.
    2. However, if I say, "I ain't gonna do no work," it, in no way, means that I am going to do work.
  B. If students learned this history of the rules of grammar, it is possible that the prestige and superiority felt by many speakers of Standard English might be lessened.

IV. Second, many teachers fail to recognize a difference between written English and spoken English.
   A. According to Dr. Rai Noguchi in his book *Grammar and the Teaching of Writing*, the growing influence of the oral culture and the accompanying decline of writing complicate grammar instruction.
      1. As people read less, they have less exposure to the conventions of writing.
      2. Thus, the conventions of writing (as opposed to those of speech) often go unnoticed and must be taught formally in the schools.
   B. Similar to how scientists and doctors use specialized language to avoid ambiguity, writing in an academic context should be standardized.
      1. This is the reason for grammar instruction.
      2. When educators fail to recognize the difference between spoken English and written English, they marginalize specific groups within their classroom.

(Transition): Now that we've examined the implications of this phenomenon and looked at the reasons why we enforce standardization, let's look at some solutions to end this problem.

V. Initially, there are several ways in which you can help on a personal level.
   A. Don't correct anyone's spoken English.
   B. According to the Linguistic Society of America's *Language Rights Resolution*, many of the dialects, vernaculars, and indigenous languages of the United States are severely threatened, which means the cultures that speak those languages are also threatened.
      1. Therefore, do not judge speakers (in classrooms or otherwise) based on the way they choose to use language.
      2. Also, stand up for those who are unfairly criticized.

VI. There are several institutional changes that should be made.
   A. Because the U.S. government has never and *will* never create an institution to control and standardize language, I'm not going to ask you to write your senators.
   B. However, it may help to write a letter to your high school principal or English department chair, insisting that teachers teach grammar by separating written English and spoken English, and study the differences in grammar of both styles in the classroom.

Conclusion

   1. Today, I have discussed how standardization of the English language is a major problem in society.
   2. It's clear that if nothing is done, Standard American English will only continue to marginalize certain cultural and socioeconomic communities.
   3. It is important that we, as a society, help end this severely underestimated problem.

References

Language Rights Resolution. Linguistic Society of America. Retrieved from www.lsadc.org/lsa-res-rights.

Noguchi, R. R. (1991). *Grammar and the Teaching of Writing: Limits and Possibilities.* Urbana, IL: National Council of Teachers of English.

Smith, K. A. (2010, September 23). Personal interview at Illinois State University.

Wheeler, R. S., & Swords, R. (2010). Codeswitching: Tools of Language and Culture Transform the Dialectally Diverse Classroom. Workshop on *Developing Writers, Series #5.* Christopher Newport University. Annenberg, 1–19.

A Brief Analysis of the Planning Outline

When applying a real topic to the boilerplate provided earlier, it is easy to see how the process unfolds. Note how transitions work, moving the speaker from the introduction of the speech to the body, from one main point to the next and, finally, from the body of the speech to the conclusion.

Remember, although the word transition appears in the outline, it is not stated in your speech. Transitions help connect listeners in a personal way to the subject being discussed. It also provides the thesis statement and previews the main points of the speech.

Notice that quotes are written word for word in the outline. Also, the preview is found just before the body of the speech. Once stated, the audience will know the main ideas you intend to present. As the outline moves from first- to second- to third-level headings, the specificity of details increases. The planning outline moves from the general to the specific.

Speaker's Notes

Speaker's notes are an abbreviated key-word outline, lacking much of the detail of the planning outline. They function as a reminder of what you plan to say and the order in which you plan to say it. Speaker's notes follow exactly the pattern of your planning outline, but in a condensed format.

Follow the same indentation pattern you used in your planning outline to indicate your points and subpoints. Include notations for the introduction, body, and conclusion and indicate transitions. It is helpful to include suggestions for an effective delivery. Remind yourself to slow down, gesture, pause, use visual aids, and so on. This is helpful during your speech, especially if you experience public speaking apprehension.

Guidelines for Constructing Speaker's Notes

1. **Avoid overloading your outline.** Some speakers believe that having substantial information with them at the podium will give them confidence and make them more prepared. The opposite is usually true. Speakers who load themselves with too many details are torn between focusing on their audience and focusing on their notes. Too often, as they bob their heads up and down, they lose their place.

2. **Include only necessary information**. You need just enough information to remind you of your planned points. At times, of course, you must be certain of your facts and your words, such as when you quote an authority or present complex statistical data. In these cases, include all the information you need in your speaker's notes. Long quotes or lists of statistics can be placed on separate index cards or sheets of paper (if allowed in the situation).

3. **Reduce your sentences to key phrases**. Instead of writing: "The American Medical Association, an interest group for doctors, has lobbied against socialized medicine;" write: "The AMA and socialized medicine." Your notes should serve as a stimulus for what you are going to say. If you only need a few words to remind you, then use them. For example, Therese, who had directed several high school musicals, planned to discuss aspects of directing a high school musical. Her speaker's notes could include the following key words:
    ✢ Casting
    ✢ Blocking
    ✢ Choreography
    ✢ Singing
    ✢ Acting
    Little else would be needed, since she can easily define and/or describe these aspects of directing. However, under the key word "casting," she might include "when to cast," and "how to cast." Relevant quotes or perhaps a reference to a dramatic story would be included in the notes as well.

4. **Include transitions, but in an abbreviated form**. If you included each transition, your notes would be too long, and you would have too much written on them. Look at one of the transitions from the previous speech on the standardization of American English:

    (Transition): Because most of us have learned that there is actually one form of "correct" grammar, I see a lot of confused faces in the audience. However, the perpetuation of Standard American English only serves to marginalize racial and socioeconomic groups, and should therefore be considered as only one of many acceptable forms of spoken English.

    In this speech, we will examine the problems with the standardization of spoken English, such as its promotion of racism and classism. Next, we will discuss its causes, before finally addressing its solutions.

    Instead of these two paragraphs, your speaker's notes might look like this:
    ✢ Confused faces
    ✢ SAE marginalizes
    ✢ Will discuss problems, causes, solutions
    If you practice your speech, these words should suffice as notes. Abbreviate in a way that makes sense to you. Each person will have his or her own version of shorthand.

5. **Notes must be legible**. Your notes are useless if you cannot read them. Because you will be looking up and down at your notes as you speak, you must be able to find your place

with ease at any point. Do not reduce your planning outline to eight points and paste them to note cards. If you can type your notes, make sure they are 14-point or larger. If you write your notes, take the time to write legibly. Think about this: You may have spent several hours researching, preparing, and organizing your speech. Why take the chance of reducing the impact of your speech by writing your notes at the last minute?

Following is an example of a set of speaker's notes. The transformation from planning outline to key-word outline is noticeable in terms of length and detail. Transitions, delivery hints, and the parts of the outline are emboldened.

"Revisiting Standard American English," sample speaker's notes.

Introduction   1

    I. Belief in form of English
        A. Common throughout the world
        B. Difference between spoken and written
   II. Prescriptive grammar instruction is bad
        A. Belief that "nonstandard" English is wrong
        B. Marginalizes groups
(Look around room. Make eye contact. Slow down.)
(Standard English is racist and classist. We will examine the problems, causes, and solutions.)

Body *(Slow down)*   2

    I. Racist and classist
        A. Smith quote on racism
        B. Codeswitching
   II. Students miss cultural perspectives
        A. Other forms are legitimate
           1. "aks"
           2. Not wrong, different
        B. Teaches to ignore history of language

(Equally important to understand causes)   3

 III. Formal speech = Intelligent speech
        A. Jonathan Swift
           1. Concept of the double negative
           2. "I ain't gonna do no work" ≠ "I'm gonna do work"
        B. Don't know history of rules

IV. No perceived difference between spoken and written   4
    A. Dr. Rai Noguchi quote
        1. Less exposure to conventions
        2. Must be taught formally
    B. Writing should be standardized
        1. This is the reason for SAE
        2. Separate written and spoken English

(Let's look at solutions)   5

V. Personal solutions
    A. Do not correct
    B. Threat to dialect
        1. Do not judge
        2. Stand up for others
VI. Institutional solutions
    A. Do not write to Congress
    B. Write to school

Conclusion   6

  I. Discussed problems, causes, and solutions
  II. No change, SAE will always be bad
  III. Help
(Pause. Wait for applause.)

A Brief Analysis of Speaker's Notes

Including your specific purpose and thesis statement in your speaker's notes is unnecessary. Speaker's notes follow exactly the pattern of the planning outline so you maintain the organizational structure and flow of your speech. The introduction, body, and conclusion are labeled, although it is possible you might need only the initial letters "I," "B," and "C" to note these divisions. Nonessential words are eliminated, although some facts are included in the speaker's notes to avoid misstatement. Delivery instructions can provide helpful reminders.

The more experience you have as a speaker, the more you will come to rely on both your planning outline and speaker's notes, as both are indispensable to a successful presentation.

☞ Summary

The first step in organizing your speech is to determine your main points. Organize your efforts around your specific purpose and thesis statement, then brainstorm to generate specific ideas, and finally, group similar ideas.

Your second step is to use supporting material to develop each main point. In step 3, choose an organizational pattern. Arrange your ideas in chronological order, use a spatial organizational pattern, follow a pattern of cause and effect, look at a problem and its solutions, or choose a topical pattern. Your final step is to connect your main ideas through transitions, internal previews, and internal summaries.

As you develop your speech, your primary organizational tool is the planning outline, which includes most of the information you will present. The outline uses a traditional outline format, which establishes a hierarchy of ideas. The number of main points developed in your speech should be between two and five. The planning outline uses complete sentences, labels transitions, and includes a reference list.

Speaker's notes, the notes you use during your presentation in an extemporaneous speech, are less detailed than the planning outline. They serve as brief reminders of what you want to say and the order in which you say it. They may include complete quotations and statistical data as well as important delivery suggestions. Speaker's notes are organized around phrases, not sentences, and they use the same format as the planning outline.

☞ References

Clarke, M. L. (1963). *Rhetoric at Rome: Historical Survey*. New York: Barnes & Noble.

Creating and Using Presentation Note Cards. Retrieved September 2, 2011 from www.wisc-online.com/objects/ViewObject.aspx?ID=SPH3102.

Daniels, T. D., & Witman, R. F. (1981). The Effects of Message Structure in Verbal Organizing Ability upon Learning Information. *Human Communication Research, Winter*, 147–160.

Horner, W. B. (1988). *Rhetoric in the Classical Tradition*. New York: St. Martin's Press.

Lemonick, M. D. (2007, July 5). How We Get Addicted. *Time*. Retrieved February 15, 2011 from time.com.

Makay, J., & Fetzger, R. C. (1984). *Business Communication Skills: Principles and Practice*, 2nd Ed. Englewood Cliffs, NJ: Prentice-Hall.

Sprague, J., & Stuart, D. (1992). *The Speaker's Handbook*, 3rd Ed. San Diego: Harcourt Brace Jovanovich.

Supporting a Speech. Retrieved September 2, 2011 from www.hawaii.edu/mauispeech/html/supporting_materials.html.

Tardiff, E., & Brizee, A. (2011). Four Main Components of an Effective Outline. Retrieved September 8, 2011 from www.owl.english.purdue.edu/owl/resource/544/01.

Turner, F. H., Jr. (1970). The Effects of Speech Summaries on Audience Comprehension. *Central States Speech Journal, Spring*, 24–39.

Willerton, D. R. (1999, December). *Toward a Rhetoric of Marketing for High-Tech Service*. Published Master's Thesis, University of North Texas. Retrieved August 31, 2011 from digital.library.unt.edu/ark:/67531/metadc2432/m1/1/high_res_d/thesis.pdf.

Chapter 6

Introducing and Concluding Your Speech

"The White Rabbit put on his spectacles. 'Where shall I begin, please your Majesty?' he asked. 'Begin at the beginning,' the King said gravely, 'and go on till you come to the end: then stop.'"
— Lewis Carroll's *Alice's Adventures in Wonderland*

SPEECH: General Douglas MacArthur — Duty, Honor, Country

General Douglas MacArthur (1880–1964) had a long career in the U.S. Army, which included active and distinguished duty in World War I, World War II, and the Korean Conflict. He served as an aide to President Theodore Roosevelt and as Chief of Staff of the U.S. Army for Presidents Herbert Hoover and Franklin Roosevelt. Gen. MacArthur delivered this speech on May 12, 1962 to the cadets of the U.S. Military Academy at West Point. Gen. MacArthur received the Sylvanus Thayer Award, which recognized him as an outstanding citizen for his lifetime of service and accomplishments that exemplified the ideals of West Point's motto: Duty, Honor, Country.

Sources: http://www.macarthurmemorial.org/DocumentCenter/View/1689
https://www.westpointaog.org/thayerward

Duty, Honor, Country

No human being could fail to be deeply moved by such a tribute as this [Thayer Award]. Coming from a profession I have served so long and a people I have loved so well, it fills me with an emotion I cannot express. But this award is not intended primarily to honor a personality, but to symbolize a great moral code-a code of conduct and chivalry of those who guard this beloved land of culture and ancient descent. For all hours and for all time, it is an expression of the ethics of the American soldier. That I should be integrated in this way with so noble an ideal arouses a sense of pride, and yet of humility, which will be with me always.

Duty, honor, country: Those three hallowed words reverently dictate what you ought to be, what you can be, what you will be. They are your rallying point to build courage when courage seems to fail, to regain faith when there seems to be little cause for faith, to create hope when hope becomes forlorn.

Unhappily, I possess neither that eloquence of diction, that poetry of imagination, nor that brilliance of metaphor to tell you all that they mean.

The unbelievers will say they are but words, but a slogan, but a flamboyant phrase. Every pedant, every demagogue, every cynic, every hypocrite, every troublemaker, and, I am sorry to say, some others of an entirely different character, will try to downgrade them even to the extent of mockery and ridicule.

But these are some of the things they do. They build your basic character. They mold you for your future roles as the custodians of the Nation's defense. They make you strong enough to know when you are weak, and brave enough to face yourself when you are afraid.

They teach you to be proud and unbending in honest failure, but humble and gentle in success; not to substitute words for actions, not to seek the path of comfort, but to face the stress and spur of difficulty and challenge; to learn to stand up in the storm, but to have compassion on those who fall; to master yourself before you seek to master others; to have a heart that is clean, a goal that is high; to learn to laugh, yet never forget how to weep; to reach into the future, yet never neglect the past; to be serious, yet never to take yourself too seriously; to be modest so that you will remember the simplicity of true greatness, the open mind of true wisdom, the meekness of true strength.

They give you a temperate will, a quality of the imagination, a vigor of the emotions, a freshness of the deep springs of life, a temperamental predominance of courage over timidity, of an appetite for adventure over love of ease.

They create in your heart the sense of wonder, the unfailing hope of what next, and joy and inspiration of life. They teach you in this way to be an officer and a gentleman.

And what sort of soldiers are those you are to lead? Are they reliable? Are they brave? Are they capable of victory?

Their story is known to all of you. It is the story of the American man-at-arms. My estimate of him was formed on the battlefield many, many years ago, and has never changed. I regarded him then, as I regard him now, as one of the world's noblest figures; not only as one of the finest military characters, but also as one of the most stainless.

His name and fame are the birthright of every American citizen. In his youth and strength, his love and loyalty, he gave all that mortality can give. He needs no eulogy from me; or from any other man. He has written his own history and written it in red on his enemy's breast.

But when I think of his patience in adversity of his courage under fire and of his modesty in victory, I am filled with an emotion of admiration I cannot put into words. He belongs to history as furnishing one of the greatest examples of successful patriotism. He belongs to posterity as the instructor of future generations in the principles of liberty and freedom. He belongs to the present, to us, by his virtues and by his achievements.

In 20 campaigns, on a hundred battlefields, around a thousand camp fires, I have witnessed that enduring fortitude, that patriotic self-abnegation, and that invincible determination which have carved his statue in the hearts of his people.

From one end of the world to the other, he has drained deep the chalice of courage. As I listened to those songs [of the glee club], in memory's eye I could see those staggering columns of the first World War, bending under soggy packs on many a weary march, from dripping dusk to drizzling dawn, slogging ankle deep through the mire of shell-shocked roads to form grimly for the attack, blue-lipped, covered with sludge and mud, chilled by the wind and rain, driving home to their objective, and for many to the judgment seat of God.

I do not know the dignity of their birth, but I do know the glory of their death. They died, unquestioning, uncomplaining, with faith in their hearts, and on their lips the hope that we would go on to victory.

Always for them: Duty, honor, country. Always their blood, and sweat, and tears, as we sought the way and the light and the truth. And 20 years after, on the other side of the globe, again the filth of murky foxholes, the stench of ghostly trenches, the slime of dripping dugouts, those boiling suns of relentless heat, those torrential rains of devastating storms, the loneliness and utter desolation of jungle trails, the bitterness of long separation from those they loved and cherished, the deadly pestilence of tropical disease, the horror of stricken areas of war.

Their resolute and determined defense, their swift and sure attack, their indomitable purpose, their complete and decisive victory-always through the bloody haze of their last reverberating shot, the vision of gaunt, ghastly men, reverently following your password of duty, honor, country.

The code which those words perpetuate embraces the highest moral law and will stand the test of any ethics or philosophies ever promulgated for the things that are right and its restraints are from the things that are wrong. The soldier, above all other men, is required to practice the greatest act of religious training — sacrifice. In battle, and in the face of danger and death, he discloses those divine attributes which his Maker gave when He created man in His own image. No physical courage and no greater strength can take the place of the divine help which alone can sustain him. However hard the incidents of war may be, the soldier who is called upon to offer and to give his life for his country is the noblest development of mankind.

You now face a new world, a world of change. The thrust into outer space of the satellite, spheres, and missiles marks a beginning of another epoch in the long story of mankind. In the five or more billions of years the scientists tell us it has taken to form the earth, in the three or more billion years of development of the human race, there has never been a more abrupt or staggering evolution.

We deal now, not with things of this world alone, but with the illimitable distances and as yet unfathomed mysteries of the universe. We are reaching out for a new and boundless frontier. We speak in strange terms of harnessing the cosmic energy, of making winds and tides work for us, of creating unheard of synthetic materials to supplement or even replace our old standard basics; to purify sea water for our drink; of mining ocean floors for new fields of wealth and food; of disease preventatives to expand life into the hundred of years; of controlling the weather for a more equitable distribution of heat and cold, of rain and shine; of spaceships to the moon; of the primary target in war, no longer limited to the armed forces of an enemy, but instead to include his civil populations; of ultimate conflict between a united human race and the sinister forces of some other planetary galaxy; of such dreams and fantasies as to make life the most exciting of all times.

And through all this welter of change and development your mission remains fixed, determined, inviolable. It is to win our wars. Everything else in your professional career is but corollary to this vital dedication. All other public purposes, all other public projects, all other public needs, great or small, will find others for their accomplishment; but you are the ones who are trained to fight.

Yours is the profession of arms, the will to win, the sure knowledge that in war there is no substitute for victory, that if you lose, the Nation will be destroyed, that the very obsession of your public service must be duty, honor, country.

Others will debate the controversial issues, national and international, which divide men's minds. But serene, calm, aloof, you stand as the Nation's war guardian, as its lifeguard from the raging tides of international conflict, as its gladiator in the arena of battle. For a century and a half you have defended, guarded, and protected its hallowed traditions of liberty and freedom, of right and justice.

Let civilian voices argue the merits or demerits of our processes of government: Whether our strength is being sapped by deficit financing indulged in too long, by Federal paternalism grown too mighty, by power groups grown too arrogant, by politics grown too corrupt, by crime grown too rampant, by morals grown too low, by taxes grown too high, by extremists grown too violent; whether our personal liberties are as thorough and complete as they should be.

These great national problems are not for your professional participation or military solution. Your guidepost stands out like a ten-fold beacon in the night: Duty, honor, country.

You are the leaven which binds together the entire fabric of our national system of defense. From your ranks come the great captains who hold the Nation's destiny in their hands the moment the war tocsin sounds.

The long, gray line has never failed us. Were you to do so, a million ghosts in olive drab, in brown khaki, in blue and gray, would rise from their white crosses, thundering those magic words: Duty, honor, country.

This does not mean that you are warmongers. On the contrary, the soldier above all other people prays for peace, for he must suffer and bear the deepest wounds and scars of war. But always in our ears ring the ominous words of Plato, that wisest of all philosophers: "Only the dead have seen the end of war."

The shadows are lengthening for me. The twilight is here. My days of old have vanished — tone and tint. They have gone glimmering through the dreams of things that were. Their memory is one of wondrous beauty, watered by tears and coaxed and caressed by the smiles of yesterday. I listen vainly, but with thirsty ear, for the witching melody of faint bugles blowing reveille, of far drums beating the long roll.

In my dreams I hear again the crash of guns, the rattle of musketry, the strange, mournful mutter of the battle-field. But in the evening of my memory always I come back to West Point. Always there echoes and re-echoes: Duty, honor, country.

Today marks my final roll call with you. But I want you to know that when I cross the river, my last conscious thoughts will be of the corps, and the corps, and the corps.

I bid you farewell.

The text of this speech is reproduced from Department of Defense Pamphlet GEN-1A, US Government Printing Office, 1964.
http://www.au.af.mil/au/awc/awcgate/au-24/au24-352mac.htm

Imagine your classmate is about to give a persuasive speech on intercultural communication, and is mulling over an almost unlimited number of ways to start. Consider the following three possibilities:

* Bonjour! Parce que ma presentation s'agit d'une question de la communication inter-culturelle, j'ai décidé de presenter completement en français! D'accord? Bien. La communication interculturelle est un grand probleme dans l'Etats Unis et d'autres nations ont beaucoup souffert. In other words, intercultural communication, or rather, lack thereof, is a huge problem that has plagued America as well as other foreign countries across the world.

* How many of you have finished your foreign language requirement for college graduation? How many of you feel that you are fluent in another language? Do you realize that it's not unusual for our European counterparts to speak four languages? Intercultural communication or rather, lack thereof, is a huge problem that has plagued America as well as foreign countries across the world.
* Intercultural communication or rather, lack thereof, is a huge problem that has plagued America as well as foreign countries across the world.

Which beginning do you find most creative? Least creative? Most engaging? Least engaging? Which one would be the easiest to develop? The most difficult? Which is most direct?

As you look at the above examples, a final question comes to mind. Are all three examples acceptable ways to begin a speech? The answer may certainly be yes. The way you begin and end your speech is critical to your overall success. Expending effort on your introduction is time well spent.

This chapter approaches introductions and conclusions in relation to how your speech can make a lasting impression. Two topics are considered: how to engage your audience at the beginning of your speech so they will be motivated to listen to the rest of it, and how to remind your audience at the end of your speech what you said and why it was relevant. For both introducing and concluding your speech, strategies and pitfalls are identified to help you craft your best start and finish.

The primacy/recency effect, explained in the previous chapter, sheds light on the importance of effective speech beginnings and endings. This theory suggests that we tend to recall more vividly the beginning and ending, and less of the middle of an event. When several candidates are interviewing for a job, the first and last candidates have an advantage because the interviewer is most likely to remember more about these two than the others. This theory also holds true for speeches: Your audience will likely recall more of the beginning and ending of your speech than the content in the middle.

The familiar speaker adage, "Tell them what you are going to say, say it, and then tell them what you said," addresses this truth. Beginning and ending a speech well helps your audience remember and, later use, the ideas you present. Let's begin with a closer look at introductions.

Introductions

If done well, an **introduction** helps your audience make a smooth transition to the main points of your speech, create a positive first impression, and set an appropriate tone and mood for your talk. If done poorly, your audience may prejudge your topic as unimportant or dull and stop listening.

Consider the following example. As part of a conference for a group of business executives, business consultant Edith Weiner was scheduled to deliver a speech on the unequal distribution of world resources—admittedly, a topic with the potential to put her listeners to sleep. She was experienced enough as a speaker, though, to realize that the last thing her listeners wanted to hear at the beginning was a long list of statistics comparing the bounty of North America to the paucities in other parts of the world. Her speech would never recover from such a dull start. The challenge she faced was to capture the audience's attention at the outset.

Arriving at the auditorium early on the morning of her speech, Weiner marked off different-sized sections of the hall to represent, proportionately, the continents. She allotted coffee, pastries, and chairs according to the availability of food and income in each. Then she assigned audience members to these areas according to actual world population ratios.

What happened was memorable. While 30 people in the area representing Africa had to divide three cups of coffee, two pastries, and two chairs, the 17 people assigned to North America had more coffee and pastries than they could eat in a week, surrounded by 40 chairs. As participants took their seats (with those in Asia and Africa standing), they did so with a new perspective on world hunger and poverty, and with a desire to listen to whatever Weiner had to say. She began:

> I wanted to speak … about a topic most people tire of, but you, being so important to the financial community, cannot ignore. …
>
> Hunger and poverty aren't comfortable, are they? Neither is bounty when you realize the waste and mismatch of people and resources. …
> (Interview with Edith Weiner, October 10, 1989)

Edith Weiner's risky introduction grabbed the attention of all audience members in a powerful way.

Functions of Introductions

The emphasis on strong opening comments has long been held as important. In the first century Roman philosopher Quintillian noted that for a speech to be effective, an introduction must do four things (Corbettt & Connor, 1999). Introductions must:

1. Capture attention and focus
2. Provide a motive for the audience to listen
3. Enhance the credibility of the speaker
4. Preview the message and organization

Edith Weiner's introduction was effective because it accomplished each of these objectives, as we shall see.

Capture Attention and Focus

Every experienced speaker knows that the first few moments are critical to the success of the entire speech. It is within these minutes that your listeners decide whether they care enough to continue listening. You want your listeners to think, "This is interesting," or "I didn't know that," or "That was really funny." The common denominator in each of these responses is piqued audience interest.

Many introductions contain a personalized greeting. This acknowledges the audience and tells listeners that you see the speech as an opportunity to communicate your point of view. William Kamkwamba (2009) was invited to speak before participants at a TED (technology, entertainment, and development) conference to tell how, at 14 years of age, he invented a windmill from scraps in his poverty-stricken country. He began his message in this way: "Two years ago I stood on the TED stage in Arusha, Tanzania. I spoke very briefly about one of my proudest creations. It was a simple machine that changed my life."

Kamkwamba's first appearance at TED two years earlier was unsuccessful because he was too nervous and overwhelmed. At that first speech, his only words were "I tried, and I made it." In his address two years later, he referenced this failure in his introduction, explaining: "Before that time I had never been away from my home in Malawi. I had never used a computer. I had never seen an Internet. On the stage that day, I was so nervous. My English lost, I wanted to vomit. [(Laughter)] I had never been surrounded by so many azungu, white people. [Laughter)]"

Such self-effacing humor and honest, vulnerable explanation created a bond with his audience and piqued their interest in what he would have said two years earlier. Kamkwamba continued with: "There was a story I wouldn't tell you then. But, well, I'm feeling good right now. I would like to share that story today."

As you capture the attention and focus of your audience, you also need to set the mood and tone of your speech. The **mood** of a speech refers to the overall feeling you hope to engender in your audience. **Tone** is the emotional disposition of the speaker as the speech is being delivered. Tone is created verbally by the words and ideas you select and nonverbally, by the emotions you communicate.

Imagine observing the following scenario: Angela stood behind the podium beside the closed casket as she delivered the eulogy to tearful faces. Her sentimental message of grief was appropriate in every way except that she delivered it with a smile. The whole speech! The disconnect between her words and facial expressions was unsettling, to say the least. Angela later confessed that she smiled because she wanted to communicate that she was glad to be there and honored to perform such an important duty. Unfortunately, Angela did not create an appropriate tone and mood in her introduction.

Consider the desired mood and adjust your tone appropriately in the introduction. In this way, you ensure that your tone matches your reason for speaking and that your speech creates the desired mood in your audience.

Provide a Motive to Listen

An effective speaker quickly establishes a reason for audience members to listen. Edith Weiner's introduction helped build that critical relationship with her public speaking audience. She wanted her listeners to care about her message. She wanted them to decide from the outset that what she was saying had meaning and importance. Although the introduction also helped make her point with its physical demonstration of world food problems, its primary purpose was to build a psychological bridge that would last throughout the speech.

Her well-designed demonstration led her audience to care about her topic because Weiner had effectively related the topic of her speech to something the audience cared about, their own hunger.

The introduction should seek to establish common ground with the audience. By focusing on something you and your audience can share and announcing it early, you help people identify with your topic. When people perceive that your message is meant for them and is relevant to their lives, they will listen attentively.

Enhance Credibility

During your introduction, your listeners make important decisions about you. They decide whether they like you and whether you are credible. Your **credibility** as a speaker is judged, in large part, on the basis of what you say during your introduction, how you say it, and how you carry yourself.

Edith Weiner (1989) became a credible speaker by demonstrating, in a participatory way, that she understood the problems of world food distribution and that she cared enough about her audience—and topic—to come up with a creative way to present her ideas. Credibility also increases as you identify, early on, what qualifies you to speak about a topic. Weiner might have said, "I want to talk to you about world resources because for several years I have studied how your investments overseas can have important impacts on your future economic well-being." Similarly, Angela, the inappropriately smiling mourner, might have mentioned early on that she was close to the deceased, knew her for 30 years, and thought of her as a sister. Offering an explanation linking you to the topic you are covering helps your audience believe in you and trust your ideas.

Audiences may have an initial sense of your credibility even before you speak. Your introduction is an ideal place to enhance that impression. As we discuss later in the text, you can think of your credibility in terms of your perceived competence, concern for your audience, dynamism, and personal ethics. Put another way, if you know your subject, care about your audience, offer an enthusiastic delivery, and communicate a sense of ethical integrity, your audience's impression of your credibility will likely be positive. The content and delivery of your introduction must maximize these four aspects if you want your audience to listen attentively throughout your speech.

Preview Your Message and Organization

Finally, Weiner used her introduction to tell her audience what she would talk about during the rest of her speech. In a sentence, she previewed her focus. ("I intend to explore several options [for maximizing your role and gain] during the rest of my speech.") This simple statement helped her listeners make the intellectual connections they needed to follow her speech. Instead of wondering, "What will she talk about?" or "What is her point of view?" they were ready for her speech to unfold.

As we said in the opening of this chapter, your audience will recall your message more fully if you tell them what you are going to say, say it, and then tell them what you said.

Repeating key ideas helps us recall important information. But the first part, telling them what you are going to say, also provides a preview of the organization you intend to use. If your audience knows the main points you intend to develop in your speech, they are less likely to be confused and distracted. So, an effective introduction might offer a preview statement similar to "Today it is important that we better understand the nature of world hunger, explore creative solutions to this problem, and finally, see if some of these solutions might also be profitable to your business." In this example, the audience learns that there will be three main points to the message.

Here is how Agnes, a student at an international university in Manila, Philippines, started her informative speech on child obesity and junk food at home. The preview statement is italicized:

> In July, 2011, McDonald's announced changes to their well-known "Happy Meals" to offer healthier food. Happy Meals target children. United States First Lady Michelle Obama, who has been campaigning against childhood obesity, has commended McDonald's for their action.
>
> Following suit, the National Restaurant Association in the U. S. announced their Kids Live Well program. This means dozens of restaurant chains, including Burger King and Denny's, committed to offering healthier meals for children, too. Great, right? But what about candy, soda, pizza, and other snacks at home?
>
> Changes have been made and are starting to be made across the globe, but many individuals are not taking action here in Manila. More parents need to get involved in this movement because it will better the lives of many children. *Today, I will more clearly define "junk food," discuss the health issues it creates for our kids, and offer easy alternatives to junk food in your home.*

When Agnes finished this statement, her audience had no doubt what her speech would cover. When you preview your message, your audience will listen and understand with increased clarity and will remember more of your message later.

Developing Effective Introductions

There are many ways to accomplish Quintillion's four functions of an introduction. Following are 10 techniques often used in introductions. You might consider using one or combining several to provide the initial impact you want. This is one area where a little creativity can go a long way. Keep your audience in mind. A few of these techniques may be more appropriate or attention-getting for your specific audience and specific purpose.

Startling Facts/Intriguing Statements

Some introductions seem to force listeners to pay attention. They make it difficult to think of other things because of the impact of what is being said. The effectiveness of these introductions in part, comes from the audience's feeling that the speaker's message is directed at them.

Here is how Lady Gaga began her speech at a rally in Portland, Maine in September 2010 to repeal the military's Don't Ask, Don't Tell policy. After noting that the title of her speech was "The Prime Rib of America" she stated:

> I do solemnly swear, or affirm, that I will support and defend the Constitution of the United States, against all enemies foreign and domestic, and I will bear true faith and allegiance to do the same, and I will obey the orders of the president of the United States and the orders of the officers appointed over me, according to regulations and the uniform code of military justice, so help me God.
>
> Unless, there's a gay soldier in my unit, sir.

Starting with this oath served as an intriguing statement, since it wasn't clear initially why she would include it in her speech. Her last statement is startling, and quickly gets to the heart of the issue. In this case, she took the familiar and turned it on its side to arouse audience emotions.

Startling statements often challenge the listener. Instead of revealing the expected, the speaker takes a slightly—or perhaps even a radically—different turn.

Dramatic Story/Build Suspense

Closely related to the startling statement is the dramatic story, which involves listeners in a tale from beginning to end. Shortly after returning from a winter vacation break, Shannon delivered a speech to her classmates that began this way:

> My friends and I were driving home from a day at the ski slopes when suddenly, without warning, a pair of headlights appeared directly in front of our car. To avoid a collision, I swerved sharply to the right, forcing our car off the road into a snow-filled ditch.
>
> It's funny what comes into your mind at moments like this. All I could think of was how Justin Mentell, who used to be on *Boston Legal*, one of my favorite TV shows, died on icy roads just a month ago. And he was only 27. I thought I was going to die, too, just because of another driver's stupidity and carelessness.
>
> Obviously, I didn't die or even suffer any serious injuries. And my friends are safe, too, although my car was totaled. I'm convinced that we are all here today because we were locked into place by our seat belts. Justin Mentell might have been here, too, had he bothered to buckle up.

Everyone in the audience knew what it was like to be driving home with friends—feeling safe and secure—only to be shocked into the realization that they were vulnerable to tragedy. Audience attention was riveted on the speaker as she launched into her speech on seat belt use.

Quotation and/or Literature Reference

You can capture audience attention by citing the words of others. If you use an appropriate quotation, the words themselves may be compelling enough to engage your listeners. One of the most well-known quotes from Harry Potter was used by a student to introduce the subject of his speech, sarcasm:

> "You know your mother, Malfoy? The expression on her face—like she's got dung under her nose? Is she like that all the time or just because you were with her?"

This passage was selected because it is funny, clever, and sarcastic. He set the stage for a lighter look at the harms of sarcasm with this quotation.

Robert Frost, well-known American poet, is frequently quoted from his poem *The Road Not Taken*, particularly, the last three lines:

> Two roads diverged in a wood, and I—
> I took the one less travelled by,
> and that has made all the difference.

The last three lines can be the start of a speech about following your heart, choosing your own path, making your own decisions, not following the crowd.

The two examples above have been used by others to start a speech or make some point. In addition to using the words of a *well-known individual*, you could also cite the words of a *recognized authority* whose reputation enhances your credibility.

Here, for example, is how Toby, a public speaking student, began his speech to capture the attention of his audience. Quoting a knowledgeable public figure, he began:

> "Today, 12.5 million children are overweight in the United States—more than 17 percent. Overweight children are at greater risk for many serious health problems." These are the words of your U.S. Surgeon General, Dr. Regina M. Benjamin (OSG, 2011). Dr. Benjamin continues with the following facts:
> Overweight adolescents have a 70 percent chance of becoming overweight or obese adults.
> The number of overweight children has more than tripled over the past three decades.
> Studies show that nearly 34 percent of children and teens in America are either overweight or at risk of becoming overweight.
> Research has shown that parents are often their children's most important role model. If children see their caregivers enjoying healthy foods and being physically active, they are more likely to do the same.

These powerful words from a recognized expert set the stage for Toby to advocate parental involvement in combating the childhood obesity epidemic our nation faces.

In similar fashion, Christopher, another public speaking student, captured his audience's attention when speaking about the nation's health care crisis by stating:

> If a criminal has a right to an attorney, don't you have a right to a doctor? President Obama put it like this: "Everybody here understands the desperation that people feel when they're sick. And I think everybody here is profoundly sympathetic and wants

to make sure that we have a system that works for all Americans" (msnbc.com, 2011). Obama sent a clear wake-up call to Congress to get serious about health care reform in America.

Christopher introduces the topic of health care by quoting the words of our president. Although these words could have been uttered by anyone, Christopher establishes credibility at the beginning of his speech by using a recognized authority.

Humor

At the beginning of a speech, humor helps break down the psychological barriers that exist between speaker and audience. Here is how Karen used humor at the start of a classroom speech on the problem of divorce in America:

> Janet and Lauren had been college roommates, but had not seen each other in the 10 years since graduation. They were thrilled when they ran into each other at a college reunion and had a chance to talk.
>
> "Tell me," asked Janet, "has your husband lived up to the promises he made when he was dating you in college?"
>
> "He certainly has!" said Lauren. "He told me then that he wasn't good enough for me and he's proven it ever since."
>
> The class laughed, Karen waited, then:
>
> I laughed, too, when I heard that story. But the fact remains that about half the marriages in our country end in divorce and one of the major reasons for these failures is that one partner can't live up to the expectations of the other.

Humor works in this introduction for two reasons. First, the story is genuinely funny; we chuckle when we hear the punch line. And, second, the humor is tied directly to the subject of the speech; it is appropriate for the topic and the occasion. It also provides an effective transition into the speech body.

Humor *can* work when it's self-deprecating. Rahm Emanuel, mayor of Chicago, was known for his profanity-laced communication. At a commencement ceremony at George Washington University in 2009, he made reference to that at the beginning of his speech:

> Congratulations. I also want to thank George Washington University for bestowing this honorary degree. This is actually the second honorary degree I've received this year. Just last week I was awarded an honorary degree for my contribution in the field of linguistics, particularly my work in four-letter words.

Again, humor makes the audience snicker, giggle, or cackle, and it can set the right tone for your speech. Make sure you *can* do humor. At the 2011 Academy Awards, the loudest laughter came when Billy Crystal took the stage away briefly from hosts Anne Hathaway and James Franco, who were *trying* to be funny. If you are not comfortable with humor and elect to force it, both you and your listeners will feel awkward.

Rhetorical Question

When you ask your audience, "How many of you ate breakfast this morning?" you expect to see people raise their hands. When you ask a *rhetorical* question, however, you do not expect an answer. What you hope is that your question will cause your listeners to start thinking about the subject of your speech.

Imagine a speech about the negative effects of snoring. It could start like this:

> Have you ever been told you snore? Have you ever had to sleep in the same room with someone who has a loud snore? Have you been told you have a "cute" little snore?

These are all rhetorical questions. The speaker is not expecting someone to answer these questions aloud. The purpose is to get the audience to start thinking about the topic. Hopefully, the speaker has their attention. Then the speaker continues:

> If you don't snore, be grateful. If you do snore, you need to hear this. If you don't snore, but you marry "a snorer," well, good luck! Studies show that married couples argue about snoring as much as they do money; snoring couples have less sex than nonsnoring couples, and over 20 percent of couples regularly sleep apart due to snoring. Ouch! Oh, and there's more. The nonsnorer faces difficulties from sleep deprivation. In the next few minutes I'm going to describe the economic consequences of being sleep deprived, including increased health care costs, automobile accidents, workplace accidents, and decreased job performance.

The speaker linked the rhetorical questions and startling facts to audience, and previewed the main points in her speech. The best rhetorical questions are probing in a personal way. They mean something to every listener and encourage active participation throughout your speech.

Illustrations, Examples, and Anecdotes

Speakers often begin with an interesting comment about the immediate surroundings or some recent or historical event. These openings are even more powerful when the speaker carefully plans these comments. Through the skillful use of *illustrations* ("In the short time I will be talking with you, 150 violent crimes will have been committed in our nation"), *examples* ("Lisa was a young woman from our community whose life was forever altered on January 18th"), and *anecdotes* ("Once, while traveling on the subway, I noticed a shifty looking man carefully watching each passenger enter and leave the car"), speakers gather our attention to them and their message.

Physically Involve the Audience

An example of this technique regularly occurs at sales seminars, where the speaker offers a gift, usually money, to the first person in the audience who will simply leave his/her seat and come to the front to get it. Eventually some brave soul approaches, takes the money, and returns to his/her seat. Then everyone else in the audience realizes they could have had the gift themselves if they had only been willing to act instead of sitting passively.

In a speech about the importance of eating a good breakfast, a speaker could start by asking all students who ate breakfast to raise their hands. Then, the speaker could ask how many of those ate at fast food, or ate eggs or fruit. Depending on how the speaker defined a good breakfast, the questions could lead the speaker to comment that "Only a few of you had a good breakfast today. I hope to make a difference for tomorrow."

Some speakers may ask the audience to yell "Good morning" until they've been loud enough. A speaker talking about the need for exercise may ask the audience to jump up and down for a few moments. At a graduation speech in 2003 at the University of Wisconsin, after thanking the administration, director and movie producer Jerry Zucker involved the audience physically when he started his speech with the following:

> Before I start my remarks, I'd like everyone just to do something for me. Very simply— so everyone can kind of just get to know everyone else—on the count of three, I'd like everyone to turn around and shake the hand of the person sitting right behind you. One, two, three—right now, everybody, please do that.

Relate Personal Experience

Sharing a story or several examples from your past with your listeners can be an effective start. Be sure your personal experiences will not hurt your credibility and that they relate directly to your topic. Recently, a student giving a "speech of presentation" started this way:

> It was the end of my third week of college, and the problem was getting harder and harder to ignore. I, like so many people today, had no idea where to turn, or who to talk to. So, I took to the streets. I walked up 4th, walked around the Courthouse, and then headed due east. Finally, on 9th Street, I found hope again ... In the form of Terry's Clip and Chip Barbershop. You see, my hair had started tickling the backs of my ears, and I was getting that abhorrent ring-around-the-collar phenomenon ...

The student's speech was to present a Small Business award to the barbershop/golf repair shop. He continued to describe his experience as an illustration of why Terry's Clip and Chip deserved the award. It was a humorous beginning with a personal story that related directly to the topic.

Use a Visual or Media Aid

Before the president of the United States speaks, the broadcast feed from the White House shows the presidential seal. This is no accident; it helps to draw attention to the upcoming speech and also helps reinforce the president's credibility. But you do not have to be the president to use this technique. Beginning your speech with an interesting sound recording, visual, or prop is guaranteed to draw attention to the beginning of your speech, too. Showing the world population clock or the U.S. debt clock grabs attention, as would some funny or startling YouTube video. One student brought a garbage bag filled with one week's worth of used diapers for one child to demonstrate how much waste is produced.

Refer to the Situation

Skilled public speakers often begin with a positive comment related to the occasion, the person who spoke before them, the audience, the date, or even the physical location. Each of these may be more appropriate at one time than at another. For example, a commencement speaker at her alma mater might start, "It's hard for me to believe that 25 years ago I sat in those seats listening to the commencement speaker." Or, if an audience was waiting outside in the rain to hear a Democratic candidate who was late, the candidate might start, "I bet there isn't a more committed group of voters than those of you here who have been standing in the rain waiting for me." When you are planning a speech, ask yourself if referencing the event, a prior speaker, the audience, or the significance of this date in history would create interest and gather attention.

Each of these is an option for opening a speech. Keep in mind that your attention-gaining device must relate in some way to your topic or you run the risk of confusing your audience. Your choice should be guided by several other factors. First, consider the mood you are attempting to create. Second, consider your audience's expectations of you and the occasion. Third, consider how much time and resources each approach will require. Finally, consider your strengths and weaknesses—you may not be as strong at joke telling as recalling a powerful story.

Five Guidelines and Suggestions for Introductions

As you focus on crafting your introduction for your next speech, consider how you can create a strong and effective message. Remember, as in any recipe, no ingredient stands on its own. Attention to each part of the process leads to an excellent final product. After choosing the most appropriate beginning, consider these general guidelines as you prepare and deliver your introduction.

1. Prepare After the Body of the Speech

Your introduction will take form more easily after you have created an outline of the body of your speech. When speakers attempt to create the introduction first, they inevitably rewrite it several times as they continue to change the body of their message. However, some students find that writing the introduction after selecting a thesis and main points helps to "jump start" the rest of the creative process. In either case, the direction and key ideas are in place before the introduction is considered.

2. Make It Creative and Easy to Follow

Whether you are offering a startling statistic or asking a question, keep things simple. When you offer your thesis and even when you preview your main points, look for ways to be concise and straight-forward. Recently, a student beginning his persuasive speech started with his arms open in a pleading gesture, zealously urging the class, "Please! Please I beg of you—stop washing your hands!" He then briefly noted the dangers of too much cleansing and stated his thesis.

His enthusiastic approach and startling plea made for a creative introduction that was simple and easy to understand.

Consider your introduction as an invitation to creativity. The more creative your introduction, the more likely your audience will listen to the entire message. One student turned the lectern around on the table so the top sloped toward his audience, climbed up, and perched himself atop with legs dangling, and paused. His audience chuckled at his odd behavior. Then he forcefully announced, "Science has discovered a link between nonconformity and intelligence." His audience roared! His speech about nonconformity and intelligence was well received, but his attention-gaining strategy was risky. Sometimes creativity can backfire. Be sure your strategy suits your occasion and audience expectations of the speaker.

3. Communicate High Energy by Being Well Practiced

The most important part of your speech to practice thoroughly is the introduction, followed by the conclusion, and then the body. The first impression created by a well-practiced introduction lays the foundation for your ultimate success. Rehearse your introduction many times. Your introduction should be delivered enthusiastically. Since introductions are relatively short, put your heart, mind, and energy into it. If you are truly engaged in the introduction, your audience is more likely to become involved in your message.

It is difficult to communicate high energy if you are dependent on notes. Strive to avoid looking at notes during your introduction. Rehearsing your introduction helps you accomplish this.

4. Engage Audience Nonverbally Before You Start

Poise counts! Recall that your speech actually begins as you rise to speak and eyes fall on you. Create a confident, energetic approach to the front. Once there, pause, catch and hold your audience's eye contact for a moment, and take a deep breath. Each of these measures is critical to beginning your speech effectively. You want your audience to know you are interested in the speech and that you want them to be part of the experience. Your nonverbal messages are the first part audiences receive as they form a first impression of you. It may help to picture a favorite speaker or actor whom you admire for their effective posture, poise, and presence. Can you embed these traits in your nonverbal approach?

5. Consider Time Constraints and Mood

When giving a five-minute speech, telling a protracted, dramatic story would be inappropriate. The same is true of showing a one-minute video clip. Alternately, when delivering a 45-minute lecture, such a beginning would be wholly acceptable. The mood you are hoping to create in your audience must be related to the tone you adopt as a speaker. The introduction is your best chance to establish your tone and alter the mood of your audience. Carefully consider what effects different introductions might have on mood. Capture the nonverbal elements of voice and body that reflect the best tone for you to deliver your message.

Common Pitfalls of Introductions

Excuse the cliché, but as they say, you never get a second chance at a first impression. Here is a list of problematic approaches to avoid during your introduction.

1. **Beginning with an apology.** Do not use your introduction to apologize for mistakes you are likely to make, for inadequate visual aids, being ill prepared, or even just plain ill. Apologies set a negative tone that is hard to overcome.
2. **Being too brief or too long.** Do not jump into the body of the speech or spend too much time setting up the speech. Your introduction should take between 10 and 20 percent of your total allotted speaking time. Not adhering to this guideline means violating an audience expectation and potentially annoying them.
3. **Giving too much away.** While the introduction should provide a road map for your speech, you do not want to give the substance of your speech in your preview. Instead, use general terms to tell your audience what you intend to cover.
4. **Reading.** We have advised you to rehearse your introduction thoroughly. Do not read your introductory remarks to your audience. Your script becomes a barrier between you and your audience. Worse yet, you will likely sound more like a reader than a public speaker. Avoid reading extensively in the introduction (or anywhere else).
5. **Relying on shock tactics.** Your victory will be short lived if you capture audience attention by screaming at the top of your lungs, pounding the table, telling a bawdy joke, or using material that has nothing to do with your speech. Your audience will trust you less because of the way you manipulated their attention. Using an innovative approach can be effective as long as it is tied directly to the topic of your speech and is not over-the-top.
6. **Promising too much.** Some speakers, fearful that their speech says too little, promise more than they can deliver, in the hope that the promise alone will satisfy their listeners. It rarely does. Once you set expectations in the introduction, the body of your speech has to deliver or you lose credibility.
7. **Using unnecessary prefatory remarks.** Resist the urge to begin with "I'm so nervous," "I can't believe I have to do this speech," or "Okay, deep breath, here we go." Even if you feel these things, such verbal adaptors are likely to make you even more nervous and hurt your credibility. Instead, begin with your planned opening statement.
8. **Using long-winded poems, quotations, and prose.** We understand that for full effect, an entire piece of prose or poetry should be read. We also know that editing a poem or piece of prose may not be easy. However, it is possible to find an appropriate nugget embedded within the piece that is perfect for your speech. Consider paraphrasing or moving longer passages to the body of your speech.

9. **Becoming someone else**. Because your initial credibility is being established in the introduction, avoid histrionics and melodrama. Being true to yourself will earn the respect of your listeners.

10. **Overusing some techniques**. Often overused are simple questions, rhetorical questions, and startling, catastrophic stories. This is made worse by relying on trite phrases. Spend some time thinking about how to begin your speech. Think about what might be most effective with your particular audience. Seek originality and creativity.

☞   Conclusions

Think of your **conclusion** as the pinnacle of your speech—the words you want your listeners to remember as they leave the room. Too often, speakers waste the opportunity with endings like "That's it," "I guess I'm finished now," or "I'm through. Any questions?" Or they simply stop talking, giving the audience no indication that they have finished their speech. Just as an introduction sets a first impression, a well-delivered conclusion leaves a lasting imprint on your audience.

A conclusion should not be viewed as an afterthought. Understand that the conclusion is your last opportunity to have an impact. Just as the introduction should be clear and flow smoothly to the body of the speech, the body should flow smoothly to the conclusion. Following are three functions of conclusions to consider as you think about the transition from the body to the conclusion and determine how to create the greatest effect on your audience.

Functions of Conclusions

Strong endings to speeches summarize important information, motivate listeners, and create a sense of closure. President George W. Bush addressed the nation in the evening following the tragic events in New York City on what has become known simply as 9/11. After talking about the terror that so many Americans experienced, he explained how the rescuers responded, and what the government planned to do to prevent another attack. His conclusion was designed to touch the emotions of all Americans, and he provided closure at the end by stating the following:

> Tonight, I ask for your prayers for all those who grieve, for the children whose worlds have been shattered, for all whose sense of safety and security has been threatened. And I pray they will be comforted by a Power greater than any of us, spoken through the ages in Psalm 23:
> *Even though I walk through the valley of the shadow of death, I fear no evil for you are with me.*
> This is a day when all Americans from every walk of life unite in our resolve for justice and peace. America has stood down enemies before, and we will do so this time. None of us will ever forget this day, yet we go forward to defend freedom and all that is good and just in our world. Thank you. Good night. And God bless America.

Summarizing Important Information

The transition from the body to the conclusion is pivotal in signaling the impending end of your speech. Your instructor and your own personal preference may help you decide how to tell your audience you are ending. Whether you use a formal "In conclusion …" or prefer something less formal, such as "Now, to wrap this up today …," you want your audience to be clear that you are about to finish. Audiences know that when you give them that signal, they are about to get an important recap of your key ideas.

According to speech communication professor John Baird Jr. (1974), "Summaries may be effective when presented at the conclusion of a speech [because] they provide the audience with a general structure under which to subsume the more specific points of the speech" (pp. 119–127). Research indicates that in some instances summaries are not essential, but if your audience is unfamiliar with the content of your speech, or if the speech is long or complex, a summary reinforces your main points.

Iceland's Prime Minister, Johanna Sigurdardottir, spoke at official ceremonies on June 17, 2011 in honor of National Day, the celebration of the nation's independence. Her speech is a patriotic one that highlights the country's progress, and specifically identifies Jon Siguardsson's contributions in the struggle for independence. She concluded her speech by saying:

> Fellow Icelanders: Energy, thrift, foresight and persistence, were the words Jon Sigurdsson chose to rally his nation in the early nineteenth century. His rallying cry is no less appropriate today, and we should honor the memory of this great campaigner by making them our watchwords. Let us be energetic and thrifty, show foresight and persistence, and work together in unity to build a healthy and robust society. The summer awaits us, and there are definitely brighter times ahead for the Icelandic nation. May all of you enjoy this National Day and bicentennial year.

In the process of ending, an effective conclusion reinforces the main idea of the speech. The Prime Minister's speech summarizes the main points of her speech, so the audience has one more opportunity to process her main ideas.

Motivating Listeners

Great speakers do more than summarize in their conclusions; they motivate their audiences. In motivating your audience, you might accomplish three things: relate your topic to your listeners, communicate a feeling, and broaden the message.

1. **Relate your topic to your listeners**. Your speech will achieve the greatest success if your listeners feel you have helped them in some concrete way. Consider making this connection in your conclusion. At the Virginia Statewide Housing Conference in November 2010, U.S. Secretary of Housing and Urban Development Shaun Donovan drew his speech to end with the following remarks:

   > For me, for President Obama, and for Senator Sanders, all this work comes down to a very simple belief: That no matter where you live, when you choose a home, you don't

just choose a home. You also choose schools for your children and transportation to work. You choose a community—and the choices available in that community. A belief that our children's futures should never be determined—or their choices limited—by the zip code they grow up in.

Like our President, I know change is never easy—that revitalizing our nation's communities, rural, urban, and suburban won't happen overnight. Nor will it happen because of any one policy or the work of any one agency or one party. But working together, in common purpose—in partnership—we can tackle our toughest challenges. We can push back on this crisis. We can build upon the remarkable change and sense of possibility you're catalyzing in communities across the state.

And most important of all, we can create a geography of opportunity for every American—and every family. Ensuring we do is our goal today. Let us rise to meet it.

In this brief passage, Donovan uses the word *community* four times. His use of the inclusive "we" is yet another way to establish a group identity and a sense of community. Donovan's conclusion clearly serves to motivate listeners to continue to work to improve living conditions in the United States.

2. **Communicate a feeling**. The conclusion sets the psychological mood listeners carry with them from the hall. A student speaking against aspartame noted at the beginning of her speech that she believed aspartame contributed to her previous depression and weight gain. She ended her speech by noting that eliminating aspartame from her diet lifted her depression and led to significant weight loss. Her passion about the topic and the relief she feels were clearly communicated.

3. **Broaden your message**. Finally, the conclusion can be used to connect your topic to a broader context. If in your speech you talk about the responsibility of every adult to vote on election day, you can use your conclusion to tie the vote to the continuation of our democratic system. If your speech focuses on caring for aging parents, you can conclude with a plea to value rather than discard the wisdom of the elderly.

Creating Closure

Good conclusions create a sense of closure for the speech. The audience feels a sense of satisfaction that you have completed and accomplished something important. If you are having dinner with others, the dessert often completes the dining experience. So, when speaking, it is not enough to simply stop with a comment: "Well, that's it, I guess I can see if anyone has a question," thus leaving the audience without a sense of closure. An effective conclusion tells your listeners your speech has ended. Next we offer four techniques speakers use to create a memorable closing.

Developing Memorable Conclusions

Thanking as Transition

Although saying thank you at the end of the speech indicates you are finished, it is no substitute for a statement that brings your discussion to a close. You can, however, use the "thank you" statement as a **transition** into your concluding remarks. For example, Oprah Winfrey received the first Bob Hope Humanitarian Award at the 54th Emmy Awards in September, 2002.

After saying thank you, Winfrey explained why she was thanking people. Rather than ending by saying thank you to several individuals, she gave the speech more impact by quoting Maya Angelou and leaving the audience with a final thought by asserting that she planned to make herself worthy of the honor by continuing to give to the world.

Call to Action

As you wrap up your speech, you can make a direct appeal to your listeners by urging them to take a specific action or to change their attitudes. In a persuasive speech, the conclusion is the most forcible and memorable place to position your final appeal.

Living in an age of mass media, Americans hear calls to action every time we turn on the television. Advertisers plead with us to drop everything and buy their products NOW! We see 1–800 numbers flash across the screen, urging us to order knives or DVDs or diet aids. Televangelists urge us to contribute to their mission. Internet sites and service station pumps now force us to tune in to the sales pitch of the day. As annoying as these pleas can be, the fact that we are accustomed to calls to action makes them a natural conclusion to a speech.

In a speech designed to persuade her audience that industrial hemp should be grown in the United States, Mary, a public speaking student, ended her speech with a call to action:

> It is easy to get excited about this crop. What other plant can give you so many products? Industrial hemp can make jeans and milk and just about everything in between. And what plant has such a rich and diverse history?
>
> I've only given you a small amount of information, and I'm sure you will be hearing more about industrial hemp in the future. States have stopped waiting for the federal government to legalize it and have begun passing their own bills. Industrial hemp won't save the world, but it will make a big difference. The possibilities are endless, so call your representative today. Tell him or her that the time has come for American to again grow Hemp for Victory.

Mary makes her last persuasive appeal, and then asks the audience to do something about it. Her call could have been stronger and more specific if, for example, she had prepared letters for her colleagues to sign and mail in an addressed, stamped envelope. More letters would be sent because Mary would not be relying on her audience to remember to create and mail their letters later.

Here is how a professor of Political Science might conclude a lecture:

> I have explained my thoughts on the implications of the changes that are now taking place in the Middle East. As you review them, keep this in mind: What we are witnessing is nothing less than a change in world politics. In the days ahead, think about these changes and about how it will affect each and every one of us in the Western democracies.

The call to action, in this case, involves mental activity—reflection, rather than some physical action. This is a perfectly acceptable final statement.

Use a Dramatic Illustration

Ending your speech with a dramatic story connected to your speech's thesis reinforces the theme in your listeners' minds. It is the last message of your speech the audience will hear and, as a story, it is the most likely to be remembered.

German Chancellor Angela Merkel spoke to the U.S. Congress on the 20th anniversary of the falling of the Berlin Wall on November 2009. In her speech, she thanked Americans for their support and for their role in helping to end the Cold War. She also reminded U.S. politicians that the world will be looking to America and Europe for leadership in forging a global climate change agreement. She ended her speech with the following:

> I am convinced that, just as we found the strength in the 20th century to tear down a wall made of barbed wire and concrete, today we have the strength to overcome the walls of the 21st century, walls in our minds, walls of short-sighted self-interest, walls between the present and the future.
>
> Ladies and gentlemen, my confidence is inspired by a very special sound—that of the Freedom Bell in the Schöneberg Town Hall in Berlin. Since 1950 a copy of the original American Liberty Bell has hung there. A gift from American citizens, it is a symbol of the promise of freedom, a promise that has been fulfilled. On October 3, 1990 the Freedom Bell rang to mark the reunification of Germany, the greatest moment of joy for the German people. On September 13, 2001, two days after 9/11, it tolled again, to mark America's darkest hour.
>
> The Freedom Bell in Berlin is, like the Liberty Bell in Philadelphia, a symbol which reminds us that freedom does not come about of itself. It must be struggled for and then defended anew every day of our lives. In this endeavor Germany and Europe will also in future remain strong and dependable partners for America. That I promise you.

Conclude with a Quotation

Closing a speech with the words of others is an effective and memorable way to end your presentation. One of the most famous moments in presidential oratory was the conclusion of President Ronald Reagan's address to the nation from the Oval Office on the Challenger disaster, January 29, 1986:

> The crew of the space shuttle *Challenger* honored us by the manner in which they lived their lives. We will never forget them, nor the last time we saw them—this morning, as they prepared for their journey, and waved good-bye, and "slipped the surly bonds of earth" to "touch the face of God."

As in this example, quotations can be interwoven into the fabric of the speech without telling your listeners that you are speaking the words of others, in this case *High Flight*, by American poet John Magee. If you use this technique, and you are not the president, we recommend that you use the quotation's words exactly and attribute it to the writer.

Conclude with a Metaphor That Broadens the Meaning of Your Speech

You may want to broaden the meaning of your speech through the use of an appropriate **metaphor**—a symbol that tells your listeners that you are saying more. Mao Tse-Tung, also known as Chairman Mao and identified by *Time* magazine as one of the 100 most influential individuals of the 20th century, spoke at the opening of the Party School of the Central Committee of the Communist Party of China on February 1, 1942. He used a medical metaphor in his closing statement:

> But our aim in exposing errors and criticizing shortcomings, like that of a doctor curing a sickness, is solely to save the patient and not to doctor him to death. A person with appendicitis is saved when the surgeon removes his appendix.
>
> So long as a person who has made mistakes does not hide his sickness for fear of treatment or persist in his mistakes until he is beyond cure, so long as he honestly and sincerely wishes to be cured and to mend his ways, we should welcome him and cure his sickness so that he can become a good comrade.
>
> We can never succeed if we just let ourselves go, and lash out at him. In treating an ideological or a political malady, one must never be rough and rash but must adopt the approach of "curing the sickness to save the patient," which is the only correct and effective method.
>
> I have taken this occasion of the opening of the Party School to speak at length, and I hope comrades will think over what I have said.

Without saying it directly, his use of figurative analogy implied that disagreement with the government is a sickness, a disease, and is separate from the afflicted patient. His conclusion was that government must offer a gentle cure for a willing patient. His speech was not about one person being sick, but about a larger context: how China and its citizens grapple with global politics and ideological dissention. His metaphor helps his audience find a new way to conceive of these broader issues by relating them to something basic and familiar.

Conclude with Humor

If you leave your listeners with a humorous story, you will leave them laughing and with a reservoir of good feelings about you and your speech. To be effective, of course, the humor must be tied to your core idea.

A Hollywood screenwriter, invited to speak to students in a college writing course about the job of transforming a successful novel into a screenplay, concluded her speech with the following story:

> Two goats who often visited the set of a movie company found some discarded film next to where a camera crew was working. One of the goats began munching on the film.
>
> "How's it taste?" asked the other goat, trying to decide whether to start chomping himself.
>
> "Not so great," said the first goat. "I liked the book better."

The audience laughed in appreciation of the humor. When the room settled down, the speaker concluded her speech:

> I hope in my case the goat isn't right and that you've enjoyed the films I've written even more than the books on which they were based.
> Thank you for inviting me to speak.

Humor at the end of the speech is especially effective if it corresponds to the introduction.

Encourage Thought with a Rhetorical Question

Rhetorical questions encourage thought. At the end of a speech, they leave listeners with a responsibility to think about the questions raised after your speech is over. Your question can be as simple as "Can our community afford to take the step of hiring 50 new police officers? Perhaps a better question is, Can we afford not to?" Rhetorical questions have the power to sway an audience with their emotional impact.

Refer to Your Introduction

In your conclusion, you can refer to an opening story or quotation or answer the rhetorical questions you raised. Here is how Shannon closed her speech on seat belt safety:

> One thing I didn't tell you at the beginning of my speech about my accident was that for years I resisted wearing my belt. I used to fight with my parents. I felt it was such a personal decision. How could they—or the state government, for that matter—dare tell me what to do?
> Thank goodness I had the sense to buckle up that day. And you can be sure that I will never get into a car without wrapping myself securely with my belt of life. I hope that my experience will be enough to convince you to buckle up, too.

Like matching bookends, closing your speech with a reference to your introduction provides intellectual and emotional symmetry to your remarks.

How to Conclude the Same Speech in Different Ways

Just as many topics lend themselves to different types of introductions, they also lend themselves to various methods of conclusion. Here three techniques are used to conclude a speech on learning to deal more compassionately with the elderly:

> **Example 1:** A quotation that personalizes your message.
> In 1878, in a poem entitled *Somebody's Mother*, poet Mary Dow Brine wrote these words:
> She's somebody's mother, boys, you know, For all she's aged and poor and slow.

Most of us are likely to be somebody's mother—or father—before we die. And further down the road, we're likely to be grandparents, sitting in lonely places, hoping that our children have figured out a more humane way to treat us than we have treated our elderly relatives.

Example 2: A dramatic story that also serves as a metaphor.

Not too long ago, I had a conversation with a doctor who had recently hospitalized an 82-year-old woman with pneumonia. A widow and the mother of three grown children, the woman had spent the last seven years of her life in a nursing home.

The doctor was called three times a day by these children. At first their calls seemed appropriate. They wanted to be sure their mother was getting the best possible medical care. Then, their tone changed. Their requests became demands; they were pushy and intrusive.

After several days of this, the doctor asked one of the children—a son—when he had last visited his mother before she was admitted to the hospital. He hesitated for a moment and then admitted that he had not seen her for two years.

I'm telling you this story to demonstrate that we can't act like these grown children and throw our elderly away, only to feel guilty about them when they are in crisis.

Somehow we have to achieve a balance between our own needs and the needs of our frail and needy parents—one that places reasonable demands on ourselves and on the system that supports the elderly.

Example 3: Rhetorical questions.

Imagine yourself old and sick, worried that your money will run out and that your family will no longer want you. You feel a pain in your chest. What could it be? You ask yourself whether your daughter will be able to leave work to take you to the hospital—whether your grandchildren will visit you there—whether your medical insurance will cover your bills—whether anyone will care if you live or die.

Imagine asking yourself these questions and then imagine the pain of not knowing the answers. We owe our elderly better than that.

By providing these three examples, we note that each has a different feel that surely influences the final mood of the audience. It takes time and effort to create an effective conclusion, just as with an introduction. Both activities are centered on discovering how to best reach your audience.

Common Pitfalls of Conclusions

Knowing what *not* to do is almost as important as knowing what *to* do. Here is a list of approaches to avoid during your conclusion.

1. **Don't use your conclusion to introduce a new topic**. Develop your main and subordinate points in the body of your speech, not in the conclusion.
2. **Don't apologize**. Even if you are unhappy with your performance, do not apologize for your shortcomings when you reach the conclusion. Remarks like, "Well, I guess I didn't

have that much to say," or "I'm sorry for taking so much of your time" are unnecessary and usually turn off the audience.

3. **Don't end abruptly.** Just because you have made all your points does not mean that your speech is over. Your audience has no way of knowing you are finished unless you provide closure. A one-sentence conclusion is not sufficient closure.

4. **Don't change the mood or tone.** If your speech was serious, do not shift moods at the end. A humorous conclusion would be inappropriate and lessen the impact of your speech.

5. **Don't use the phrases "in summary" or "in conclusion" except when you are actually at the end of your speech.** Some speakers use these phrases at various points in their speech, confusing listeners who expect an ending rather than a transition to another point.

6. **Don't ask for questions.** Never risk asking, "Any questions?" Think about it, if there are no questions, you will be creating an awkward silence—hardly the climactic conclusion you were hoping for. Also, most speech days in class are designed to have a number of speakers fill the class period. Answering questions or taking comments may interfere with the instructor's schedule.

    If there is to be a question-and-answer session, consider it as a separate event from the speech. Complete your entire conclusion, receive your well-earned applause, and *then* field any questions.

7. **Don't ignore applause.** Graciously accept the praise of your audience by looking around the room and saying, "thank you."

8. **Don't forget to thank your audience and host.** Part of your lasting positive impression will come from a sincere thanks offered to both your audience for their attention and your host for allowing you the opportunity to speak. This is true in many speaking situations, but does not apply to the general public speaking class.

9. **Don't run away.** Remember to keep your poise as you confidently make your retreat from the speaking platform. Being in too big a rush to sit down gives the appearance that you are glad it is over. You may be ready to leave, but stifle the urge to flee abruptly from the podium.

10. **Don't read it.** Just as with the introduction, the delivery of the conclusion is important. Practice it enough that you are not dependent on your speaker's notes. Eye contact with your audience as you wrap up your message will reinforce your perceived credibility as well as your message's importance. Having to rely heavily on notes, or worst of all, reading your conclusion makes the ending of your message less satisfying to your audience.

☞   Summary

The primacy/recency effect, which suggests that people attend to either the first information they receive or the last information they receive, underscores the importance of strong introductions and conclusions. Introductions serve several functions: they focus attention, provide a motive for the audience to listen, build speaker credibility, and preview the topic of your speech.

Several techniques can be used to capture audience attention in the introduction. Among these are startling statements, dramatic stories, quotations and/or literature references, humor, rhetorical questions, illustrations, examples, anecdotes, audience involvement, personal experience, visual aids, and making reference to your speaking situation.

Your introduction will be successful if you follow established guidelines including preparing it after the body of the speech, making it clear and easy to follow, communicating high energy by practicing it as many times as needed, engaging the audience nonverbally before you start, and considering time constraints and mood. Your introduction will be more effective if you avoid 10 common pitfalls.

The conclusion of your speech should summarize, motivate, and communicate closure. An effective conclusion reinforces your message, acts as a summary, relates your message to your listeners' lives, and connects your message to a broader context.

Among the techniques you can use to conclude your speech are a call to action, a dramatic story, a closing quotation, a metaphor that broadens meaning, humor, rhetorical questions, and a reference to the introduction. Your conclusion will benefit from avoiding 10 common pitfalls such as poor eye contact and apologies.

References

Baird, John E., Jr. (1974). The Effects of Speech Summaries upon Audience Comprehension of Expository Speeches of Varying Quality and Complexity. *Central States Speech Journal, Summer*, 119–127.

Bush, George W. (2001). *Speech to the Nation on 9/11.* Retrieved September 8, 2011 from www.americanrhetoric .com/speeches/gwbush911addresstothenationon.htm.

Childhood Overweight and Obesity Prevention Program: Fact Sheet. (2011). Retrieved September 7, 2011 from www .surgeongeneral.gov/obesityprevention/factsheet/index.html

Corbett, E., & Connor, R. (1999). *Classical Rhetoric for the Modern Student*, 4th Ed. London: Oxford University Press.

Donovan, Shaun. (2010, November 18). *Speech Given at the Virginia Housing Conference.* Retrieved September 8, 2011 from portal.hud.gov/hudportal/HUD/press/speeches_remarks.2010.htm.

Emanuel, Rahm. (2009). *Commencement Speech at George Washington University.* Retrieved September 8, 2011 from www.blogs.gwhatchet.com/newsroom/2009/05/17/transcript-of-rahm-emanuels-commencement-address/.

Firth, Colin. (2011). *Oscar Acceptance Speech 2011.* Retrieved September 8, 2011 from www.nowpublic.com/colin-firth-oscar-acceptance-speech-2011-video-transcript.2761763.html.

Jagland, Thorbjorn. (2010). *Nobel Peace Prize Speech.* Retrieved September 8, 2011 from www.nobelprize.org/prizes_peace/presentation-speech.html.

Kamkwamba, William. (2009). How I Harnessed the Wind. *TED: Ideas Worth Spreading.* Retrieved July 28, 2011 from www.ted.com/talks/william_kamkwamba_how_i_harnessed_the_wind.html.

Lady Gaga. (2010, September). *The Prime Rib of America* (Speech). Retrieved September 8, 2011 from www.mtv .com/news/articles/1648304/lady-gagas-don't-ask-don't-tell-speech-full-transcript.jhtml.

Merkel, Angela. (2009, November 3). *We Have No Time to Lose* (Speech). Retrieved March 2, 2011 from www .spiegel.de/international/europe.

Notable Quotes from HealthCare Summit. (2010, February 25). Retrieved September 7, 2011 from www.msnbc.msn .com/id/35585513/ns/politics/t/notable-quotes-health-care-summit/.

Reagan, Ronald. (1986). *Challenger* (Speech). Retrieved September 8, 2011 from www.americanrhetoric.com/speeches/ronaldreaganchallenger.htm.

Shapiro, L. (1990, February 26). The Zap Generation. *Newsweek*, 56.

Sigurdardottir, J. Address of the Prime Minister of Iceland at official ceremonies on the parliament square Austurvollur, 17 June 2011. Retrieved on Februrary 2, 2012 on http://www.forsaetisraduneyti.is/.

Tse-tung. Mao. (1942, February 1). *Rectify the Party's Style of Work* (Speech). Retrieved March 2, 2011 from www.marxists.com.

Weiner, Edith. (1989, October 10). Personal interview.

Winfrey, Oprah. (2002, September 22). *Speech*. Retrieved September 8, 2011 from www.famousquotes.me.uk/speeches/Oprah-Winfrey/.

Zucker, Jerry. (2003). *Commencement* (Speech). Retrieved September 8, 2011 from www.news.wisc.edu.8682.

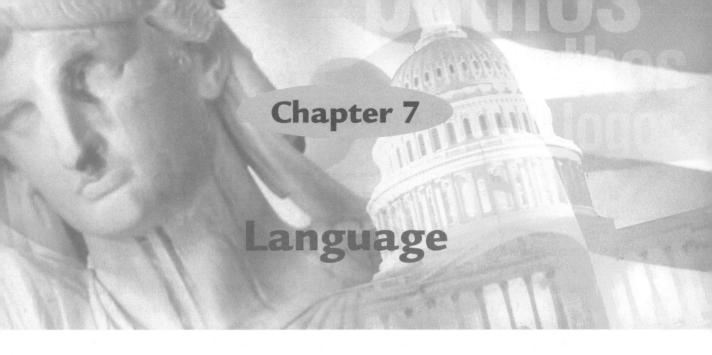

Chapter 7

Language

"It is not enough for language to have clarity and content: it must also have a goal and an imperative."

René Daumal

SPEECH: Sojourner Truth—Ain't I a Woman

Sojourner Truth (née Isabella Baumfree) (1797–1883) was born into slavery in New York. The New York Anti-Slavery Law of 1827 should have ensured her freedom, however, her master did not honor his promise to free her, so she left his estate. In the years that followed, she experienced a religious conversion, became an itinerant preacher and, in 1843, changed her name to Sojourner Truth. During this period, she became actively involved in the antislavery movement. By the 1850s, she was also involved in the women's rights movement. Sojourner Truth attended the Women's Rights Convention in Akron, Ohio on May 29, 1851. Men and women were in the audience. Some supported the resolutions to address the need for equal rights of women under the law, with explicit attention to labor and education. Some, notably clergy, opposed what were seen as radical notions. Mrs. Frances D. Gage, who chaired the convention, introduced Sojourner Truth to a hostile audience. The power of Sojourner Truth's rhetoric and ethos transformed the angry mob's mentality to one of respect and admiration. The version of the speech presented below is based on Mrs. Gage's eyewitness account of Truth's extemporaneous speech.

Sources: https://www.nps.gov/wori/learn/historyculture/sojourner-truth.htm

Andrews, James and Zarefsky, David (1989). American Voices: Significant Speeches in American History, 1640–1945. New York: Longman, pp. 218–219.

Sojourner Truth (1797–1883): *Ain't I A Woman?*
Delivered 1851
Women's Rights Convention, Akron, Ohio

Well, children, where there is so much racket there must be something out of kilter. I think that 'twixt the negroes of the South and the women at the North, all talking about rights, the white men will be in a fix pretty soon. But what's all this here talking about?

That man over there says that women need to be helped into carriages, and lifted over ditches, and to have the best place everywhere. Nobody ever helps me into carriages, or over mud-puddles, or gives me any best place! And ain't I a woman? Look at me! Look at my arm! I have ploughed and planted, and gathered into barns, and no man could head me! And ain't I a woman? I could work as much and eat as much as a man - when I could get it - and bear the lash as well! And ain't I a woman? I have borne thirteen children, and seen most all sold off to slavery, and when I cried out with my mother's grief, none but Jesus heard me! And ain't I a woman?

Then they talk about this thing in the head; what's this they call it? [member of audience whispers, "intellect"] That's it, honey. What's that got to do with women's rights or negroes' rights? If my cup won't hold but a pint, and yours holds a quart, wouldn't you be mean not to let me have my little half measure full?

Then that little man in black there, he says women can't have as much rights as men, 'cause Christ wasn't a woman! Where did your Christ come from? Where did your Christ come from? From God and a woman! Man had nothing to do with Him.

If the first woman God ever made was strong enough to turn the world upside down all alone, these women together ought to be able to turn it back, and get it right side up again! And now they is asking to do it, the men better let them.

Obliged to you for hearing me, and now old Sojourner ain't got nothing more to say.

https://www.nps.gov/wori/learn/historyculture/sojourner-truth.htm

Language matters. It is so powerful that it can move us to tears. Consider this story attributed to professor, author, and speaker Leo Buscaglia (2007) about a contest he once judged:

> "The purpose of the contest was to find the most caring child. The winner was a four-year-old child whose next door neighbor was an elderly gentleman who had recently lost his wife. Upon seeing the man cry, the little boy went into the old gentleman's yard, climbed onto his lap, and just sat there. When his Mother asked what he had said to the neighbor, the little boy said, "'Nothing, I just helped him cry.'"

Language provokes us. Language can move us to tears, leave us bewildered, make us laugh, or awkwardly blush. More accurately, speakers *using* language influence our emotions and behavior. Your language will in large part determine the success of your speech. Through words, you create the vivid images that remain in the minds of your audience after your speech is over. Moreover, your choice of words and style of language influence your credibility as a speaker. By choosing language that appeals to your audience—by moving your audience intellectually and emotionally through the images of speech—you create a climate that enhances your credibility, encourages continued listening, and ensures retention of key ideas.

The three Cs for public speaking are: Clear, Concise, and Colorful. In this chapter, we explore tools that help your presentations ring clear, concise, and colorful. First, we identify characteristics of spoken language that differentiate it from written language. Then we provide guidelines for using spoken language more effectively. Finally, we end our discussion of language by considering several common pitfalls that detract from the message.

Characteristics of Spoken Language

If you wrote a paper in a Sociology or English class on "Trafficking of Women in Eastern Europe," using it as the basis for an informative speech would be expedient. It would certainly save time and effort, particularly on researching and gathering supporting materials. But be careful. A written report can be used as the foundation for a speech, but it requires major adjustments. The needs of written language and spoken language are different because listeners process information differently than readers. Imagine your instructor speaking for a minute. Then imagine what it would be like if your instructor were reading these comments from a manuscript. It would be remarkably boring. The spoken and written language differ in many ways, including word order, rhythm, and signals. Simply reading a written report would be violating many such spoken language norms.

Word Order

The first characteristic of spoken language is word order, which relates to the order in which ideas should be arranged in a sentence. In general, the last idea presented is the most powerful. Consider this famous line spoken by John F. Kennedy at his inauguration: "Ask not what your country can do for you, ask what you can do for your country." Inverted, the sentence loses its power: "Ask what you can do for your country, ask not what your country can do for you." Because speech is slower than silent reading, individual words take on more importance, especially those appearing at the end of the sentence.

Comedians rely on this technique by making the last word in a punch line the key to the joke. Every "knock knock" joke does the same. Watch for this rule of comedy and see how often the strategy appears and is effective.

Rhythm

The second characteristic of spoken language is rhythm. Rhythm in music and poetry distinguishes these genres from others. The rhythm of a piece of music creates different moods. The rhythm may create a sense of calm and serenity that allows us to listen and reflect, or the rhythm may create the urge to dance like a maniac. Rhythm is important in spoken language, also. It is the speech flow or pattern that is created in many ways, including variations in sentence length, the use of parallel structure, and the expression of images in groups of three.

Read aloud Patrick Henry's famous line, "Give me liberty or give me death," to illustrate the importance of rhythm (Tarver, 1988):

I know not what course others may take. But as for me, give me liberty or death.

Now read the original, and notice the greater impact:

I know not what course others may take. But as for me, give me liberty or give me death.

By taking out one of the repetitive "give me" phrases, the rhythm—and impact—of the sentence changes. As you develop your speech, consider the following ways you can use rhythm to reinforce your ideas and to maintain audience attention.

Vary sentence length. First, create rhythm by varying sentence length. The rhythm of speech is affected by how well you combine sentences of varying lengths. Long sentences can be confusing and short sentences might be dull and simple, but a combination of long and short sentences adds rhythmic interest. On June 1, 1997, Mary Schmich, columnist for the *Chicago Tribune*, wrote an essay she described as a commencement speech called "Wear Sunscreen." In addition to imploring graduates to wear sunscreen, Schmich provides several words of advice, including the following:

> Sing.
> Don't be reckless with other people's hearts. Don't put up with people who are reckless with yours.
> Floss.
> Don't waste your time on jealousy.

Schmich's commencement speech is filled with humor and advice, but its impact is due, in part, to the variation in sentence structure. Rhythm is a critical element. The rhythm of this speech is so engaging, it captured the attention of musical artists who developed their own version of Schmich's advice, including Baz Luhrmann's *Everybody's Free (to Wear Sunscreen)* and John Safran's *Not the Sunscreen Song*.

Use parallel structure. Second, create rhythm by using parallel structure. Parallelism involves the arrangement of a series of words, phrases, or sentences in a similar form. Classically, this is done in two ways: anaphora and epistrophe.

Anaphora is the repetition of the same word or phrase at the *beginning* of successive clauses or sentences, as in these two examples:

> In his first inaugural speech, President Richard M. Nixon stated, "Where peace is unknown, make it welcome; where peace is fragile, make it strong; where peace is temporary, make it permanent" (Detz, 1984, p. 69).
>
> Barack Obama's 2009 inaugural address also made effective use of parallel structure in many places, including anaphora in the memorable: "We will harness the sun and the winds and the soil to fuel our cars and run our factories. And we will transform our schools and colleges and universities to meet the demands of a new age" (Phillips, 2009).

A non-inaugural example of parallel structure can be seen when Tina Fey accepted the Mark Twain Prize for American humor at the Kennedy Center in November 2010. Her repetition of "I am proud" gives rhythm to her speech and allows her to make important points succinctly.

I'm so proud to represent American humor, I am proud to be an American, and I am proud to make my home in the '"not real"' America. And I am most proud that during trying times, like an orange [terror] alert, a bad economy, or a contentious election that we, as a nation, retain our sense of humor." (Farhi, 2010)

Epistrophe is the repetition of a word or expression at the *end* of phrases, clauses, or sentences. Lincoln used this device in the phrase, "of the people, by the people, for the people." It is an effective technique for emphasis. On January 8, 2008 in his presidential bid, then–Senator Barack Obama delivered an inspired "Yes, We Can" speech. Obama's audience was so captivated by his use of the tag line "Yes, we can" at the end of key sentences that they called back the phrase with him each time he repeated it. Parallel structure emphasizes the rhythm of speech. When used effectively, it adds a harmony and balance to a speech that can verge on the poetic.

Use three as a magic number. Third (yes, we intentionally provided three points!), rhythm can be created by referring to ideas in groups of three. Winston Churchill once said, "If you have an important point to make, don't try to be subtle or clever. Use a pile driver. Hit the point once. Then come back and hit it again. Then hit it a third time—a tremendous whack." Experienced speakers know that saying things three times gets their point across in a way saying it once cannot—not simply because of repetition, but because of the rhythmic effect of the repetition. Many presidents use this device during important speeches. You can hear the emotional impact of Abraham Lincoln's words in his Gettysburg address when he said, "We cannot dedicate, we cannot consecrate, we cannot hallow this ground (Detz, 1984, pp. 68–69).

Re-examine the words quoted above from Barack Obama and Tina Fey, and you will note they freely use the rule of three. Try this in your speeches. For example, in a speech of tribute, you might say, "I am here to honor, to praise, and to congratulate the members of the volunteer fire department."

Signals

A third specific characteristic of spoken language involves using signals. You may reread an important passage in a book to appreciate its meaning, but your audience hears your message only once—a fact that may make it necessary to signal critical passages in your speech. The following signals tell your listeners to pay close attention:

* This cannot be overemphasized …
* Let me get to the heart of the matter …
* I want to summarize …
* My three biggest concerns are …

Although all speakers hope to capture and hold listeners' attention throughout their speech, wise speakers draw people back to their message at critical points. Signals are more necessary in spoken language than in print.

☞   Guidelines for Language and Style

As you strive to be precise, clear, and understandable, keep in mind the difference between denotative and connotative definitions. A dictionary provides the literal, objective, **denotative** definition of the word. **Connotation** is the meaning we ascribe to words as framed by our personal experiences. These often lie in the realm of our subjective, emotional responses. For example, the American flag can be described denotatively by its color and design, but connotatively, the meaning varies around the world. Americans, in general, see the flag as a symbol of freedom and democracy, whereas some from other cultures may view our flag as a symbol of Western imperialism or immorality. Whether the audience favors or disfavors your view, ensure they understand what you mean and what you believe to be the facts that support your ideas. This next section provides six guidelines for effective use of language.

Be Concrete

On a continuum, words range from the most concrete to the most abstract. Concrete language is rooted in real-life experience—things we see, hear, taste, touch, and feel—while abstract language tells us little about what we experience, relying instead on more symbolic references. Compare the following:

Table 7.1

Abstract	Concrete
Bad weather	Hail the size of golf balls
Nervousness	Trembling hands; knocking knees
An interesting professor	When she started throwing paper airplanes around the room to teach us how air currents affect lift, I knew she was a winner.

Concrete words and phrases create pictures in listeners' minds and can turn a ho-hum speech into one that captures listener attention. Winston Churchill understood this premise when he said, during World War II, "We shall fight them on the beaches," instead of "Hostilities will be engaged on the coastal perimeter" (Kleinfeld, 1990). Consider the differences between these two paragraphs:

Version 1:

On-the-job accidents take thousands of lives a year. Particularly hard hit are agricultural workers who suffer approximately 1,500 deaths and 140,000 disabling injuries a year. One-fifth of all agricultural fatalities are children. These statistics make us wonder how safe farms are.

Version 2:

Farmers who want to get their children interested in agriculture often take them on tractors for a ride. About 150 children are killed each year when they fall off tractors and are crushed underneath. These children represent about half the children killed in farm accidents each year—a statistic that tells us farms can be deadly. About 1,500 people die each year on farms, and an additional 140,000 are injured seriously enough that they can no longer work.

In Version 2 the images and language are more concrete. Instead of wondering "how safe farms are," Version 2 declares that "farms can be deadly." Instead of talking about "disabling injuries," we are told that workers "are injured seriously enough that they can no longer work." Concrete language produces an emotional response in listeners because it paints a more vivid picture, allowing the audience to imagine the situation on a more emotional level.

Complete Your Thoughts and Sentences

Focus on completing every sentence you start. This may seem like common sense, but many people do not follow this advice when speaking before groups. Although we accept the fact that many sentences trail off in conversational speech, we are more likely to lose confidence when a speaker continually does this. From the mouth of a public speaker, this language is disconcerting:

In many states, your signature on your driver's license makes you a potential organ donor. If you are killed … According to the laws in these states, if you are killed in an auto accident, the state has the right … Your organs can be used to help people in need of organ transplants. There are sick people out there who need the kidneys, corneas, and even the hearts of people killed. Think about it. When you are dead, you can still give the gift of life.

On the other hand, we encourage you to *violate* this rule by incorporating sentence fragments, where relevant. Keep in mind that carefully chosen sentence fragments can contribute to clear communication. Here is an example:

Is Christmas too commercial? Well, maybe. It wasn't that long ago when the holiday season began after Thanksgiving. Now the first Christmas catalogs reach shoppers in September. Before summer is over. Before the temperature has dropped below 90 degrees. Even before Labor Day.

Do not confuse sentence fragments with the incomplete thoughts and sentences we discussed earlier. In the case above, the fragments are intentional and are used effectively to create drama and emphasis.

Use the Active Voice

A direct speaking style involves the use of the active rather than passive voice as often as possible or preferable. The following example demonstrates the difference between the passive and active voice:

Version 1: Passive voice.

Students in an English class at Long Beach City College were asked by their teacher to stand in line. After a few minutes, the line was broken by a student from Japan who walked a few yards away. The behavior demonstrated by the student shows how cultural differences can affect even the simple act of waiting in line. In this case, the need for greater personal space was felt by the student who considered it impolite to stand so close.

Version 2: Active voice.

An English teacher at Long Beach City College asked the class to stand in line. After a few minutes, a Japanese student broke the line and walked a few yards away. The student's behavior demonstrated how cultural differences affect even the simple act of waiting in line. In this case, the student felt the need for more personal space because the Japanese culture considers it impolite to stand so close.

In the active voice structure, the subject is identified first and it performs the action implied by the verb (Purdue OWL, 2011). Here are two shorter examples: "The cat scratched the girl" is active because the subject (cat) is identified first in the sentence and is performing the action (scratch). "The speaker explored her subject thoroughly before she crafted her speech" is active because the subject (speaker) comes before, and performs the action of the verb (explored). In addition to using fewer words, the active voice is more direct, easier to follow, and more vigorous.

There are times when you may prefer the passive voice because it has the ability to create a shift the tone in your message and the moods in your audience. For example, in "rules are made to be broken" the rhythm created by a passive structure is so powerful that we would use it over an active version, like "Authorities make rules to be broken (Purdue OWL, 2011). Passive voice is also used when we want the importance of the subject to be deemphasized or omitted. In our "rules are made to be broken" example, the subject (authorities) is left out altogether because the emphasis is really on breaking rules rather than on authorities. To create rhythm or alter emphasis, we sometimes elect to use the passive over the active voice.

Use Language to Create a Theme

A key word or phrase can reappear throughout your speech to reinforce your theme. Each time the image is repeated, it becomes more powerful and is more likely to stay with your listeners. When addressing women's rights in Africa, First Lady Michelle Obama used her husband's now famous "Yes, We Can" speech to conclude her remarks in a powerful way while reinforcing her theme: "And if anyone of you ever doubts that you can build that future, if anyone ever tells you that you shouldn't or you can't, then I want you to say with one voice—the voice of a generation—you tell them, Yes, we can. [Applause] What do you say?" "Yes, we can." [Applause] "What do you say?" "Yes, we can!" (Mooney, 2011).

When something works, the Obama's stick with it! By referring to a key phrase several times in a speech, the message is often more effective and memorable (Berg & Gilman, 1989).

Use Language That Fits Your Personality and Position

If you are delivering a speech on advances in microsurgery, a casual, flippant tone is inappropriate, though it might work for a speech on naming the family dog. Audiences are perceptive. They quickly know whether you are comfortable with your speaking style or whether you are trying to be something or someone you are not. It is hard to fake an emotional presentation if you are a cool, non-emotional person. If you are naturally restrained, it is difficult to appear daring and impulsive.

Some try to be more formal or articulate than they are comfortable with by choosing big, complicated, rarely heard words. While it can have a comedic pay-off, this is rarely the goal of most speakers. The language you choose mirrors who you are, so choose carefully. Let your language reflect what you want others to know about you, and keep it real.

Use Varying Language Techniques to Engage Listeners

A carpenter uses a saw, a hammer, and nails to construct a building. A speaker uses language to construct a speech. Words are literally the tools of a speaker's trade. A speaker has numerous tools to choose from when building a speech.

When constructing your speech, consider using a variety of language techniques to enhance imagery. **Imagery** involves creating a vivid description through the use of one or more of our five senses. Using imagery can create a great impact and lasting memory. Mental images can be created using many devices, including metaphors, similes, and figures of speech.

Metaphors

Metaphors state that something *is* something else. Through metaphors we can understand and experience one idea in terms of another. For example, if you ask a friend how a test went, and the friend responded, "I scored a home run," you would know that your friend thought the test went well for him. In his "Sinews of Peace" speech to Westminster College in Fulton, Missouri, Prime Minister Winston Churchill used the following metaphor on March 5, 1946: "An iron curtain has descended across the continent." During his inaugural address, President Bill Clinton said, "Our democracy must not only be the envy of the world but also the engine of our own renewal." Metaphors create "idea marriages" that bring new insights to listeners.

Similes

Similes create images as they compare the characteristics of two different things using the words "like" or "as." Here are two examples. "Speed reading Charlie Sheen's autobiography would be like a trip through a sewer in a glass-bottom boat." "Watching presentations at this conference is like watching a WNBA playoff game; you are practically the only one there and the rest of the world does not care." Both metaphors and similes rely on concrete images to create meaning and insights, and both invite the imagination out to play. Although these can enliven your speech, guard against using images that are trite, odd, or too familiar.

Figures of Speech

Figures of speech connect sentences by emphasizing the relationship among ideas and repeating key sounds to establish a pleasing rhythm. Among the most popular figures of speech are alliteration, antithesis, asyndeton, and personification.

Alliteration is the repetition of the initial consonant or initial sounds in series of words. Tongue twisters such as "Peter Piper picked a peck of pickled peppers" are based on alliteration. With "Peter Piper" the P sound is repeated multiple times. Alliteration can be used effectively in speeches, such as in Martin Luther King's 1963 "I have a dream" speech, when he said, "We have come to our nation's capital to cash a check." Alliteration occurs with the repetition of C in "capital to cash a check."

Antithesis is the use of contrast, within a parallel grammatical structure, to make a rhetorical point. Jesse Jackson told an audience of young African Americans: "We cannot be what we ought to be if we push dope in our veins, rather than hope in our brains" (Gustainis 1987, p. 218). During a press conference in November 2008, President Obama used antithesis when he said, "If we are going to make the *investments we need*, we also have to be willing to shed the *spending that we don't need*" (*New York Times*, 2008). Antithesis is powerful because it is interesting; it is the analogy turned on its head to reveal insights by the pairing of two opposite things.

Asyndeton is the deliberate omission of conjunctions between a series of related clauses. Saying "I came, I saw, I conquered" rather than "I came, then I saw, and finally I conquered" is a good choice and excellent use of this figure of speech.

Personification is investing human qualities in abstractions or inanimate objects either through metaphor, simile, or analogy. General Douglas MacArthur, addressing West Point cadets confessed: "In my dreams I hear again the crash of guns, the rattle of musketry, the strange, mournful mutter of the battlefield." The general personifies the inanimate battlefield by ascribing to it human mournful mutters. This personification creates a much stronger emotional appeal.

Many other linguistic and stylistic devices are available to you. Because ancient Greek and Roman rhetoricians delighted in identifying and naming them, a rich heritage of figures of speech is waiting for you to come and explore.

Use Humor with Care

Nothing brings you closer to your audience than well-placed humor. Humor reveals your human side. It relaxes listeners and makes them respond positively. Through a properly placed anecdote, you let your audience know that you are not taking yourself—or your subject—too seriously. Even in a serious speech, humor can be an effective tool to emphasize an important point.

Research has shown the favorable impact humor has on an audience. In particular, humor accomplishes two things. First, when appropriate humor is used in informative speaking, the humor enhances the speaker's image by improving the audience's perception of the speaker's character (Gruner, 1985). Second, humor can make a speech more memorable over a longer time. In a research study, two groups of subjects were asked to recall lectures they heard six weeks earlier. The group who heard the lecture presented humorously had higher recall than the group who heard the same lecture delivered without humor (Kaplan & Pascoe, 1977).

In another experiment, students who took a statistics course given by an instructor who used humor in class lectures scored 15 percent higher on objective exams than did students who were taught the same material by an instructor who did not (Ziv, 1982).

Humor works only if it is carefully used and is connected to the thesis of your speech, the occasion, audience, or yourself in a meaningful way. Here are five guidelines for using humor in a speech.

1. Use Humor Only If You Can Be Funny

Some speakers do not know how to be funny in front of an audience. On a one-on-one basis they may be funny, but in front of a group, their humor vanishes. They stumble over punch lines and their timing is bad. These people should limit themselves to serious speeches or "safe" humor. For example, former Maine senator Ed Muskie made his audience laugh by describing the shortest will in Maine legal history—a will that was only 10 words long: "Being of sound mind and memory, I spent it all" (Rackleff, 1987, p. 313). If you are not sure you can make your planned humor work, have a short practice session among friends and see if they laugh. Not naturally very funny? This is a skill, like any other.

2. Laugh at Yourself, Not at Others

In his humble acceptance speech for Best Actor at the 2011 Academy Awards, Colin Firth's humorous comments included a few jabs at himself. His first words were "I have a feeling my career has just peaked" (NowPublic.com, 2011). After thanking the Academy, he remarked:

> I'm afraid I have to warn you that I'm experiencing stirrings somewhere in the upper abdominals which are threatening to form themselves into dance moves. Joyous as they may be for me, it would be extremely problematic if they make it to my legs before I get off stage.

Research has shown that speakers who make themselves the object of their own humor often endear themselves to their listeners. In one study, students heard brief speeches from a "psychologist" and an "economist," both of whom explained the benefits of their professions. While half the speeches were read with mildly self-deprecating humor directed at the profession being discussed, the other half were read without humor. Students rated the speakers with the self-deprecating humor higher on a scale of "wittiness" and "sense of humor," and no damage was done to the perceived character or authoritativeness of the speaker (Chang & Gruner, 1981).

Jokes at one's own expense can be effective but telling a joke at the expense of others is in poor taste. Racial, ethnic, or sexist jokes are rarely acceptable, nor are jokes that poke fun at the personal characteristics of others. Although stand-up comics like Dane Cook, Jeff Foxworthy, and Chris Rock may get away with such humor, public speakers typically cannot.

3. Understated Anecdotes Can Be Effective

An economist speaking before a group of peers starts with the following anecdote:

> I am constantly reminded by those who use our services that we often turn out a ton of material on the subject but we do not always give our clients something of value. A balloonist high above the earth found his balloon leaking and managed to land on the edge of a green pasture. He saw a man in a business suit approaching and very happily said: "How good it is to see you. Could you tell me where I am?"
>
> The well-dressed man replied: "You are standing in a wicker basket in the middle of a pasture." "Well," said the balloonist, "You must be an economist." The man was startled. "Yes, I am, but how did you know that?"
>
> "That's easy," said the balloonist, "because the information you gave me was very accurate—and absolutely useless" (Valenti, 1982, pp. 80–81).

This anecdote is funny in an understated way. It works because it is relevant to the audience of fellow economists. Its humor comes from the recognition that the speaker knows—and shares—the foibles of the audience.

4. Find Humor in Your Own Experiences

The best humor comes from your own experiences. Humor is all around you. You might want to start now to record humorous stories for your speeches so that you will have material when the need arises. If you decide to use someone else's material, you have the ethical responsibility to give the source credit. You might start with, "As Jerry Seinfeld would say …" This gives appropriate source citation and makes clear that line or story is meant as a joke. Usually you will get bigger laughs by citing their names than if you tried to convince your audience that the humor was original.

5. Avoid Being *Not* Funny

We chose the double negative to make a point. When humor works and the audience responds with a spontaneous burst of applause or laughter, there is little that will make you feel better—or more relaxed—as a speaker. Its effect is almost magical. However, when the humor is distasteful to the audience or highly inappropriate, a speaker may find no one is laughing.

Ricky Gervais hosted the 2010 Golden Globe awards, and his humor received mixed reviews. Without making specific reference to Mel Gibson's 2006 drunk driving arrest, Gervais quipped, "I like a drink as much as the next man … unless the next man is Mel Gibson" (www.dailymail.co.uk).

Just before introducing Colin Farrell, Gervais remarked, "One stereotype I hate is that all Irishmen are just drunk, swearing hell raisers. Please welcome Colin Farrell" (www.dailymail .co.uk). He also made reference to Paul McCartney's expensive divorce and Hugh Hefner's marriage to a woman 60 years younger than he. While some jokes were well-received, some felt that he stepped over the line, even for a comedian, because the tone of special occasions should be kept positive.

Often humor is based on direct or implied criticism though. We laugh at things people do, what they say, how they react, and so on. In fulfilling our ethical responsibilities, however, while someone or some event is being mocked, the speaker needs to do so with taste and appropriateness.

So, to avoid being *not* funny, audience analysis is vital. As a beginning public speaker, we urge you to err on the side of caution. It is better to avoid humor than to fail at it. While most humor is risky, there are certain things you can be fairly sure your audience will find funny. Stick with those, and try riskier humor as you gain confidence and experience. You might also check with a friend or classmate if you have any question about the humor of a line or story.

Language Pitfalls

Although your speaking style—the distinctive manner in which you speak to produce the effect you desire—like your style of dress, is a personal choice, some aspects of style enhance communication while others detract. You may have a great sense of humor, but used too much and some may be put off by your lack of seriousness. You may be very bright and reflective, but your overly quiet tone may tire many in your audience. You have read several language guidelines for creating an effective speech. Following are five language pitfalls to avoid.

Long and Unnecessary Words

Using long and unnecessary words violates the first principle of language usage, which is to be simple and concrete. When you read, you have the opportunity to reread something or to look up a word you do not understand. In a speech, you do not have the rewind option, and if the audience does not understand, they lose interest.

When Mark Twain wrote popular fiction, he was often paid by the word, a fee schedule that led him to this humorous observation:

> By hard, honest labor, I've dug all the large words out of my vocabulary ... I never write *metropolis* for seven cents because I can get the same price for *city*. I never write *policeman* because I can get the same price for *cop*.

The best speakers realize that attempting to impress an audience by using four- or five-syllable words usually backfires. We prefer "row, row, row your boat" to "maneuver, maneuver, maneuver your craft" most days of the week. The IRS has been called out to simplify its tax language so it is more readable to the common taxpayer. Translation: Lose the legalese. The Plain Language

Act of 2009 (H.R. 946) requires the IRS to write tax documents in "plain writing." Gina Jones, president of the National Association of Enrolled Agents said, "The regulations are not in plain language. For example, the definition of a qualifying child: You almost have to be an attorney to understand where all of the instances apply. If they could make it a little simpler, it would be a tremendous benefit for taxpayers and tax professionals" (Duarte, 2011). It might be wise to audit your use of long and unnecessary words in your presentations.

Here are a few multisyllabic words and their simpler alternatives.

Table 7.2

Words to Impress	Words to Communicate
Periodical	Magazine
Utilize	Use
Reiterate	Repeat
Commence	Start
Discourse	Talk

Unnecessary words are as problematic as long words. Spoken language requires some redundancy, but when people are forced to listen to strings of unnecessary words, they may find comprehension difficult. When the listening process becomes too difficult, they stop paying attention. Here is an example of unfocused rambling:

> Let me tell you what I did on my summer vacation. I drove down to Memphis in my car to take part in the dozens of memorial ceremonies marking the anniversary of the death of Elvis Presley. There were about 40,000 or 50,000 other people at the ceremony along with me.
>
> I took a tour of the mansion Elvis lived in before his death, known as Graceland, and I visited the new museum dedicated solely to his cars. The museum holds 20 different vehicles, including the favorite of Elvis's mother: a pink 1955 Cadillac Fleetwood.

Here is a simpler version:

> During summer vacation, I drove to Memphis to celebrate the anniversary of Elvis Presley's death. With about 40,000 or 50,000 other people, I toured Graceland, Elvis' home, and visited the museum dedicated to his 20 vehicles, including his mother's favorite, a pink 1955 Cadillac Fleetwood.

Not only does the second version eliminate almost half of the words, it also sharpens the message and helps listeners focus on the important points.

Using Euphemisms: Language That Masks or Muddles

As a speaker, be clear and provide something meaningful for your audience. Avoid sentences that lack content, mask meaning, or include euphemisms because they can do damage to your credibility. Using a **euphemism** involves substituting a mild, vague, or indirect word or phrase for a more harsh, blunt, or inciting, yet more accurate, word or phrase. Rather than use the word "war" when the U.S. had troops fighting in Vietnam, government officials used the word "conflict" (a term some still maintain is technically correct). Also, "collateral damage" is a euphemism for civilian deaths that occur during a military action. When someone dies, we hear euphemisms such as "passed," "passed away," "gone," as well as "she is no longer with us." A medical procedure may involve "harvesting" an organ instead of "removing" an organ.

While most of us use euphemisms in our everyday speech, we generally do so to avoid offending our listeners or making them uncomfortable. As a speaker, though, it is important that we do not confuse our listeners. Language that masks or muddies rather than clarifies meaning can confuse listeners. Former President George W. Bush comes to mind here. While he is a capable and intelligent man, he became known for, among many other things, his public muddlings. Here are four noteworthy examples (Kurtzman, n.d.) where the language of the military is combined with the language of diplomacy.

> "Too many good docs are getting out of the business. Too many ob-gyns aren't able to practice their love with women all across this country."—Poplar Bluff, Missouri, September 6, 2004
>
> "They misunderestimated me."—Bentonville, Arkansas, November 6, 2000
>
> "Rarely is the question asked: Is our children learning?"—Florence, South Carolina, January 11, 2000
>
> "Our enemies are innovative and resourceful, and so are we. They never stop thinking about new ways to harm our country and our people, and neither do we."—Washington, D.C., August 5, 2004

An effective speaker avoids using language that is unclear, makes an audience uncomfortable, or confuses the listeners. Using euphemisms is not recommended.

Jargon, Slang, and Profanity

Jargon is the host of technical terms used by special groups. For example, the jargon of the publishing business includes such terms as "specs," "page proofs," "dummy stage," and "halftones." Although these terms are not five syllables long, they may be difficult to understand if you are unfamiliar with publishing.

A special kind of jargon involves the use of acronyms—the alphabet soup of an organization or profession. Instead of saturating your speech with references to the FDA, PACs, or ACLI on the assumption that everyone knows what the acronyms mean, define these abbreviations the first time they are used. Tell your listeners that the FDA refers to the Food and Drug Administration; PACs, political action committees; and the ACLI, the American Council of Life Insurance.

Jargon can be used effectively when you are *sure* that everyone in your audience understands the reference. Therefore, if you are the editor-in-chief of a publishing company addressing your editorial and production staffs, publishing jargon requires no definition. However, if you deliver a speech about the publishing business to a group of college seniors, definitions are needed.

Slang is the use of informal words and expressions that are not considered standard in the speaker's language. For example, instead of saying "marijuana," one might hear slang terms such as "weed," "dope," "pot," and "ganja" (among others). Some words endure over decades (cool) whereas other words or phrases have a shorter life-span (bee's knees). Slang is generally spoken by the young, but this is not true in all cases. It may be news to you that your parents grew up when "thongs" were the name for "flip-flops," and "peddle-pushers" were what is now known as "capris."

Slang helps individuals identify with their peers, but it is not often appropriate within the formal speaking environment. Grammatical structures such as "ain't" and "you guys" should be used *only* for specific effect. In public discourse, slang used in any way can violate an audience's sense of appropriateness—or propriety.

Profanity is seldom appropriate within the public speaking context. Listeners almost always expect a degree of decorum in a formal speech, requiring that certain language be avoided. Even celebrities are expected to avoid certain profanity in public situations. For example, Melissa Leo dropped the f-bomb during her acceptance speech for Best Supporting Actress at the 2011 Academy Awards ceremony. She quickly apologized for her error during backstage interviews.

Robert Pattinson, while presenting a career achievement award at the MTV Movie Awards in 2011 to actress Reese Witherspoon, his co-star in the film *Water for Elephants*, dropped the f-bomb. This gaffe slipped through the censors. While many individuals use profanity with their peers, when we listen to speakers in a public setting, we have a different set of expectations.

Exaggeration and Clichés

Exaggerations are statements made to impress at the expense of accuracy. Instead of telling your classmates that you "always" exercise an hour a day, tell them that you exercise an hour a day "as often" as you can. Some of your classmates may know you well enough to realize that "always" is stretching the truth. Instead of saying that you would "never" consider double parking, tell your listeners that you would consider it "only as a last resort in an emergency." Obvious exaggerations diminish your credibility as a speaker.

Clichés, according to communication professors Eugene Ehrlich and Gene R. Hawes (1984), are the "enemies of lively speech." They explain:

> They are deadwood: the shiny suits of your word wardrobe, the torn sandals, the frayed collars, the scuffed shoes, the bobby socks, the fur pieces, the Nehru jackets, the miniskirts—yesterday's chewing gum (p. 48).

Clichés can lull your listeners into a state of boredom because they suggest that both your vocabulary and imagination are limited. Here is a section of a speech purposefully altered with slang and clichés:

> Two years ago, the real estate market was weak. *At that point in time* I would *guesstimate* that there were 400 more houses on the market than there are today. For us, it was

time to *put our noses to the grindstone. We toughed it out and kept our eyes on the prize.* The winning *game plan* we should follow from now on is to convince potential buyers that we *have a good thing going* in this community—good schools, good libraries, a good transportation system. We should also convince them that we're a *community with a heart.* We're here to help each other when we're *down and out.* It's a *win-win* relationship we're after today, as …

Imagine listening to this entire speech. Even if the speaker has something valuable to say, it is virtually impossible to hear it through the clichés. Clichés are unimaginative and add unnecessary words to your speech.

Phrases That Communicate Uncertainty

Speakers should avoid phrases that communicate uncertainty. Language can communicate a sense of mastery of your subject or it can communicate uncertainty. Compare the following paragraphs:

Version 1:

Sometimes I think that too many students choose a career solely on the basis of how much they are likely to earn. It seems to me, they forget that they also have to somewhat enjoy what they are probably going to spend the rest of their work lives doing, in my estimation.

Version 2:

Too many students choose a career based solely on how much they would earn. They forget that enjoying what they spend the rest of their work lives doing is important, too.

Version 1 contains weakening phrases: "sometimes I think", "likely", "it seems to me", "somewhat", "probably", and "in my estimation," adding nothing but uncertainty to the speaker's message. At least it is phrased in an active voice, which does communicate confidence. If you have a position, state it directly without crutch words that signal your timidity to the audience.

☞ Summary

Spoken language differs from written language in several important ways. In many cases, spoken language requires redundancy; it affects the order of ideas, and requires that the speaker pay attention to rhythm. Spoken language may also require that you signal your audience before you present important material.

The most effective language is simple, clear, and direct. Use short, common words instead of long, unusual ones; avoid euphemisms and jargon; eliminate unnecessary words that pad your speech; be direct and concrete, and avoid exaggeration.

Engage the imagination of your listeners through the use of metaphors, similes, and other figures of speech that paint memorable word pictures. Use language to create a theme. Regardless of the choices you make, be certain your language fits your personality, position, and the needs of your audience. The effective use of humor requires that you have confidence in your ability to make people laugh. Be cautious with humor, particularly if you are not typically a funny person. Laugh at yourself, not others. Use understated anecdotes. And remember, humor is everywhere. Find humor in your own experiences.

To improve your speaking style, avoid long and unnecessary words, clichés, and inappropriate euphemisms. Edit out profanity, slang, and jargon, drop exaggeration and clichés, as well as sentences that say nothing or communicate uncertainty. Removing these common pitfalls will enhance your language prowess.

☞   References

Berg, K., & Gilman, A. (1989). *Get to the Point: How to Say What You Mean and Get What You Want*. New York: Random House.

Buscaglia, Leo. (2007). *I Helped Him Cry*. Children's Thoughts on Love. Utah Government Document. Retrieved July 28, 2011 from www.schools.utah.gov/cte/documents/.../6_8ChildrensThoughtsOnLove.

Burton, G. O. (n.d.). Silva Rhetoricae: *The Trees of Rhetoric* (Online resource). Brigham Young University. Retrieved September 1, 2011 from rhetoric.byu.edu/.

Chang, M., & Gruner, C. R. (1981). Audience Reaction to Self-Disparaging Humor. *Southern Speech Communication Journal, 46*, 419–426.

Colin Firth Oscar Acceptance Speech 2011: Video, Transcript. Retrieved September 3, 2011 from www.nowpublic.com/culture/colin-firth-oscar-acceptance-speech-2011-video-transcript-2761763.html.

Derose, S. (2011). *Business Meeting Bingo*. Retrieved August 1, 2011 from www.derose.net/steve/resources/papers/Bingo.html.

Detz, J. (1984). *How to Write and Give a Speech*. New York: St. Martin's Press.

Dosomething.org. (2011). *Tips and Tools, 11 Facts About the BP Oil Spill*. Retrieved August 1, 2011 from www.dosomething.org/tipsandtools/11-facts-about-bp-oil-spill.

Duarte, N. (2011). *Congress, Preparers Urge IRS to Clarify Publications by Using Plain Language*. Retrieved July 28, 2011 from www.tax.com/taxcom/features.nsf/Articles/054E880A97191EFF852576E3006878C5?OpenDocument.

Ehrlich, E., & Hawes, G. R. (1984). *Speak for Success*. New York: Bantam Books.

Farhi, P. (2010, November 15). PBS Edits Tina Fey's Remarks from Twain Event. *The Washington Post Online*. Retrieved September 3, 2011 from www.voices.washingtonpost.com/arts-posts/2010/11/by_paul_farhi_tina_fey.html.

Gruner, C. R. (1985, April). Advice to the Beginning Speaker on Using Humor—What the Research Tells Us. *Communication Education, 34*, 142.

Gustainis, J. J. (1987). Jesse Louis Jackson. In B. K. Duffy & H. R. Ryan (Eds.), *American Orators of the Twentieth Century: Critical Studies and Sources*. New York: Greenwood Press.

Harrell, A. (1997). *Speaking Beyond the Podium: A Public Speaking Handbook, 2nd Ed*. Harcourt Brace College Publishing: Fort Worth.

Kaplan, R. M., & Pascoe, G. C. (1977). Humorous Lectures and Humorous Examples: Some Effects upon Comprehension and Retentions. *Journal of Educational Psychology, 69*, 61–65.

Kleinfeld, N. R. (1990). Teaching the 'Sir Winston' Method. *New York Times, March 11*, 7.

Knowlton, B. (2008). Obama Vows to Cut Budget Waste. *New York Times. November 25*. Retrieved September 3, 2011 from www.newyorktime/2008/11/26/us/politics/25-cnd-transition/html.

Kurtzman, D. (n.d.). *Political Humor, Top 10 Bushisms*, About.com. Retrieved July 29, 2011 from politicalhumor.about.com/cs/georgewbush/a/top10bushisms.htm.

Mooney, A. (2011, June 22). Michelle Obama Brings 'Yes, We Can' to Africa. *CNN Politics, The 1600 Report*. Retrieved July 29, 2011 from whitehouse.blogs.cnn.com/2011/06/22/michelle-obama-brings-yes-we-can-to-africa/.

Phillips, M. (2009, January 21). President Barack Obama's Inaugural Address. *The White House Blog*. Retrieved July 29, 2011 from www.whitehouse.gov/blog/inaugural-address/.

Purdue OWL. (2011). *Active and Passive Voice*. Purdue Online Writing Lab, Purdue University. Retrieved July 29, 2011 from owl.english.purdue.edu/owl/resource/539/4/.

Rackleff, R. B. (1987, September 26). The Art of Speech Writing: A Dramatic Event (Speech). Reprinted in *Vital Speeches of the Day*, March 1, 1988.

Schmich, M. (1997). Advice, Like Youth, Probably Just Wasted on the Young. *Chicago Tribune, June 1*. Retrieved June 10, 2007 from www.chicagotribune.com.

Tarver, J. (1988, March 2). Words in Time: Some Reflections on the Language of Speech. Reprinted in *Vital Speeches of the Day*, April 15, 410–412.

Valenti, J. (1982). *Speak Up with Confidence*. New York: William Morrow and Company, Inc.

Ziv, A. (1982). Cognitive Results of Using Humor in Teaching. Paper presented at the *Third International Conference on Humor*, Washington, DC. (Cited in Gruner, Advice to the Beginning Speaker, p. 144).

Chapter 8

Being Audience-Centered

"Eloquence not only considers the subject, *but also the* speaker *and the* hearers, *and both the subject and the speaker for the sake of the hearers."*

George Campbell

SPEECH: Elizabeth Cady Stanton— Seneca Falls Keynote Address

In 1840, Elizabeth Cady Stanton (1815–1902) attended an antislavery convention in London, England, where women were excluded from participating in discussions and only allowed to observe the proceedings from the gallery. The controversy over the role of women in the abolitionist movement, in addition to legal changes in New York regarding the right of women to hold property, motivated Elizabeth Cady Stanton and others (in particular, Lucretia Mott, Martha Wright, and Mary Ann McClintock) to organize the first women's rights convention held in Seneca Falls, New York in 1848. The rhetoric in this speech is clearly analogous to the rhetoric of the American Revolution as demonstrated in the Declaration of Independence.

Source: Reid, Ronald F. (1995). American Rhetorical Discourse (2nd ed.). Prospect Heights, IL: Waveland Press, pp. 380–381.

First Woman's Rights Convention

Seneca Falls, NY 19-20 July 1848

DECLARATION OF SENTIMENTS

When, in the course of human events, it becomes necessary for one portion of the family of man to assume among the people of the earth a position different from that which they have hitherto occupied, but one to which the laws of

---

nature and of nature's God entitle them, a decent respect to the opinions of mankind requires that they should declare the causes that impel them to such a course.

We hold these truths to be self-evident: that all men and women are created equal; that they are endowed by their Creator with certain inalienable rights; that among these are life, liberty, and the pursuit of happiness; that to secure these rights governments are instituted, deriving their just powers from the consent of the governed. Whenever any form of government becomes destructive of these ends, it is the right of those who suffer from it to refuse allegiance to it, and to insist upon the institution of a new government, laying its foundation on such principles, and organizing its powers in such form, as to them shall seem most likely to effect their safety and happiness. Prudence, indeed, will dictate that governments long established should not be changed for light and transient causes; and accordingly all experience hath shown that mankind are more disposed to suffer, while evils are sufferable, than to right themselves by abolishing the forms to which they were accustomed. But when a long train of abuses and usurpations, pursuing invariably the same object, evinces a design to reduce them under absolute despotism, it is their duty to throw off such government, and to provide new guards for their future security. Such has been the patient sufferance of the women under this government, and such is now the necessity which constrains them to demand the equal station to which they are entitled.

The history of mankind is a history of repeated injuries and usurpations on the part of man toward woman, having in direct object the establishment of an absolute tyranny over her. To prove this, let facts be submitted to a candid world.

He has never permitted her to exercise her inalienable right to the elective franchise.

He has compelled her to submit to laws, in the formation of which she had no voice.

He has withheld from her rights which are given to the most ignorant and degraded men — both natives and foreigners.

Having deprived her of this first right of a citizen, the elective franchise, thereby leaving her without representation in the halls of legislation, he has oppressed her on all sides.

He has made her, if married, in the eye of the law, civilly dead.

He has taken from her all right in property, even to the wages she earns.

He has made her, morally, an irresponsible being, as she can commit many crimes with impunity, provided they be done in the presence of her husband. In the covenant of marriage, she is compelled to promise obedience to her husband, he becoming, to all intents and purposes, her master — the law giving him power to deprive her of her liberty, and to administer chastisement.

He has so framed the laws of divorce, as to what shall be the proper causes, and in case of separation, to whom the guardianship of the children shall be given, as to be wholly regardless of the happiness of women — the law, in all cases, going upon a false supposition of the supremacy of man, and giving all power into his hands.

After depriving her of all rights as a married woman, if single, and the owner of property, he has taxed her to support a government which recognizes her only when her property can be made profitable to it.

He has monopolized nearly all the profitable employments, and from those she is permitted to follow, she receives but a scanty remuneration. He closes against her all the avenues to wealth and distinction which he considers most honorable to himself. As a teacher of theology, medicine, or law, she is not known.

He has denied her the facilities for obtaining a thorough education, all colleges being closed against her.

He allows her in Church, as well as State, but a subordinate position, claiming Apostolic authority for her exclusion from the ministry, and, with some exceptions, from any public participation in the affairs of the Church.

He has created a false public sentiment by giving to the world a different code of morals for men and women, by which moral delinquencies which exclude women from society, are not only tolerated, but deemed of little account in man.

He has usurped the prerogative of Jehovah himself, claiming it as his right to assign for her a sphere of action, when that belongs to her conscience and to her God.

He has endeavored, in every way that he could, to destroy her confidence in her own powers, to lessen her self-respect, and to make her willing to lead a dependent and abject life.

Now, in view of this entire disfranchisement of one-half the people of this country, their social and religious degradation — in view of the unjust laws above mentioned, and because women do feel themselves aggrieved, oppressed, and fraudulently deprived of their most sacred rights, we insist that they have immediate admission to all the rights and privileges which belong to them as citizens of the United States.

In entering upon the great work before us, we anticipate no small amount of misconception, misrepresentation, and ridicule; but we shall use every instrumentality within our power to effect our object. We shall employ agents, circulate tracts, petition the State and National legislatures, and endeavor to enlist the pulpit and the press in our behalf. We hope this Convention will be followed by a series of Conventions embracing every part of the country.

http://utc.iath.virginia.edu/abolitn/abwmat.html

At the end of the second week of public speaking, two students approached their teaching assistant, Mr. Wyckoff, and tentatively asserted themselves:

"Why do you use so many baseball examples?" Liz asked. "I know it's the national pastime and all that, and I realize that the San Francisco Giants just won the World Series, but neither of us *care* for the sport."

"Yeah," Sarah added, "we don't get all the references, and to be perfectly honest, we lose interest and start tuning you out."

Mr. Wyckoff, momentarily caught off guard at the realization that the whole world did not share his enthusiasm for the sport, explained, "Oh, I've been involved with baseball since I first played t-ball, and I've umpired for the last 10 years. But thanks for the heads-up. I'll work on variety," adding with a laugh, "assuming there *is* life outside of baseball."

Mr. Wyckoff was able to make adjustments to his lecture by incorporating a variety of examples that related to his audience, and he received more positive reinforcement from his class as a whole.

Whether in a large auditorium, a corporate board room, or a classroom, audiences are usually self-centered. Listeners want to know "What's in it for me?" That is, they want to understand what they can learn from a speech or how they can take action that will, in some way, enhance their lives. If you show your audience you understand their needs and help them achieve their goals, they will want to listen. Being **audience-centered** and **adapting** to their needs are critical factors in creating effective presentations. These two concepts are the focus of this chapter.

Know Your Audience

How do you prepare and deliver a speech that will mean enough to your audience to capture their attention and convince them to listen? Begin by learning as much as you can about your listeners so you can identify and focus on their concerns.

Audience-Centeredness

Making your intended audience central in your message formation will result in a stronger, more tailored speech that resonates with your listeners. This is desirable because you can feel and respond positively to the energy and enthusiasm that a receptive and captivated audience exudes. In essence, if you are audience centered, both you and your audience benefit greatly.

Early in your speech, telling your audience what's in it for them and letting them know they were front and center in your mind as you worked on your message is a great way to help establish your credibility, common ground, and build their interest in your topic. Knowing what your audience needs is the first step to being audience-centered.

Audience Analysis

Jon Favreau, who is credited with creating Obama's campaign slogan, "Yes we can," assumed the position of director of speechwriting when Obama took office. Before being hired, the then–presidential candidate asked, "What is your theory of speechwriting?" Favreau admitted:

> I have no theory. But when I saw you at the [2004] convention, you basically told a story about your life from beginning to end, and it was a story that fit with the larger American narrative. People applauded not because you wrote an applause line but because you touched something in the party and the country that people had not touched before. Democrats haven't had that in a long time (Quoted from Richard Wolfe, *Newsweek*, 2008).

Favreau's observation serves to confirm that Obama's approach to the 2004 speech was audience-centered. The speech "touched" people, both at the convention and those watching the proceedings.

In discussing the primaries, Favreau shared his impression of Obama's campaign speech:

> The message out of Iowa was one of unity and reaching out across party lines. We knew we were going to do well with independents, young people and first-time voters. We knew the message was similar to what he said at the 2004 convention.

In creating a message of "unity" and "reaching out across party lines," Favreau identifies the targeted audience characteristics: independents, young people, and first-time voters. Obama's success in the primaries as well as the general election confirms his ability during that campaign to analyze his audience effectively.

You need not be a presidential speechwriter to understand your audience. All speakers can create a sketch of their listeners by analyzing them in terms of key demographic and psychographic characteristics.

Demographics include age, gender, race and ethnicity, education/knowledge, group affiliation, occupational group, socioeconomic status, religious background, political affiliation, and geographic identifiers. Depending on your general and specific purposes, certain demographics may be more important than others for any given speech.

Psychographics include lifestyle choices, attitudes, beliefs, and values of your listeners. In many cases these are more difficult to ascertain unless the audience is known for their attitudes, beliefs, and values. Information that emerges from demographic and psychographic analyses is the raw material for a successful speaker–audience connection (Woodward & Denton, 2004).

Demographic Analysis

We need a good fit within the various aspects of our speech, such as supporting material, thesis and main points, and audience characteristics. Depending on the speaking situation, ascertaining demographics may be easily accomplished. At your disposal are up to four approaches to determine audience characteristics. First, you may make some assumptions about the audience as a whole. If you were asked to give a speech on patriotism, think about the differences in demographics between the Daughters of the American Revolution and Vietnam Veterans Against the War. We can make certain logical assumptions about each of these audience's demographics; in this instance, that includes age, gender, and group affiliation.

Second, you may have the opportunity to observe the audience in advance and learn first-hand what their demographics are. Third, you could interview someone who knows the audience well. Finally, a fourth strategy involves creating a simple audience analysis survey that you can adapt. Later in this chapter we cover types of questions you might use to uncover demographics. Whether through knowledge of the group the audience represents, direct observation, interview, or survey, it's important to gain insight into your audience before you construct your speech. Ten key demographics are identified as follows.

1. Age. Try to determine the age of your audience and if there is a large or a small variation in age. Examples and stories you provide need to relate to your audience. Think about how you might foster a feeling of inclusion among all ages present. Ask yourself, "How does my age potentially impact my audience's perceptions of me?" Perhaps certain stereotypes exist based solely on their assessment of your age. If you believe your age may influence their response to you, reflect on how you might make these assumptions work in your favor instead of against you.

   One brave student, Vicky, was enraged about proposed tuition increases and decided to speak to the college's board of trustees about the issue. Knowing well that the board was made up of individuals who were on average 30 years her senior, Vicky used examples and illustrations appropriate for their age demographic, including a brief reference to the GI Bill and The Great Society, as well as an impassioned anecdote about a share-cropper family whose son would change the world for migratory farmers: Cesar Chavez. Vicky's message was better received because her audience could identify with her examples. Her tactic was unexpected and appreciated by an audience who thought they were about to hear a whining diatribe with little real substance. Vicky was able to make age-related assumptions work in her favor and serve her ultimate goals for speaking.

When taking into consideration your age and the age(s) of your audience, we suggest the following:

- **Avoid assumptions about the average age of your audience**. If you are speaking to a group of students, do not assume they will all be in your age bracket. Today, millions of nontraditional students are enrolled in four-year colleges. On any campus, you will meet 40-year-old sophomores seeking a new career or returning to school after their children are grown and 60-year-old freshmen returning because they love learning. Whereas we know that Vietnam Veterans Against the War must fit into a certain age group, to be a member of the Daughters of the American Revolution, a female must be 18 or older. You would need to find other ways to discover the age range of this audience.

- **Focus on your speech, not your age**. In many cases, there is no reason to bring attention to your age. Doing so may detract from your message. Business consultant Edith Weiner started to deliver speeches to senior-level executives at the age of 23. "I was much younger than people thought I was going to be," said Weiner. "When I got up to speak, they didn't know what to make of me." Weiner's response was to focus on her message. "If I did well in the first three minutes, not only did I surprise the audience, I created fans. Expectations were so low that when I came across as confident and funny and comfortable, the audience was hooked into the rest of my speech" (personal interview, 1989). Her speech may have come across differently if she had apologized for her youth or made excuses.

- **Avoid dating yourself with references or language**. If you are addressing a group of teenagers on the topic of popular culture, talk about their current favorite rock group, not the New Kids on the Block. If you are addressing a group of middle-aged executives, do not assume that they know what college students are thinking. Avoid purposefully using current terms or phrases that might come off as sounding patronizing and condescending.

2. **Gender**. Some topics may have broader appeal to men, in general, while others may be of greater interest to women, in general. Gender role differences do exist, however, and generalizations based on these differences are not necessarily wrong. Therefore, if you are addressing a group of young men who you know are likely to enjoy professional sports, it's fair to use a sports analogy to make your point—not because you are a fan but because talking about the Cleveland Browns or the Dallas Cowboys helps you connect with your listeners.

Consider the composition of your next audience. Is it mixed or is there a majority of males or females? Also, while we do not identify sexual orientation as one of the 10 demographics, it is closely related. Every audience will likely contain members who are gay, lesbian, bisexual, or transgender. Maintaining this awareness by using sensitive and inclusive language and examples goes a long way toward fostering common ground, inclusiveness, and a more positive response your message. Language sensitivity and inclusiveness are topics that are covered in greater detail in Chapter 7.

Regarding gender, we do suggest that you *structure your speech so you are inclusive*. Avoid unfairly categorizing or stereotyping members of the audience. For example, airlines no longer have "stewardesses," but "flight attendants." "Car salesmen" are no longer only men; that term has been replaced by "sales associates." Departments on college and university campuses are no longer headed by a "chairman" but rather by a "chair" or a "chairperson." For the most part, speakers should avoid relying on the masculine pronoun and find ways to include men *and* women in their audiences.

3. **Race and ethnicity**. Long ago, the image of the United States as a melting pot gave way to the image of a rainbow of diversity—an image in which African Americans, Hispanics, Asians, Greeks, Arabs, and Europeans define themselves by their racial and ethnic ties as well as by their ties to the United States. Within this diversity are cultural beliefs and traditions that may be different from your own.

Even now, over half a century after the most sweeping civil rights legislation in American history was passed by Congress and signed into law by the President, racial issues and differences spawn controversy. In 2005, Hurricane Katrina devastated much of the southern shoreline of America. Charges were made by a variety of leaders essentially declaring that if the majority of the population of New Orleans had been white, there would have been much greater and quicker efforts to move citizens to safe places with ample food and water.

If you deliver a speech on the topic of communication failures and the devastation of Hurricane Katrina, you need take into account the considerable problems faced by black citizens in New Orleans and along the southern shoreline. If you do not, you are likely to fail in achieving your specific purpose for your speech and you will make your presentation unacceptable to some of your listeners. This is not to suggest that you change your views if they are carefully conceived and supported. However, if your topic includes racial and ethnic issues that you fail to acknowledge during your speech, you can expect members of your audience to be offended or dismissive.

While most of us can grasp the concept of race, given that it has a biological basis, understanding ethnicity is somewhat more difficult. A Latino speaker recently noted in his opening comments to a largely Anglo Midwestern audience that he was pleased to be the lone representative from the "real south." His comment brought both laughter and an appreciation for his unique point of view. He made the most of an obvious contrast with his audience (ethnicity) by addressing it quickly and then dismissing it with humor. Notice, though, that he left it at that. Going too far with racial and ethnic comments can create more tension and discomfort. Noting the obvious is welcomed by audiences, as long as it is handled deftly and with tact.

As you develop your speech, we ask that you avoid invoking **stereotypes** related to race, ethnicity, or nationality, even if these groups are not present in your audience. Even when couched in humor, such comments are deeply offensive and unethical. Appreciation of different people and ways can help you avoid several critical errors in your speech. Any of these gaffes will surely compromise the connection you are trying to create.

Understand also, that **ethnocentrism**, which is the belief that one's own culture is superior to other cultures, comes into play when we express a bias for the way we do things. Unfortunately, some or many individuals who might be identified as ethnocentric have little experience with other cultures. Therefore, an accurate comparison is difficult to make. A speaker should try to avoid being offensive or unfair by examining his/her language usage as well as the examples, stories, and illustrations he/she is contemplating incorporating into a speech.

4. **Education/knowledge**. Are the members of your audience high school or college graduates, experts with doctorates in the field, or freshmen taking their first course? Knowing the educational level of your audience will aid in the construction of your message. If you're speaking to elementary students about Queen Elizabeth I, you can safely assume they need to be provided with some historical background. But to a group of European historians such information would not be necessary.

    Ideally, your audience will have some knowledge of your subject matter on which your message will build. It may be more difficult to develop a speech for an audience that has no knowledge of your topic, since they may not have much interest. To determine your audience's knowledge of your topic and desire for additional information, you might explore surveying, interviewing, and observing them.

    In addition to determining what type of background information or explanation is needed, another consideration is language. You want to speak *to* your audience, not over their heads or at such a basic level that you sound condescending. We have the following two suggestions that highlight how important it is to analyze your audience's needs:

    - **Do not assume that expertise in one area necessarily means expertise in others**. For example, if you are a stockbroker delivering a speech to a group of scientists about investment opportunities, you may have to define the rules that govern even simple stock trades. Although the more educated your audience, the more sophisticated these explanations can be, explanations must still be included for your speech to make sense.
    - **Be careful about assuming what your audience knows—and does not know—about technical topics**. Mention a server to people who know nothing about computers, and they may be baffled. Define it for a group of computer experts, and they will wonder why you were asked to speak to them. In both cases, you run the risk of losing your audience; people who are confused or who know much more about a subject may simply stop listening.

5. **Group affiliation**. Listeners may identify themselves as members of formal and informal interest groups. An informal interest group generally doesn't require signing up or paying for membership, or making any type of formal commitment. Examples include YouTube watchers, Starbucks customers, and residents of an inner-city neighborhood. A formal interest group usually requires an official commitment, such as signing a membership form or paying dues. Examples include members of Future Farmers of America, the Chamber of Commerce, or a LISTSERV on alternative treatments for Alzheimer's.

Members of your audience may be members of labor organizations or service clubs. Perhaps they volunteer for a local or national organization. They may identify themselves as being Republican, Democratic, Independent, Green, or a member of the Tea Party. Maybe they are active members of the Chinese Student and Scholars Association on your campus. If they belong to any of these groups, these affiliations may well affect choices they make.

If you are addressing members of the Sierra Club, you can be sure the group has a keen awareness of environmental issues. Similarly, if you are addressing an exercise class at the local Y, you can be sure that physical fitness is a priority of everyone in the room. It is important to know something about the group you are speaking to so you can adapt your message to their interest.

Our main suggestion with regard to group affiliation is to *avoid assuming that all members of a group have similar attitudes.* All members of the International Students group on campus do not share the same set of values or beliefs. They represent different countries with different political and religious practices. Their one shared demographic is that they come from a country outside of the United States. While our two-party system in the United States classifies individuals as either Democrat or Republican, we know that there are conservatives and liberals in both parties. Knowing group affiliation may help us construct our main points and identify appropriate supporting material. We need to take caution, however, and avoid stereotyping the group.

6. **Occupational groups**. You may find an occasion that involves speaking to a specific occupational group, such as teachers, students, doctors, lawyers, union representatives, miners, or factory workers. Occupational information can often tell you a great deal about listeners' attitudes. An audience of physicians may be unwilling to accept proposed legislation that would strengthen a patient's right to choose a personal physician if it also makes it easier for patients to sue for malpractice. A legislative speaker might need to find creative ways to convince the doctors that the new law would be in the best interests of both doctors and patients.

Knowledge of what your listeners do for a living may also tell you the type of vocabulary appropriate for the occasion. If you are addressing a group of newspaper editors, you can use terms common to the newspaper business without bothering to define them. Do not use job-related jargon indiscriminately, but rather, use it to your advantage.

When conducting your audience analysis, try to determine what your listeners do for a living. The speaking occasion often makes this clear. You may be invited by a group of home builders to speak about the dangers of radon, or a group of insurance agents may ask you to talk about the weather conditions associated with hurricanes. Knowing the occupations of your audience may lead you to decide not only what type of information to include, but what specific statistics, examples, or illustrations would be most effective for the particular group.

Our suggestion regarding occupational groups is to *avoid too little analysis or too much analysis of the importance of occupational affiliation to your audience members.* When you ask people to describe themselves, what is the first thing they say? It might be "I'm a white female," "I'm a gay activist," "I'm the mother of four young children," or "I'm a lawyer." Some people *define* themselves by their occupation; others view their jobs as a way to feed a family and maintain a reasonable lifestyle. By determining how important the occupational group characteristic is to your audience, you can create an on-target message that meets their needs.

7. **Socioeconomic status.** Depending on the situation, it may be difficult to determine whether members of your audience earn more than $100,000 a year or less than $30,000. However, this demographic characteristic may influence how you develop your speech and create common ground with your audience. When Rabbi Harold Kushner (2002) talks to groups about his book *When All You've Ever Wanted Isn't Enough*, he learns the group's socioeconomic status in advance. He explains:

> Generally, if I'm addressing affluent business executives, I concentrate on the downside of economic success and on the spiritual nature of affluence. When the group is less affluent, I talk about learning to cope with economic failure and with the feeling of being left behind.

This statement illustrates how one person adapts to his audience based on socioeconomic status. Knowing whether the economic situation has changed recently for your audience or whether there is likely to be another change soon may influence your approach to your topic. For example, when speaking to a group of incoming freshmen at a public university in 2012, it might be wise to spend more time on financial aid than a speaker would have in 2002. Topics such as welfare, socialized medicine, and social security will be approached differently based on whether your audience comes from a wealthy background or one of poverty.

We suggest you be *mindful of your audience's financial status while framing your message*. Giving a speech linking high credit card debt to filing for bankruptcy would need to be adapted to an audience that has no debt. However, those facing financial ruin do not need to hear a "holier-than-thou" lecture on the dangers of credit card debt.

8. **Religious background.** According to the article "Where We Stand on Faith," many people in the United States consider themselves spiritual and religious (*Newsweek*, September 6, 2005). Suppose your topic is in-vitro fertilization, one of medicine's generally effective techniques to help infertile couples have children. Your presentation goes well, but the faces of your listeners suggest you hit a nerve. Without realizing it, you may have offended your audience by failing to deal with the potential religious implications of such procedures.

Speakers seldom intend to offend their audiences. However, when it comes to religion, speakers can offend unwittingly. Please consider that *religious beliefs may also define moral attitudes*. When speaking on issues such as abortion, premarital sex, birth control, gay marriage, and gays in the military, we risk alienating our audience. By no means are we suggesting you avoid such topics. However, failing to acknowledge and address the religious beliefs of your listeners when your speech concerns a sensitive topic sets up barriers to communication that may be difficult to overcome.

So, what do you do if you are religious? What if your comments are framed in that specific moral attitude? Explaining your frame of reference and personal biases is ethical and builds rapport, even with those who don't share your convictions. Audiences expect and respect honesty. One student handled her religious frame of reference directly: "Now I am a Christian, and the in-vitro procedure I received was in a Catholic hospital. I understand there are many other ways to look at the ethics of my decision, but I want to put that aside for now and focus only on the process." Where possible, remove stumbling blocks for your audience by being forthright and truthful about your own religious convictions while also communicating tolerance and open-mindedness to other perspectives.

9. **Political affiliation**. In an election year, our interest in political affiliation is heightened. Whether you self-identify as Libertarian, a mainstream Democrat or Republican, or a member of the Tea Party or the Green Party, political affiliation may influence how you respond to a given speaker. If you are fundraising for the homeless, you will probably give a different speech to a group with liberal beliefs than to a group of conservatives. Consider these variations of a message based on political affiliation:

To a group of political liberals

> We are a nation of plenty—a nation in which begging seems as out of place as snow in July. Yet our cities are filled with poor citizens who have no food or lodging. They are the have-nots in a nation of haves. I ask for your help tonight because we are a nation built on helping one another escape from poverty. No matter how hard you work to cement your own success, you will never achieve the American Dream if one person is left on the streets without a home.

To a group of political conservatives

> It is in your best interest to give money to homeless causes. I'm not talking about handouts on the street but money that goes into putting a roof over people's heads and into job training. In the long run, giving people dignity by giving them a home and training them for productive work will mean fewer people on welfare and lower taxes. Is it a leap of faith to see this connection or just plain common business sense?

Acknowledging political differences has been important in America since its founding. You will not compromise your values when you accept the fact that political differences exist. Rather, you will take the first step in using these differences as the starting point for communication.

We cannot stress enough that *all members of a particular party do not share the same attitudes, beliefs, and values.* Find out how to connect to the diversity of your audience. Your speech as a conservative Republican addressing a group of conservative Republicans will sound different than when addressing an audience that represents the Republican spectrum.

10. **Geographic identifiers**. We have a variety of ways to discuss geographic identifiers. One is directional differences, such as north/south or east/west. Think how an audience comprised largely of people from the Deep South might vary from an audience of individuals from the Northwest. A second geographic identifier is upstate vs. downstate. For example, Illinois is divided into two general areas, Chicago and Downstate (everything

south of Chicago). This also alludes to the geographic identifier of urban versus rural. You may have an audience that lives in the same community, or you may have an audience that represents a number of communities. A third geographic identifier relates to terrain, such living near mountains, lakes, oceans, or as one of your authors describes herself, living near corn and bean fields and being a "flatlander."

Your authors suggest that understanding geographical identifiers as well as *focusing your message as much as possible on geographical areas of concern will enhance your message's impact and your credibility with your audience*. You may need to adapt your message to accommodate not only differences in language, speech rate, and references, but also specific interests and issues.

Psychographic Analysis

Psychographics refer to the behaviors, attitudes, beliefs, and values of your listeners. Although an analysis of demographic characteristics will give you some clue as to how your listeners are likely to respond to your speech, it will not tell you anything about the speaking occasion, why people have come together as an audience, how they feel about your topic, or about you as a speaker. This information emerges from the second stage of analysis—psychographics—and centers on the speaking situation specifically.

Behaviors. Your lifestyle choices say something about you. Do you walk, bike, drive, or take public transportation to work? Perhaps you avoid driving because walking and biking are "greener" and viewed as healthier. If you choose to be a city dweller who lives in a 22nd-story studio apartment, you probably have less inclination to experience nature than if you opt to live on a 50-acre farm in Vermont. If you put in 12-hour days at the office, your career is probably more important to you than if you choose to work part-time. Behavioral choices are linked to the attitudes, beliefs, and values of your listeners.

Attitudes, beliefs, and values. **Attitudes** are predispositions to act in a particular way that influences our response to objects, events, and situations. Attitudes tend to be long lasting, but can change under pressure. They are often, but not always, related to behavior. If I like vegetables, I am likely to bring a vegetable tray to a party. If I don't like big business, I'm less likely to shop at Walmart. Someone who doesn't care about the environment is less likely to recycle.

Beliefs represent a mental and emotional acceptance of information. They are judgments about the truth or the probability that a statement is correct. Beliefs are formed from experience and learning; they are based on what we perceive to be accurate. To be an effective speaker, you must analyze the beliefs of your audience in the context of your message. For example, if you are dealing with people who believe that working hard is the only way to get ahead, you will have trouble convincing them to take time off between semesters. Your best hope is to persuade them that time off will make them more productive and goal directed when they return. By citing authorities and providing examples of other students who have successfully followed this course, you have a chance of changing their mind-set.

Values are deep-seated abstract judgments about what is important to us. According to Rokeach's (1968) seminal work, we have both terminal and instrumental values. *Terminal values* are those we would like to achieve within our lifetime. These include national security, family security, equality, and freedom. *Instrumental values* help us achieve the terminal values, such as intellect, ambition, self-control, responsibility, and independence. Values separate the worthwhile from the worthless and determine what we consider moral, desirable, important, beautiful, and worth living or dying for.

An audience of concerned students that values the importance of education might express this value in the belief that "a college education should be available to all qualified students" and the attitude that "the state legislature should pass a tuition reduction plan for every state college." If you address this audience, you can use this attitude as the basis for your plea that students picket the State Capitol in support of the tuition reduction plan. Understanding your listeners' attitudes, beliefs, and values helps you put your message in the most effective terms.

Adapting to Different Audiences and Situations

Throughout this chapter and this textbook, you will read the words "it may" or "it might," or "perhaps." We are equivocal because audiences behave differently and have different expectations depending on their characteristics *and* the context or situation. An effective speaker adapts his/her message based on audience characteristics, both demographic and psychographic, and the situation that brings the audience together. A politician may give a speech in New York City, then tweak it before appearing at a gathering in America's heartland. Adapting a speech may be easy or difficult. In your public speaking class, it is important to keep in mind that your teacher is part of the audience. As such, you might need to make a few minor changes to be inclusive.

At a funeral, we know the mood is somber, but depending on the person being remembered and the individuals congregated, there may also be smiles and laughter. The circumstances may call for fond memory of a person's idiosyncrasies, or in case of a tragic death, laughter may be inappropriate. Also, if seven people are giving eulogies, then each one should be relatively brief, but if only two or three are speaking, more time can be allotted to each person. At a political rally, a speech given to an audience that has just seen its candidate soundly defeated would sound different than a speech given by someone on behalf of the winning candidate.

Interest Level and Expectations

Discovering the interest level in your topic and your audience's expectations helps you adapt to your audience. Interest level often determines audience response. High school seniors are more likely than high school freshmen to listen when someone from the financial aid office at the local college discusses scholarships, grants, and financial aid possibilities. People who fly frequently are less likely to pay attention to the flight attendant's description of safety procedures than individuals who have seldom flown. We tend to pay attention to things that are timely and that we know will affect us.

Experienced and successful professionals who speak frequently to audiences around the country collect information that will tell them who their listeners are and what they want and expect from their presentations. Robert Waterman Jr., coauthor of the successful book *In Search of Excellence*, indicates he spends a day or two before a speech observing his corporate audience at work. What he learns helps him address the specific concerns of his listeners (Kiechel, 1987). Waterman achieved success as a professional speaker in part because he assumed little about the characteristics of his prospective audience. To analyze an audience, questionnaires and observation are techniques that can be used successfully.

Accessing Audience Information

To adapt our message to a particular audience within a specific situation, we need to gather information. Three ways to access your audience's demographic and psychographic characteristics as well as their interest level and expectations include creating a questionnaire, observing, and interviewing.

Using a Questionnaire

Public opinion polls are an American tradition, especially around election time. Just about anything is up for analysis, from views on candidates and their issues, opinions on U.S. foreign policy, health care reform, taxes, and legalizing drugs to ice cream preferences and brand recognition.

A questionnaire can determine the specific demographic characteristics of your listeners as well as their perceptions of you and your topic. It can also tell you how much knowledge your listeners have about your topic and the focus they would prefer in your speech.

By surveying all your classmates, sampling every fourth person in your dorm, or emailing selected members of your audience to ask them questions, you can find out information about your audience in advance. These methods are simple and effective. In addition, and depending on the age of your intended audience, online survey creation and response tabulation companies like SurveyMonkey.com now make it easier to poll a group of people via the Internet.

The first step in using a questionnaire is to design specific questions that are likely to get you the information you need. Three basic types of questions are most helpful to public speakers: fixed-alternative questions, scale questions, and open-ended questions (Churchill, 1983).

Fixed-alternative questions limit responses to specific choices, yielding valuable information about such demographic factors as age, education, and income. Fixed-alternative questions can offer many responses, or they can offer only two alternatives, such as yes/no questions. Following is an example of a fixed-alternative question focusing on attitudes:

Do you think all professional athletes should be carefully tested for drugs and steroids? (Choose one)

Professionals should be carefully tested for drugs and steroids.
Professional athletes should be tested for the use of drugs and steroids in selected sports.
Professional athletes should never be required to test for drugs and steroids.
No opinion.

This type of question is easy to answer, tabulate, and analyze. These questions yield standardized responses. For example, it would be more difficult to ask people, "How many times a week do you eat out?" without supplying possible responses, because you may receive answers like "regularly," "rarely," "every day," and "twice a day." Interpreting these answers is more difficult.

Fixed alternative questions avoid confusion. When asking for marital status, consider providing specific choices. Do not ask marital status if it is irrelevant to your topic.

What is your marital status?
Single
Widowed
Married
Divorced

The disadvantage of using fixed-alternative questions is that it may force people to respond to a question when they are uncertain or have no opinion, especially if you fail to include "no opinion" as a possible response.

Scale questions are a type of fixed-alternative question that ask people to respond to questions set up along a continuum. For example:

How often do you vote?

Always   Regularly   Sometimes   Seldom   Never

If you develop a continuum that can be used repeatedly, several issues can be addressed quickly. For example, you can ask people to use the same scale to tell you how frequently they vote in presidential elections, congressional elections, state elections, and local elections. The disadvantage of the scale question is that it is difficult to get in-depth information about a topic.

In an **open-ended question**, audience members can respond however they wish. For example:

How do you feel about a 12-month school year for K–12 students?

In response to this question about extending the school year, one person may write, "Keep the school year as it is," while another may suggest a workable plan for extending the year. Because the responses to open-ended questions are so different, they can be difficult to analyze. The advantage to these questions is that they allow you to probe for details and you give respondents the opportunity to tell you what is on their minds. Here are some guidelines for constructing usable questions.

Guidelines for Survey Questions

Avoid leading questions. Try not to lead people to the response you desire through the wording of your question. Here are two examples of leading questions:

Do you feel stricter handgun legislation would stop the wanton *killing* of innocent people?
Do you believe able-bodied men who are *too lazy* to work should be eligible for welfare?

These questions should be reworded. For example, "Do you support stricter handgun legislation?" is no longer a leading question.

Avoid ambiguity. When you use words that can be interpreted in different ways, you reduce the value of a question. For example:

How often do you drink alcohol?

Frequently   Occasionally   Sometimes   Never

In this case one person's "sometimes" may be another person's "occasionally." To avoid ambiguity, rephrase the possible responses to more useful fixed-alternatives:

How often do you drink alcohol?
More than once a week
At least once a month
Less than twice every six months
Never

Ask everyone the same questions. Because variations in the wording of questions can change responses, always ask questions in the same way. Do not ask one person, "Under what circumstances would you consider enlisting in the Army?" and another, "If the United States were attacked by a foreign nation, would you consider joining the Army?" Both of these questions relate to enlisting in the military, but the first one is an open question while the second is a closed question. The answers you receive to the first question have much more information value than the second, which could be answered "yes" or "no." If you do not ask people the same questions, your results may be inaccurate.

Be aware of time constraints. Although questionnaires can help you determine interest, attitudes, and knowledge level, they also take time. If your instructor allows you to pass out a questionnaire in class, make sure it takes only a few minutes to complete. Make yours brief and clear. Ask only what is necessary and make sure the format fits your purpose. Even if there is no structured time in class for a survey, you can still catch students between classes, during group work in class, and by email. Any time spent getting to know your audience helps ensure you are audience centered.

Observe and Interview

You may find that the best way to gather information about a prospective audience is to assume the role of an observer. If you want to persuade your classmates to use reusable bottles, you might watch over a few weeks to see how many students in your class have throw-away (or recyclable) bottles, and how many are bringing reusable bottles to class. Then you could ask students who bring reusable bottles to class how long they've been using reusable bottles and why they do it. You could also interview students who bring recyclable bottles to class to ascertain their attitudes.

If you want to persuade your audience to get more involved with issues on campus, you might attend a student government meeting to see how many students attend (other than those *in* student government), and what types of issues are brought forth. Then you could interview members of the group as well as audience members to find their perceptions of student involvement on campus.

The information you gather from observing and interviewing is likely to be richer if you adopt a less formal style than you used in a traditional audience analysis questionnaire to gather information about your speech topic. By surveying, observing, and interviewing prospective audience members, your message will be well targeted, personalized, and appropriate.

Creating the Speaker–Audience Connection

It takes only seconds for listeners to tune out your message. Convince your audience your message has value by centering your message on your listeners and adapting your message to that specific audience and situation. The following suggestions will help you build the type of audience connection that leads to the message being understood and well received.

Get to the Point Quickly

First impressions count. What you say in the first few minutes is critical. Tell your listeners how you can help them first, not last. If you save your suggestions to the end, it may be that no one is listening. Experienced speakers try to make connections with their listeners as they open their speeches. For example, here is how one CEO addressed falling sales to his employees, "Good afternoon. Sales are down. Profits are gone. What's next? Jobs. I want to see all of you here again next month, but that may not happen. Let me explain how we got here and what we can do." With an opening like that, you can bet the CEO had the full attention of all employees present.

Have Confidence: They Want to Hear Your Speech

It happens frequently: Speakers with relatively little knowledge about a subject are asked to speak to a group of experts on that subject. An educator may talk to a group of athletes about intercollegiate sports. A lawyer may talk to a group of doctors about the doctor–patient relationship. When you feel your listeners know more than you do about your topic, realize they have invited you for a reason. In most cases, they want your opinion. Despite their knowledge, you have a perspective they find interesting. Athletes may want to learn how the college sports program is viewed by a professor, and doctors want to hear a lawyer's opinion about malpractice. Simply acknowledging your audience's education or intelligence and mentioning your contribution may be unique and hopefully will help create a bond of mutual respect.

Be of the People, Not Above the People

We do not want to listen to speakers who consider themselves more accomplished, smarter, or more sophisticated than we are. If speakers convey even a hint of superiority, listeners may tune them out.

On of the world's richest men and founder of Facebook, Mark Zuckerberg, demonstrated that he is "of the people" when he gave a speech to a graduating class…of a *middle* school! When Facebook moved its operation to Menlo Park, California in 2011, Zuckerberg reached out to his new neighborhood, by speaking to students and parents at Belle Haven Middle School. Wearing jeans and a t-shirt at the outdoor ceremony, Zuckerberg presented informally a message that was clearly developed for that particular audience.

> " ...I just want to share with you guys a few things that I've learned today that I think have enabled me and the people I work with to not succumb to the attitude of 'I can't.' And those things are that everything that is worth doing is actually pretty hard and takes a lot of work. That's one. The second is that you should focus on building great friendships and people that you trust because those really matter. And the third is just do what you love."

Rather than focus on his wealth, or brag about his accomplishments, he constructed a message that made him appear to be an ordinary guy with a meaningful message for the graduates.

Use Humor

Humor can help you connect with your audience and help them think of you as approachable rather than remote. Opening your speech with something that makes people smile or laugh can put both you and your listeners at ease. Consider the opening of Will Ferrell's 2003 speech at Harvard on Class Day (the day before graduation).

> This is not the Worcester, Mass Boat Show, is it? I am sorry. I have made a terrible mistake. Ever since I left Saturday Night Live, I mostly do public speaking now. And I must have made an error in the little Palm Pilot. Boy. Don't worry. I got it on me. I got the speech on me. Let's see. Ah, yes. Here we go.
> You know, when Bill Gates first called me to speak to you today, I was honored. ... Are you sure this is not the boat show?

His opening got their attention and made them laugh. Ferrell's humor pokes fun at his message and himself, not his audience. Subject and self-deprecating humor play well; insulting your audience does not. Effective humor should be related in some way to the subject of your speech, your audience, or the occasion. So, starting with a joke that is wholly unrelated to your topic is inappropriate. Also, remember that some of us have difficulty being funny. Others of us do not gauge the audience well. In either of these cases, attempts at humor may end up falling flat or offending. So be careful: Useless or ineffective humor can damage your credibility and hurt your connection with your audience. Yet, when well executed, humor is a powerful tool in your speaker arsenal.

Get Personal

Before management consultant Edith Weiner gives a speech, she learns the names of several members of her audience as well as their roles in the company. During her speech, she refers to these people and the conversations she had with them, thereby creating a personal bond with her audience. Connections can be made by linking yourself directly to the group you are addressing and by referring to your audience with the pronoun "you" rather than the third-person "they." The word "you" inserts your listeners into the middle of your presentation and makes it clear that you are focusing attention on them.

Here is an example of "you language" in a speech delivered by Jeffrey Holland (1988) as president of Brigham Young University to a group of early childhood educators:

> You are offering more than technical expertise or professional advice when you meet with parents. You are demonstrating that you are an ally in their task of rearing the next generation. In all that you do … however good your work, and whatever the quality of life parents provide, there is no comparable substitute for families. Your best opportunity to act in children's best interests is to strengthen parents, rather than think you can or will replace them. (p. 559)

Content is another way to make it personal. Stories, anecdotes, and examples from your own experience are generally appreciated. But keep in mind, there is too much of a good thing where self-disclosure is concerned. Abide by this rule: If you are not comfortable with it being put in the headlines of the local paper, leave it out of your speech.

Encourage Participation

When you invite the listeners to participate in your speech, they become partners in the event. One of the author's friends, a first-degree black belt in karate, gave a motivational speech to a group of college women at a state university in Michigan. At the beginning of her speech, and to the excitement of the crowd, she broke several boards. She talked about her childhood, her lack of self-esteem, and her struggle to become a well-adjusted businesswoman. She used the phrase "I can succeed" several times during her speech and encouraged her audience to join in with her. By the end of her speech, the group, standing, invigorated, and excited, shouted with her, "I can succeed!"

Another way to involve your listeners is to choose a member of your audience to take part in your talk—have the volunteer help you with a demonstration, do some role-playing—and the rest of the group will feel like one of its own is up there at the podium. Involve the entire audience and they will hang on your every word. While adding participation takes time away from your speaking, it is well worth the investment. And like using humor, you will find it also lightens the mood and sets a favorable tone.

Examine Other Situational Characteristics

When planning your speech, other situational characteristics need to be considered, including time of day, size of audience, and size of room. When speechwriter Robert Rackleff (1987) addressed his colleagues about the "art of speech writing," he offered this advice:

> The time of day affects the speech. In the morning, people are relatively fresh and can listen attentively. You can explain things more carefully. But in the late afternoon, after lunch …, the audience needs something more stimulating. And after dinner, you had better keep it short and have some fireworks handy (pp. 311–312).

Rackleff reminded his listeners about the intimate connection between time of day and audience response. The relationship between physical surroundings and audience response is so strong that you should plan every speech with your surroundings in mind.

Management consultant Edith Weiner says there is a vast difference between an audience of six people and an audience of dozens or even hundreds of people: In the first case, says Weiner, "I'm speaking with the audience," but in the second, "I'm speaking to the audience." The intimacy of a small group allows for a speaker-audience interchange not possible in larger groups. Small groups provide almost instantaneous feedback; large groups are more difficult to read.

Room size is important because it influences how loudly you must speak and determines whether you need a microphone. As a student, you will probably be speaking in a classroom. But in other speaking situations, you may find yourself in a convention hall, a small office, or an outdoor setting where only the lineup of chairs determines the size of the speaking space.

If you are delivering an after-dinner speech in your own dining room to 10 members of your reading group, you do not have to worry about projecting your voice to the back row of a large room. If, on the other hand, you are delivering a commencement address in your college auditorium to a thousand graduates, you will need to use a microphone. And keep in mind, proper microphone technique takes practice, preferably in the auditorium in which you will speak.

Learn as You Go

Discovering what your audience thought of your speech can help you give a better speech next time. Realizing the importance of feedback, some professional speakers hand out post-speech questionnaires designed to find out where they succeeded and where they failed to meet audience needs. At workshops, feedback is often provided through questionnaires that can be turned in at the end or at any time during the event. When you are the speaker, you may choose to interview someone, distribute questionnaires randomly to a dozen people, or even ask the entire audience to provide feedback.

Valuable information often emerges from audience feedback, which enables speakers to adjust their presentation for the next occasion. For example, let's assume you delivered a speech to a civic organization on the increasing problem of drunk boating. You handed out questionnaires to the entire audience after your message. Results indicated that your audience would have preferred fewer statistics and more concrete suggestions for combating the problem. In addition, one listener offered a good way to make current laws more easily understood, a suggestion you may incorporate into your next presentation.

Finding out what your audience thought may be simple. In your public speaking class, your fellow classmates may give you immediate, written feedback. In other situations, especially if you are running a workshop or seminar, you may want to hand out a written questionnaire at the end of your speech and ask listeners to return it at a later time. Online survey tools (i.e., SurveyMonkey, SurveyGizmo, Surveyshare) are free and can provide rich feedback for you after your speech. Here are four questions you might ask:

1. Did the speech answer your questions about the topic? If not, what questions remain?
2. How can you apply the information you learned in the presentation to your own situation?

3. What part of the presentation was most helpful? Least helpful?
4. How could the presentation have better met your needs?

To encourage an honest and complete response, indicate in the instructions that people do not have to offer their names in the questionnaire. Remember that the goal of feedback is improvement, not ego gratification. Focus on positive feedback as much as possible and take negative comments as areas for growth.

Your ability to create and maintain a strong connection with your audience is helped by a clear understanding of their demographics and psychographics. Using this information will set you on track for an exceptional experience, for you *and* your audience.

Summary

The most important relationship in public speaking is the relationship between speaker and audience. Being audience-centered means learning everything you can about your audience so you can meet its needs in your topic and your approach. Start by analyzing your audience based on demographics and psychographics. Learn the average age of your listeners, whether they are predominantly male or female, their educational level, and how much they know about your subject. Try to identify members of your audience in terms of their membership in religious, racial and ethnic, occupational, socioeconomic, and political groups. Behavioral choices can tell you a great deal about audience attitudes, beliefs, and values.

Successful speakers define the expectations that surround the speaking occasion. They learn how much interest their audience has in their topic and how much their audience knows about it before they get up to speak. Audience analysis is accomplished through the use of questionnaires based on fixed-alternative questions, scale questions, and open-ended questions. Audience analysis can also be conducted through observation and interviews.

To ensure a speaker–audience connection, show your listeners at the start of your speech how you will help them; have confidence your audience wants to hear you, even if they are more knowledgeable than you. Present yourself as fitting into the group, rather than as being superior to the group. Refer to people in your audience and involve your listeners in your speech. When your speech is over, try to determine your audience's response through a post-speech evaluation, questionnaire, or interview.

References

Brunner, B., & Haney, E. (2007). *Civil Rights Timeline: Milestones in the Civil Rights Movement.* Information Please. Retrieved August 4, 2011 from www.infoplease.com/spot/civilrightstimeline1.html.

Churchill, G. A., Jr. (1983). *Marketing Research: Methodological Foundations*, 3rd Ed. Chicago: The Dryden Press.

Clanton, J. (1988). Title unknown. *Winning Orations of the Interstate Oratorical Association.* Mankato, MN: Interstate Oratorical Association.

Griffin, J. D. (1989, July 16). To Snare the Feet of Greatness: The American Dream Is Alive (Speech). Reprinted in *Vital Speeches of the Day, September 15, 1989,* 735–736.

Holland, J. (1988). Whose Children Are These? The Family Connection (Speech). Reprinted in *Vital Speeches of the Day, July 1, 1988,* 559.

Kiechel, W., III. (1987, June 8). How to Give a Speech. *Fortune,* 179.

Kushner, Harold S. (2002). *When All You've Ever Wanted Isn't Enough: The Search for a Life That Matters.* New York: Random House.

Noonan, P. (1989, October 15). Confessions of a White House Speechwriter, *New York Times,* 72.

Pilkington, E. (2009, January 29). Barack Obama Inauguration Speech. *The Guardian.* Accessed August 4, 2011 from www.guardian.co.uk/world/2009/jan/20/barack-obama-inauguration-us-speech.

Rackleff, R. B. (1987, September 26). The Art of Speechwriting: A Dramatic Event (Speech). Reprinted in *Vital Speeches of the Day,* March 1, 1988.

Rokeach, M. (1968). The Role of Values in Public Opinion Research. *Public Opinion Quarterly, 32*(4), 547–559.

Where We Stand on Faith. (2005, September 6). *Newsweek,* 48–49.

Woodward, G. C., & Denton, R. E., Jr. (2004). *Persuasion and Influence in American Life,* 5th Ed. (pp. 173–174). Long Grove, IL: Waveland Press, Inc.

The Y, Share the Day. (2010, July 12). A Brand New Day: The YMCA Unveils New Brand Strategy to Further Community Impact. Retrieved August 4, 2011 from www.ymca.net/news-releases/20100712-brand-new-day.html.

Chapter 9

Presentational Aids in an Electronic World

"They say one of a baby's first nonverbal forms of communication is pointing. Clicking must be somewhere just after that."

Anonymous

SPEECH: Al Gore—An Inconvenient Truth (TED Talk)

Al Gore (1948–), the 45th Vice President of the United States, has long been a passionate advocate for the environment. He authored the bestsellers *Earth in the Balance* and *An Inconvenient Truth*, which is the subject of an Oscar-winning documentary. Al Gore is the co-winner, with the Intergovernmental Panel on Climate Change, of the 2007 Nobel Peace Prize for "informing the world of the dangers posed by climate change." According to the Nobel Committee, Gore is probably the single individual who has done most to rouse the public and governments to the fact that action has to be taken to meet the climate challenge. Please watch the TED Talk: The Case for Optimism on Climate Change (https://www.ted.com/talks/al_gore_the_case_for_optimism_on_climate_change?language=en) to see how Al Gore uses presentational aids to support his message.

Sources: http://www.nobelprize.org/nobel_prizes/peace/laureates/2007/gore-bio.html
http://www.nobelprize.org/nobel_prizes/peace/laureates/2007/gore-facts.html

Al Gore: The Case for Optimism on Climate Change (Filmed Feb. 2016)

I was excited to be a part of the "Dream" theme, and then I found out I'm leading off the "Nightmare?" section of it. (Laughter)

And certainly there are things about the climate crisis that qualify. And I have some bad news, but I have a lot more good news. I'm going to propose three questions and the answer to the first one necessarily involves a little bad news. But—hang on, because the answers to the second and third questions really are very positive.

So the first question is, "Do we really have to change?" And of course, the Apollo Mission, among other things changed the environmental movement, really launched the modern environmental movement. Eighteen months after this Earthrise picture was first seen on earth, the first Earth Day was organized. And we learned a lot about ourselves looking back at our planet from space. And one of the things that we learned confirmed what the scientists have long told us. One of the most essential facts about the climate crisis has to do with the sky. As this picture illustrates, the sky is not the vast and limitless expanse that appears when we look up from the ground. It is a very thin shell of atmosphere surrounding the planet. That right now is the open sewer for our industrial civilization as it's currently organized. We are spewing 110 million tons of heat-trapping global warming pollution into it every 24 hours, free of charge, go ahead.

And there are many sources of the greenhouse gases, I'm certainly not going to go through them all. I'm going to focus on the main one, but agriculture is involved, diet is involved, population is involved. Management of forests, transportation, the oceans, the melting of the permafrost. But I'm going to focus on the heart of the problem, which is the fact that we still rely on dirty, carbon-based fuels for 85 percent of all the energy that our world burns every year. And you can see from this image that after World War II, the emission rates started really accelerating. And the accumulated amount of man-made, global warming pollution that is up in the atmosphere now traps as much extra heat energy as would be released by 400,000 Hiroshima-class atomic bombs exploding every 24 hours, 365 days a year. Fact-checked over and over again, conservative, it's the truth. Now it's a big planet, but —

(Explosion sound)

That is a lot of energy, particularly when you multiply it 400,000 times per day. And all that extra heat energy is heating up the atmosphere, the whole earth system.

Let's look at the atmosphere. This is a depiction of what we used to think of as the normal distribution of temperatures. The white represents normal temperature days; 1951-1980 are arbitrarily chosen. The blue are cooler than average days, the red are warmer than average days. But the entire curve has moved to the right in the 1980s. And you'll see in the lower right-hand corner the appearance of statistically significant numbers of extremely hot days. In the 90s, the curve shifted further. And in the last 10 years, you see the extremely hot days are now more numerous than the cooler than average days. In fact, they are 150 times more common on the surface of the earth than they were just 30 years ago.

So we're having record-breaking temperatures. Fourteen of the 15 of the hottest years ever measured with instruments have been in this young century. The hottest of all was last year. Last month was the 371st month in a row warmer than the 20th-century average. And for the first time, not only the warmest January, but for the first time, it was more than two degrees Fahrenheit warmer than the average. These higher temperatures are having an effect on animals, plants, people, ecosystems.

But on a global basis, 93 percent of all the extra heat energy is trapped in the oceans. And the scientists can measure the heat buildup much more precisely now at all depths: deep, mid-ocean, the first few hundred meters. And this, too, is accelerating. It goes back more than a century. And more than half of the increase has been in the last 19 years. This has consequences.

The first order of consequence: the ocean-based storms get stronger. Super Typhoon Haiyan went over areas of the Pacific five and a half degrees Fahrenheit warmer than normal before it slammed into Tacloban, as the most destructive storm ever to make landfall. Pope Francis, who has made such a difference to this whole issue, visited

Tacloban right after that. Superstorm Sandy went over areas of the Atlantic nine degrees warmer than normal before slamming into New York and New Jersey. The second order of consequences are affecting all of us right now. The warmer oceans are evaporating much more water vapor into the skies. Average humidity worldwide has gone up four percent. And it creates these atmospheric rivers. The Brazilian scientists call them "flying rivers." And they funnel all of that extra water vapor over the land where storm conditions trigger these massive record-breaking downpours. This is from Montana. Take a look at this storm last August. As it moves over Tucson, Arizona. It literally splashes off the city. These downpours are really unusual.

Last July in Houston, Texas, it rained for two days, 162 billion gallons. That represents more than two days of the full flow of Niagara Falls in the middle of the city, which was, of course, paralyzed. These record downpours are creating historic floods and mudslides.

This one is from Chile last year. And you'll see that warehouse going by. There are oil tankers cars going by. This is from Spain last September, you could call this the running of the cars and trucks, I guess. Every night on the TV news now is like a nature hike through the Book of Revelation.

(Laughter)

I mean, really.

The insurance industry has certainly noticed, the losses have been mounting up. They're not under any illusions about what's happening. And the causality requires a moment of discussion. We're used to thinking of linear cause and linear effect — one cause, one effect. This is systemic causation. As the great Kevin Trenberth says, "All storms are different now. There's so much extra energy in the atmosphere, there's so much extra water vapor. Every storm is different now." So, the same extra heat pulls the soil moisture out of the ground and causes these deeper, longer, more pervasive droughts and many of them are underway right now.

It dries out the vegetation and causes more fires in the western part of North America. There's certainly been evidence of that, a lot of them.

More lightning, as the heat energy builds up, there's a considerable amount of additional lightning also.

These climate-related disasters also have geopolitical consequences and create instability. The climate-related historic drought that started in Syria in 2006 destroyed 60 percent of the farms in Syria, killed 80 percent of the livestock, and drove 1.5 million climate refugees into the cities of Syria, where they collided with another 1.5 million refugees from the Iraq War. And along with other factors, that opened the gates of Hell that people are trying to close now. The US Defense Department has long warned of consequences from the climate crisis, including refugees, food and water shortages and pandemic disease.

Right now we're seeing microbial diseases from the tropics spread to the higher latitudes; the transportation revolution has had a lot to do with this. But the changing conditions change the latitudes and the areas where these microbial diseases can become endemic and change the range of the vectors, like mosquitoes and ticks that carry them. The Zika epidemic now — we're better positioned in North America because it's still a little too cool and we have a better public health system. But when women in some regions of South and Central America are advised not to get pregnant for two years — that's something new, that ought to get our attention. The Lancet, one of the two greatest medical journals in the world, last summer labeled this a medical emergency now. And there are many factors because of it.

This is also connected to the extinction crisis. We're in danger of losing 50 percent of all the living species on earth by the end of this century. And already, land-based plants and animals are now moving towards the poles at an average rate of 15 feet per day.

Speaking of the North Pole, last December 29, the same storm that caused historic flooding in the American Midwest, raised temperatures at the North Pole 50 degrees Fahrenheit warmer than normal, causing the thawing of the North Pole in the middle of the long, dark, winter, polar night. And when the land-based ice of the Arctic melts, it raises sea level.

Paul Nicklen's beautiful photograph from Svalbard illustrates this. It's more dangerous coming off Greenland and particularly, Antarctica. The 10 largest risk cities for sea-level rise by population are mostly in South and Southeast Asia. When you measure it by assets at risk, number one is Miami: three and a half trillion dollars at risk. Number three: New York and Newark. I was in Miami last fall during the supermoon, one of the highest high-tide days. And there were fish from the ocean swimming in some of the streets of Miami Beach and Fort Lauderdale and Del Rey. And this happens regularly during the highest-tide tides now. Not with rain — they call it "sunny-day flooding." It comes up through the storm sewers. And the Mayor of Miami speaks for many when he says it is long past time this can be viewed through a partisan lens. This is a crisis that's getting worse day by day. We have to move beyond partisanship.

And I want to take a moment to honor these House Republicans —

(Applause)

Who had the courage last fall to step out and take a political risk, by telling the truth about the climate crisis.

So the cost of the climate crisis is mounting up, there are many of these aspects I haven't even mentioned. It's an enormous burden. I'll mention just one more, because the World Economic Forum last month in Davos, after their annual survey of 750 economists, said the climate crisis is now the number one risk to the global economy. So you get central bankers like Mark Carney, the head of the UK Central Bank, saying the vast majority of the carbon reserves are unburnable. Subprime carbon. I'm not going to remind you what happened with subprime mortgages, but it's the same thing. If you look at all of the carbon fuels that were burned since the beginning of the industrial revolution, this is the quantity burned in the last 16 years. Here are all the ones that are proven and left on the books, 28 trillion dollars. The International Energy Agency says only this amount can be burned. So the rest, 22 trillion dollars — unburnable. Risk to the global economy. That's why divestment movement makes practical sense and is not just a moral imperative.

So the answer to the first question, "Must we change?" is yes, we have to change. Second question, "Can we change?" This is the exciting news! The best projections in the world 16 years ago were that by 2010, the world would be able to install 30 gigawatts of wind capacity. We beat that mark by 14 and a half times over. We see an exponential curve for wind installations now. We see the cost coming down dramatically. Some countries — take Germany, an industrial powerhouse with a climate not that different from Vancouver's, by the way — one day last December, got 81 percent of all its energy from renewable resources, mainly solar and wind. A lot of countries are getting more than half on an average basis.

More good news: energy storage, from batteries particularly, is now beginning to take off because the cost has been coming down very dramatically to solve the intermittency problem. With solar, the news is even more exciting! The best projections 14 years ago were that we would install one gigawatt per year by 2010. When 2010 came around, we beat that mark by 17 times over. Last year, we beat it by 58 times over. This year, we're on track to beat it 68 times over.

We're going to win this. We are going to prevail. The exponential curve on solar is even steeper and more dramatic. When I came to this stage 10 years ago, this is where it was. We have seen a revolutionary breakthrough in the emergence of these exponential curves.

(Applause)

And the cost has come down 10 percent per year for 30 years. And it's continuing to come down.

Now, the business community has certainly noticed this, because it's crossing the grid parity point. Cheaper solar penetration rates are beginning to rise. Grid parity is understood as that line, that threshold, below which renewable electricity is cheaper than electricity from burning fossil fuels. That threshold is a little bit like the difference between 32 degrees Fahrenheit and 33 degrees Fahrenheit, or zero and one Celsius. It's a difference of more than one degree, it's the difference between ice and water. And it's the difference between markets that are frozen up, and liquid flows of capital into new opportunities for investment. This is the biggest new business opportunity in the history of the world, and two-thirds of it is in the private sector. We are seeing an explosion of new investment. Starting in 2010, investments globally in renewable electricity generation surpassed fossils. The gap has been growing ever since. The projections for the future are even more dramatic, even though fossil energy is now still subsidized at a rate 40 times larger than renewables. And by the way, if you add the projections for nuclear on here, particularly if you assume that the work many are doing to try to break through to safer and more acceptable, more affordable forms of nuclear, this could change even more dramatically.

So is there any precedent for such a rapid adoption of a new technology? Well, there are many, but let's look at cell phones. In 1980, AT&T, then Ma Bell, commissioned McKinsey to do a global market survey of those clunky new mobile phones that appeared then. "How many can we sell by the year 2000?" they asked. McKinsey came back and said, "900,000." And sure enough, when the year 2000 arrived, they did sell 900,000 — in the first three days. And for the balance of the year, they sold 120 times more. And now there are more cell connections than there are people in the world.

So, why were they not only wrong, but way wrong? I've asked that question myself, "Why?"

(Laughter)

And I think the answer is in three parts. First, the cost came down much faster than anybody expected, even as the quality went up. And low-income countries, places that did not have a landline grid — they leap-frogged to the new technology. The big expansion has been in the developing counties. So what about the electricity grids in the developing world? Well, not so hot. And in many areas, they don't exist. There are more people without any electricity at all in India than the entire population of the United States of America. So now we're getting this: solar panels on grass huts and new business models that make it affordable. Muhammad Yunus financed this one in Bangladesh with micro-credit. This is a village market. Bangladesh is now the fastest-deploying country in the world: two systems per minute on average, night and day. And we have all we need: enough energy from the Sun comes to the earth every hour to supply the full world's energy needs for an entire year. It's actually a little bit less than an hour. So the answer to the second question, "Can we change?" is clearly "Yes." And it's an ever-firmer "yes."

Last question, "Will we change?" Paris really was a breakthrough, some of the provisions are binding and the regular reviews will matter a lot. But nations aren't waiting, they're going ahead. China has already announced that starting next year, they're adopting a nationwide cap and trade system. They will likely link up with the European Union. The United States has already been changing. All of these coal plants were proposed in the next 10 years and canceled. All of these existing coal plants were retired. All of these coal plants have had their retirement announced. All of them — canceled. We are moving forward. Last year — if you look at all of the investment in new electricity generation in the United States, almost three-quarters was from renewable energy, mostly wind and solar.

We are solving this crisis. The only question is: how long will it take to get there? So, it matters that a lot of people are organizing to insist on this change. Almost 400,000 people marched in New York City before the UN special session on this. Many thousands, tens of thousands, marched in cities around the world. And so, I am extremely optimistic. As I said before, we are going to win this.

I'll finish with this story. When I was 13 years old, I heard that proposal by President Kennedy to land a person on the Moon and bring him back safely in 10 years. And I heard adults of that day and time say, "That's reckless, expensive, may well fail." But eight years and two months later, in the moment that Neil Armstrong set foot on the Moon, there was great cheer that went up in NASA's mission control in Houston. Here's a little-known fact about that: the average age of the systems engineers, the controllers in the room that day, was 26, which means, among other things, their age, when they heard that challenge, was 18.

We now have a moral challenge that is in the tradition of others that we have faced. One of the greatest poets of the last century in the US, Wallace Stevens, wrote a line that has stayed with me: "After the final 'no,' there comes a 'yes,' and on that 'yes', the future world depends." When the abolitionists started their movement, they met with no after no after no. And then came a yes. The Women's Suffrage and Women's Rights Movement met endless no's, until finally, there was a yes. The Civil Rights Movement, the movement against apartheid, and more recently, the movement for gay and lesbian rights here in the United States and elsewhere. After the final "no" comes a "yes."

When any great moral challenge is ultimately resolved into a binary choice between what is right and what is wrong, the outcome is fore-ordained because of who we are as human beings. Ninety-nine percent of us, that is where we are now and it is why we're going to win this. We have everything we need. Some still doubt that we have the will to act, but I say the will to act is itself a renewable resource.

Thank you very much.

(Applause)

Source: https://www.ted.com/talks/al_gore_the_case_for_optimism_on_climate_change/transcript?language=en

Few of us think of speech making in visual terms—or find ways to reach our speaking goals by turning to presentational aids. As technology has become more accessible, expectations have increased. Audiences crave dazzling multimedia presentations. Being tech savvy is clearly an advantage to the public speaker today. Although the tools may have changed, the bottom line has not: Any presentational aids you create must communicate a clear, relevant, direct, and interesting message.

This chapter examines how technology relates to public speaking in general and presentational aids in particular. First, we consider the nature of technology and presentational aids today by describing their pervasiveness and how they function. Then, we catalog the types of presentational aids available and identify ways to include them in your presentations. We end this chapter by offering guidelines for using presentational aids effectively in your speeches.

☞   The Nature of Presentational Aids Today

"We cannot *not* communicate" is a communication axiom developed by Paul Watzlawick (1967). This suggests that in face-to-face communication, even when we choose to *not* speak, we are still communicating a message through our silence and our nonverbal communication. A similar case can be made for communicating through our presentational aids. We cannot not communicate here as well. What message does a poorly designed or displayed aid communicate to an audience about the speaker? Some might draw conclusions regarding the speaker's commitment to the speech, his/her credibility to speak on the subject, or his/her ability to deliver a captivating, well-thought-out message. Worse yet, what might an audience think of a speech that had no accompanying presentational aids at all? We have come to expect the bells, whistles, and pizzazz presentational aids can bring to a speech.

Pervasiveness of Technology

Technology is ubiquitous. We see it everywhere. We use technology for all levels of communication: intrapersonal, interpersonal, group communication, mass communication, and public speaking. As it changes—and it does rapidly—we adapt. As new technology arrives, we consider how it might aid our communication.

Consider the relatively recent advent of the smartphone. People walk, drive, sit, wait, eat, and sleep with their phones. A December 2010 survey reports that 285 million Americans are mobile subscribers (CTIA–The Wireless Association). Research suggests that 91 percent of all Americans use cell phones (arstechnica.com). And it is not only an American phenomenon. In March 2009, Reuters reported that a study by the broadband company Bitkom found that Germans in their 20s are typically more willing to give up their current partners or their cars than their cell phones!

In parallel fashion, technology-based presentational aids have become not only commonplace, but of central importance to many speakers and audiences. Can you imagine a conference today without laptops and PDAs serving up glittering eye-candy: no gumdrop bullets, sweet-tart charts, or pop rocks special effects? Not likely. But has it gone too far? What is center stage, the message or the frosting?

Whether good for the message or not, presentational aids in this electronic age are here to stay. You will benefit from understanding how these technologies may function to help, or hurt, your key message.

Functions of Presentational Aids

Presentational aids operate in a variety of ways. They can satisfy an ever-escalating thirst for information and entertainment. They promise to enhance, or hinder, our presentations. They are more than afterthoughts, add-ons, or speech class requirements. Your instructor may require you to use presentational aids not only to enhance the effectiveness of your speech, but also to help you learn how to use them comfortably as you speak. But the main reason you may be required to use them is because nearly *everyone else is using them*!

Did you know greater numbers of us have been exposed to PowerPoint than any other presentation software? Today, more people use PowerPoint to accompany presentations than any other type of technology, including YouTube, video clips, and websites. In April 2006, Microsoft estimated that it had 400 million PowerPoint customers worldwide. Why? Microsoft claims that PowerPoint can improve the way "you create, present, and collaborate on presentations" (office.microsoft.com). Chances are good that you "speak" PowerPoint, too, because it is easy to learn and use, and is effective. On the other hand, foolproof systems rarely take into account the ingenuity of fools.

Poorly conceived or executed visuals like PowerPoint can bring trouble. Using presentational software like PowerPoint, Keynote, Prezi, and others is expected by today's audiences, who were largely raised in the media era (Cyphert, 2007). When developing visuals for your audience, Professor Edward Tufte, an expert in the visual representation of technical data, offers a stern warning: "[F]ailure to think clearly about the analysis and the presentation of [visual] evidence opens the door for all sorts of … mischief to operate in making decisions" (Tufte, 1997, p. 52).

Clearly, paying attention to how a visual message is received by an audience is essential. We must keep the needs of our audience in mind. The speaker–audience connection is strengthened when the speaker judiciously considers potential advantages and disadvantages of each presentational aid before placing them in a speech.

Advantages of Presentational Aids

Availability

As long as one has access to the Internet, a nearly infinite amount of presentational material is available, often without cost. As you prepare for your speech, you can create everything online and transfer it to a flash drive when you're ready. Millions of videoclips, photos and images, and clip art are available, too. Adding music, special effects, timed sequencing, and flash video, for example, may be a little trickier for the novice, but it is being used increasingly in professional and student presentations.

Engaging

Have you ever seen a lotto billboard alongside an interstate? As you approach it, you can see the jackpot amount increasing as the digital numbers change constantly. When a presentational aid is well prepared, little can compete with it to capture—and hold—audience interest. We live in a visual age. Images that surround us in the mass media make us more receptive, on conscious and unconscious levels, to visual presentations of all kinds. We are attuned to these presentations simply because they are visual—a phenomenon you can use to your advantage during a speech.

One student wanted to emphasize how fast the world's population is growing. During her speech, she accessed a website (worldometers.info) that keeps a digital tally of births, and kept the digital counter on the screen for about a minute. Then she made reference to the number of births that had occurred during that minute. This helped keep the interest of the class. A well-placed, professional-looking presentational aid draws attention to the point you are trying to make or to statistics you want your audience to process.

Persuasive

Seeing the devastation a tornado creates is more persuasive than having someone simply talk about it. Watching a video of animals being euthanized is more powerful than talking about the process. Looking at statistics that have been organized in a clear manner through graphs or charts is more persuasive than simply hearing the numbers. Presentation software adds impact to your argument.

Presentational aids have persuasive power. Business speakers, especially those in sales, have long realized that they can close a deal faster if they use visual aids. A study by the University of

Minnesota and the 3M Corporation found that speakers who integrate visuals into their talks are 43 percent more likely to persuade their audiences than speakers who rely solely on verbal images (Vogel, Dickson, & Lehman, 1986).

One of the most well-known examples of presentation software images being used to strengthen and elucidate arguments can be seen in former U.S. Vice President Al Gore's 2006 documentary film *An Inconvenient Truth*. Gore's narration is accompanied by graphs, animation, video clips, and other images derived from presentation software (Wright, 2009). An analysis of that film reveals that slides containing text alone are used only 11 times, and bullet points are used only once. Gore links his main points to events with which Americans can relate, and provides a frame of reference for understanding and comparing his statistics. His presentational aids help to create a powerful message that was persuasive to many.

Entertaining

If you are in the mood, it takes only a few minutes to surf for video that makes you laugh. Comedy abounds on the Internet and funny clips are uploaded to countless video-sharing sites continually. Notice that both appropriate, professional clips exist as well as plenty of, well, unsavory ones. If you searched the term "stupid human tricks," you will find all sorts of hijinks, some guaranteed to make you blush. In other words, speakers have a plethora of options when seeking something entertaining to support their point, but not all are appropriate.

Presentational software offers animation and sound effects, so speakers can add entertainment value to their slides. Even something simple like creating a graphic that uses stacked hamburgers to talk about the number of hamburgers sold, or stacked oranges, apples, and pears to talk about the amount of fruit sold will add visual impact and enhance meaning. With a little forethought, technology can enhance the entertainment value of your message.

Memorable

Did you read the newspaper this morning? What do you remember from it? Chances are, if you read the paper, a photo comes to mind—the picture of a fireman rescuing a child from a burning building or the president of your university getting a pie in the face at the end of a fundraiser. You may have read the articles that accompanied these pictures, but the images are likely to have had the greatest impact.

Technology gives you the power to etch permanent images into the minds of attendees. Do you recall a TV commercial asking you to assist starving children or neglected pets? These pitches are persuasive and memorable because of the tragic and compelling pictures they offer us. Using pictures, you can create lasting mental images in the minds of your audience. Moving graphics and sound effects can be catchy and add an entertainment effect so long as they are not overdone. Through video-sharing websites like YouTube, bleekr.com, and Yahoo! video, you can easily find footage of a tornado in full fury, the war in Pakistan, and police attacking civilians in the latest Middle East revolution. Such video clips are available, tend to be vivid, and may be unforgettable.

Speakers are told that the more senses you engage, the more your audience will remember. Research indicates our retention increases significantly when messages are presented both verbally and visually (Mayer, 2001). Kraus (2008) notes other research that concluded that mixed modality presentation (auditory and visual) is superior for recall, regardless of whether the presentation is concurrent or sequential or whether materials are presented once or twice. It is important to keep this in mind: Visuals should rarely stand alone. When an audience is shown the devastating effects of a tornado via video, the prudent speaker might verbally clarify, elaborate, or refer to the visual images to create the most effective message.

After a review of relevant educational psychology, education, and experimental psychology studies, the U.S. Department of Labor concluded that: "[T]hree days after an event, people retain 10 percent of what they heard from an oral presentation, 35 percent from a visual presentation, and 65 percent from a visual and oral presentation" (OSHA, 1996). Using a simple bar graph to display this information makes it easier to understand these significant differences (see **Figure 9.1**). Researchers did find an exception: When the accompanying visual is primarily text and the speaker simply reads what is projected, memory scores drop (Unnava et al., 1996). Beyond being annoying, there seems to be no memory benefit from a speaker reading bulleted text from a screen to an audience that can read it for themselves. The visuals that supplement, vivify, and contextualize a speaker's words, rather than simply repeating them, are most effective in aiding message retention.

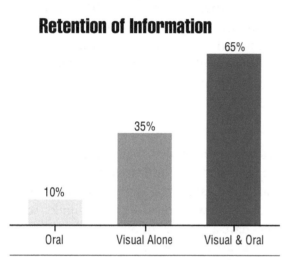

Retention of Information

Figure 9.1   This chart depicts effectiveness of visuals on audience memory 3 days after an event (osha.gov, 1996).

Clarity

A good visual design can make information clearer and more interesting (Cyphert, 2007). It also helps to emphasize key points (Kraus, 2008). Some speeches rely on many facts and statistics, which may be difficult for an audience to process. Using visuals like bar graphs, line graphs, or tables may help. Sometimes technology can lead an audience through complex material by using simple slides that highlight key points. Similarly, if you're talking about a process, such as brewing beer, for example, creating slides that identify the different steps by pairing each with photos will clarify the process.

Presentational software significantly aids teaching and learning (Kraus, 2008). Consider the last school lecture you attended. Did visuals accompany the presentation? Did they help? A study of college students' perceptions found that more than three-fourths agreed that PowerPoint presentations added clarity to an instructor's lecture and made the structure easier to follow (Nicholson, 2002). Anecdotally, they make naps easier, too, when overused.

Presentational aids have the power to clarify complex ideas. They are invaluable tools when explaining mechanical functions such as how a hot air balloon rises or how a computer stores information. They can clarify complex interrelationships involving people, groups, and institutions. They can show, for example, the stages a bill must go through before it becomes a law, and the role Congress and the president play in this process. Visuals may reduce but do not eliminate the need to explain complex details.

Presentational aids take the place of many words and, therefore, may shorten the length of a speech. They do not replace words, and one or two statements are insufficient verbal support for a series of visual displays. But presentational aids and words *in combination* reduce the amount of time you spend creating word pictures.

Makes Abstract Ideas Concrete

Abstract language can hurt your message clarity. If you are delivering a speech on the effects of the estimated 17–39-million-gallon oil spill from the BP Deepwater Horizon explosion in the Gulf of Mexico in spring and summer 2010, it may not be enough to tell your audience that the explosion killed 11 people and injured 17 more. But you can add something specific: Actual pictures of the clean-up effort of oil-saturated, sick animals.

Along with these visuals, you explain:

But people were not the only victims. Did you know that despite deploying over 5 million feet of floating barrier, the spill was allowed to drift and contaminate 125 miles of Louisiana shoreline? An estimated 30,000 first responders helped to clean up, but over a thousand animals, including endangered birds, turtles, and mammals, died. Of the animals who survived, only an estimated 6 percent have been cleaned, and biologists anticipate most will die too (Dosomething.org, 2011).

Images of specific visual pictures make the situation more relevant, personal, and easily grasped.

The image of the spill's devastating effect on wildlife provides us with specific visual pictures that make the situation more relevant, personal, and easily grasped. We need to see something concrete to process abstract ideas such as large catastrophes.

Helps Organize Ideas

As with every other aspect of your speech, presentational aids should be audience-centered. They may be eye-catching and visually stimulating, but they serve a more practical purpose. The flow and connection of a speaker's ideas are not always apparent to an audience, especially if the topic is complicated or involves many steps. Pictures, flow charts, diagrams, graphs, tables, and video clips help listeners follow a speaker's ideas. Additionally, presentational aids help keep the speaker on his/her organizational track. This benefit, however, is only realized when a speaker has rehearsed a number of times with the aids.

Disadvantages of Presentational Aids

What about when technology turns ugly? Poorly conceived or executed visuals can bring trouble. Paying attention to how a visual message is received by an audience is essential. Careful consideration of drawbacks, pitfalls, and caveats ensures the technology you use actually serves you, rather than serves to hurt you.

Access

Consider first, technology may not be available. While many colleges have computers in all classrooms, others may have them available in designated classrooms or by request only. Internet access via LAN (Local Area Network) may be out of service temporarily. What if your flash drive elects to self-destruct moments before your speech begins or you used newer, incompatible software, and the dinosaur computer you are now trying to use does not recognize your materials? Murphy's Law for the speaker who relies on technology is "If anything can go wrong, it will go wrong, during your presentation, in the worst possible way!"

Impersonal

When a speaker uses no presentational aids, the audience must focus on the speaker. One of the speaker's tasks is to create a connection with the audience through content, personality, language, and movement. When technology is used, focus often shifts. A problem exists when slides become the message rather than a means to enrich the message. When this happens we "forego an important opportunity to connect with the audience as human beings" (Alley & Neeley, 2005, p. 418). We risk losing our human connection to our audience by overusing technology.

The concern that computer-generated and projected images may hamper the speaker–audience connection is echoed by Peter Norvig, director of research at Google. He argues that a slide presentation may reduce the speaker's effectiveness, because "it makes it harder to have an open exchange between presenter and audience to convey ideas that do not readily fit into outline format" (Norvig, 2003, p. 343). Newer approaches to presentations allow the speaker to shift seamlessly from frame to frame within a larger visual context, providing more flexibility when feedback from an audience warrants this (c.f., www.prezi.com). Often, technology adds impact and clarity but can also create psychological distance and a perception of rigidity that some audience members will not appreciate.

Time Consuming

Creating slides with a standard background is fairly easy. However, finding the right video clip, creating graphs, incorporating video clips, and synchronizing music are all activities that take time and effort, and may distract you from your primary goal, which is to develop and support your ideas. Surely you have witnessed a presentation that had great visual appeal but little substance. The speaker may have spent too much time with the "bells and whistles" at the expense of developing sound arguments with ample support.

In addition to expending effort to create the slide show, setting up might take too much time before the speech. Once the computer is on and the projection equipment is warmed up (no guarantee of this actually happening when you need it to), the speaker must control volume, launch and operate software, etc. Speech classes sometimes endure lengthy gaps of dullness while an unprepared speaker bumbles with their set-up. The considerate speaker will find ways to minimize this waste of audience time.

Possible Smoke Screen

Similar to magician sleight-of-hand techniques, moving the focus from the speaker to the screen may shift attention away from a speaker's difficulties or lack of preparation. Some speakers rely heavily on 20, 40, or more slides hoping to cover up their deficiencies as a speaker (Alley & Neeley, 2005). Wright (2009) writes that "multimedia presentations can be a prop for weak presenters, but can also detract from messages delivered by competent communicators" (p. 34).

Speakers (and lecturers) who use slides for the purpose of providing the outline to their talk may find themselves less motivated or excited about the presentation. Knowing they don't have to worry about losing their place, they may spend less time practicing their speech. According to Carey (1999), "PowerPoint's reliability has lulled more than a few presenters and planners into creative complacency, resulting in audiovisual presentations that too often are monotonous, static, even boring" (pg. 47). Death by PowerPoint, as it is termed, is a painful way to go. Strike a balance by not overusing slides. One or two per minute you speak is acceptable; 20 in a five-minute speech will surely power us to the point of unconsciousness.

Potential for Reductionism

Some claim that design defaults in presentation software create the potential for reductionism because they oversimplify and fragment the subject matter (Alley & Neeley, 2005, p. 418). Only a limited amount of information can be presented on any one slide or group of slides. Abstract connections may be difficult to make, and sometimes critical assumptions are left out or relationships are not specified. Research indicates that people often begin to prepare presentations by thinking about what should appear on screen, slide by slide, and then constructing their presentations accordingly, rather than by considering what they want to say or how they can make the audience's experience better (Wright, 2009). When we reduce issues to slides of text and little pictures, we risk our audience not getting the big picture.

Messages composed mainly of bullet points and text are not always fully understood (Kalyuga et al., 1991). Furthermore, computer-based presentations can obscure messages or mislead audiences (Tufte, 2006). The focus on creating slides rather than creating arguments is problematic since the speaker's first task is to create effective messages. Relying too heavily on bullet points may reduce the richness of your ideas by limiting the information your audience focuses on, thereby fostering misinformation, misinterpretation, and mistakes in judgment.

Guaranteed Glitches and Gremlins

Having created an excellent set of slides does not guarantee an effective speech. Researchers found that listeners are most annoyed when the speaker reads the slides to his/her audience (Paradi, 2009). Your speech instructor will appreciate it if you reread that last sentence again. Out loud. Also problematic are full sentences that are too small, too long, or accompanied by different font sizes, overuse of animations, and other special effects.

Sometimes students feel compelled or coerced to use computer-based presentational software because an instructor's assignment requires it, but the resulting slides may reflect a lack of effort, conviction, or inspiration. Settling for defaults in font types, design templates, and colors can cause slide presentations to look and feel painfully similar (Alley & Neeley, 2005, p. 418). A lack of creativity often results in listeners' lack of attention, interest, and comprehension. Selecting and using the most appropriate technology for the audience, occasion, and message is the focus of the next section.

☞ Types of Presentational Aids

Presentational aids fall into four classifications: actual objects, three-dimensional models, two-dimensional reproductions, and technology-based aids. Each type has the potential to assist the speaker.

Actual Objects

Actual objects are real objects. Your authors quickly generated this list of inappropriate objects brought to their speech classes: snakes, guns, grenades, margaritas, M-80 firecrackers, marijuana, and so on. Of course, these were all bad choices. Yet good options abound. One student who had been stricken with bone cancer as a child, a condition that required the amputation of her leg, demonstrated to her classmates how her prosthetic leg functioned and how she wore it. Not one of her listeners lost interest in her demonstration.

Another student, concerned about the volumes of disposable diapers lingering in our landfills, brought to class a (heavy) week's worth of dirty diapers from one infant. In addition to visual and olfactory shock value, it left a powerfully strong image to accompany her statistics about the slow decomposition of dirty, disposable diapers.

As these examples demonstrate, objects can be effective visual aids. Because you are showing your audience exactly what you are talking about, objects have the power to inform or convince unlike any other presentational aid.

When bringing an object to class, be concerned with safety. Clear any questionable objects with your instructor. Objects you intend to use must not pose a safety risk to you or your audience. Animals, chemicals, and weapons certainly fall into this category. For example, you may think your pet Madagascar Hissing Cockroaches are snuggly-adorable, but to your instructor and some of your classmates, they may elicit terror and panic.

Three-Dimensional Models

If you decide that an actual object is too risky, a three-dimensional model may be your best choice. Models are commonly used to show the structure of a complex object. For example, a student who watched his father almost die of a heart attack used a model of the heart to demonstrate what physically happened during the attack. Using a three-dimensional replica about five times the size of a human heart, he showed how the major blood vessels leading to his father's heart became clogged and how this blockage precipitated the attack.

Models are useful when explaining steps in a sequence. A scale model of the space shuttle, its booster rockets, and the launch pad would help you describe what happens during the first few minutes after blast-off.

When considering a three-dimensional model, take into account construction time and availability. It is possible you already have the model or you know where you can borrow one, so no construction time is needed. If you need to create the three-dimensional model from a kit or your own imagination, consider how much time it will take to put it together. Here is a general rule: You do not want your presentational aid construction time to take longer than your speech preparation time.

If the three-dimensional model is in your possession, availability is not an issue. If the model is sold at the local Mega-lo-Mart, then availability is not an issue. If it is in your bedroom, attic, or garage in your hometown, you need to take travel time into account. If you have to sign your life away to borrow it, or if you have to plan six weeks or more ahead to access the model, it may not be worth your trouble.

Some replicas are easier to find, build, or buy than others. If you are delivering a speech on antique cars, inexpensive plastic models are available at a hobby shop and take little time to assemble. But if you want to show how proper city planning can untangle the daily downtown traffic snarl, you would have to build your own scaled-down version of downtown roads as they are now, and as you would like them to be. That would be too time consuming and expensive to be feasible. But a two-dimensional representation (like a map or diagram), as we see next, would be effective and affordable.

Two-Dimensional Reproductions

Two-dimensional reproductions are the most common visual aids used by speakers. Among these are photographs, diagrams and drawings, maps, tables, and graphs. Computer-projected presentations, such as Microsoft's PowerPoint, Prezi Inc.'s Prezi, or Apple's iWork Keynote, are also two-dimensional reproductions but are discussed as a separate type because of their reliance on newer, higher technologies.

Photographs

Photographs are realistic two-dimensional choices. They can have great impact. For a speech on animal rights, a photo of a fox struggling to free his leg from a trap will deliver your message more effectively than words. If you are speaking about forest fire prevention, a photo of a forest destroyed by fire is your most persuasive evidence.

Photos must be large enough for your audience to see. If a photo is important to your presentation, consider enlarging it so that the entire audience can see it. Typically, using magazine or newspaper pictures is as clear as photos.

Although photographs are effective aids, overly graphic pictures can yield negative results. If a photograph offends or disgusts your audience, some may tune you out.

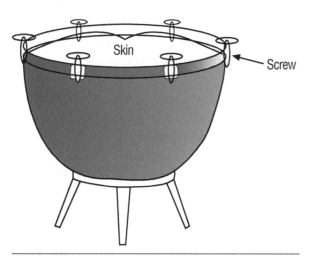

Figure 9.2   A simple diagram can show how the parts of objects such as this drum interact.

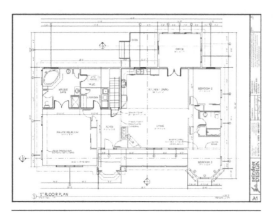

Figure 9.3   An intricate line drawing may frustrate your audience. Keep illustrations simple.

Drawings and Diagrams

When you cannot illustrate your point with a photograph—or would rather not use one—a drawing is an alternative. A drawing is your own representation of what you are describing. If you are demonstrating the difference between a kettledrum and a snare drum, a simple drawing may be all you need. If you want to extend your explanation to show how musicians are able to control the pitch of the sound made by a drum, your drawing must include more detail. The location of the screws used to tighten the skin of the drum must be shown as well as the relationship between the size of the drum and the pitch of the sound.

A detailed drawing showing the arrangement and relationship of the parts to the whole is considered a diagram. **Figure 9.2** is a simple diagram of a kettledrum. Labels are often used to pinpoint critical parts.

Do not attempt a complex drawing or diagram if you have little or no artistic ability. Neither should you attempt to produce drawings while your audience is watching. Prepare sketches in advance. Keep your audience's needs and limitations in mind when choosing diagrams. Imagine the audience's eyes as they listen to someone using **Figure 9.3** to discuss every dimension of a complex floor design. Too much detail will frustrate your audience as they strain to see the tiniest parts and labels. And when people are frustrated, they often stop listening.

Maps

Weather reports on TV news have made maps a familiar visual aid. Instead of merely talking about the weather, reporters show us the shifting patterns that turn sunshine into storms. The next time you watch a weather report, note the kind of map being used. Notice that details have been omitted because they distract viewers from what the reporter is explaining.

Too much detail will confuse your audience. For example, when talking about Europe's shrinking population, do not include the location of the Acropolis or the Eiffel Tower. Because you must focus on your specific purpose, you may have to draw a map yourself.

Figure 9.4   This map shows "blue states" and "red states," clarifying where election results stand.

Start with a broad outline of the geographic area and add to it only those details necessary for your presentation.

On election night, many news programs show a map of the United States divided into "blue states" and "red states." Blue states may be those where the majority of voters voted Democratic, and red states were Republican. Such a map (see **Figure 9.4**) gives a quick visual of where election results stand. Making a visual distinction between Republicans and Democrats began with the 2004 presidential election between John Kerry and George W. Bush, and has been so successful that the concept of "blue states" and "red states" has become part of our political vernacular.

Tables

Tables focus on words and numbers presented in columns and rows. Tables are used most frequently to display statistical data. If you were delivering a speech on the fat content of food and you note the types and percentage of fat in nuts, you could refer to a table similar to that shown in **Figure 9.5**. However, this single table should be divided into two parts because it contains too much

	Saturated	Monosaturated	Polyunsaturated	Other
Chestnuts	18%	35%	40%	7%
Brazil Nuts	15%	35%	36%	14%
Cashews	13	59	17	11
Pine Nuts	13	37	41	9
Peanuts	12	49	38	6
Pistachios	12	68	15	5
Walnuts	8	23	63	6
Almonds	8	65	21	6
Pecans	6	62	25	7
Hazelnuts	6	79	9	6

Figure 9.5   The fat content of food is measured in a single table.

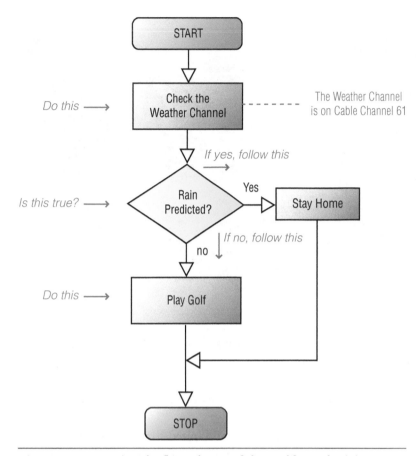

information to present in one visual. Keep in mind the audience's *information absorption threshold*—the point at which a visual will cease to be useful because it says too much.

Charts

Charts help the speaker display detailed information quickly and effectively. Charts can summarize data in an easy-to-read format, illustrate a process, and show relationships among parts.

Flow charts are used to display the steps, or stages, in a process. Each step is illustrated by an image or label. If you are an amateur cartoonist, you might give a talk on the steps involved in producing an animated cartoon. **Figure 9.6**

Figure 9.6   A simple flow chart of the golfer's decision-making process.

displays a simple flowchart of the process a golfer goes through when deciding whether to golf on a particular day. This humorous visual reveals the specific decision-making sequence.

A flow chart can make use of pictures. You might draw the pictures yourself or, if your artistic ability is limited, use selected photographs available online. Flow charts that depend on words alone should use short, simple labels that move the audience through the stages of the process.

Organizational charts reflect our highly structured world. Corporations, government institutions, schools, associations, and religious organizations are organized according to official hierarchies that determine the relationships of people as they work. You may refer to an organizational chart if you are trying to show the positions of people involved in a project. By looking at a chart like that shown in **Figure 9.7**, your audience will know who reports to whom.

Graphs

When referring to statistics or when presenting complex statistical information, a visual representation can be effective because it has the ability to simplify and clarify. Statistics may be presented in numerous ways, including bar graphs, pictographs, line graphs, and pie graphs.

In a speech urging today's college students to consider teaching social sciences or humanities in college, you want to show, graphically, that our universities will face a serious shortfall of

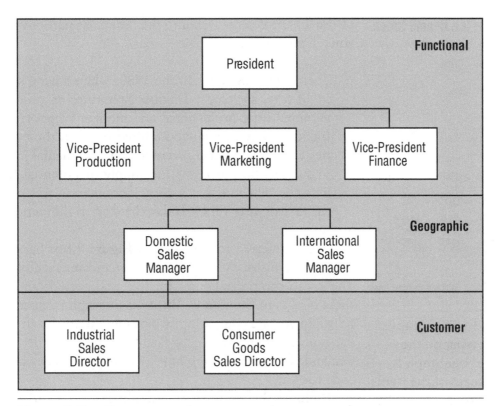

Figure 9.7   Almost every large group or company has an organizational chart to illustrate the official hierarchy and lines of access.

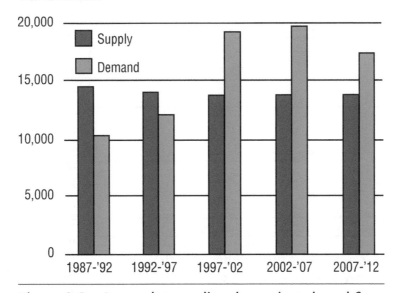

Faculty supply-and-demand projections in the social sciences and humanities

Figure 9.8   A speech to outline the projected need for new faculty in the next 30 years would be enhanced by a bar graph such as this.

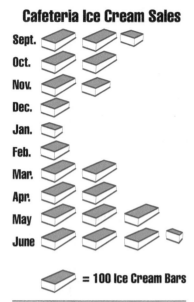

Cafeteria Ice Cream Sales

= 100 Ice Cream Bars

Figure 9.9   Pictographs provide a twist on the traditional bar graph by using pictures of the items discussed to illustrate the "bar." The pictograph should include a scale that explains what each symbol means, such as each ice cream bar sold.

liberal arts professors well into the future. As part of your speech, you tell your audience:

There were days back in the 1980s when having a Ph.D. in history, sociology, English literature, or philosophy garnered little professional and monetary opportunities. Indeed, many people who aspired to teach the humanities and social sciences were forced into menial jobs just to survive. So great was the supply of potential faculty over the demand that a new phenomenon was created: the taxi-driving Ph.D. Today, the story is different.

The visual referred to is shown in **Figure 9.8**, a bar graph displaying the history of supply and demand for faculty members. The graph compares figures for five-year periods and measures these figures in thousands. This type of graph is especially helpful when you are comparing two or more items. In this case, one bar represents the supply of faculty while the other represents demand. To make the trend even clearer, you may want to color code the bars.

Pictographs are most commonly used as a variation of the bar graph. Instead of showing bars of various lengths comparing items on the graph, the bars are replaced by pictorial representations of the graph's subject. For example, if you are giving a speech on the popularity of ice cream bars, you can use a pictograph like that shown in **Figure 9.9** to demonstrate when the most bars were sold. The pictograph must include a legend explaining what each symbol means. In this case, each ice cream bar represents 100 sold.

When you want to show a trend over time, the **line graph** may be your best choice. When two or more lines are used in one graph, comparisons are possible. **Figure 9.10** is a visual representation of the number of Irish immigrants entering the United States between 1820 and 1990. The tall peak in the graph represents the period of time when the

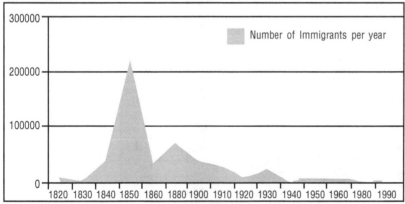

Irish Immigration to the United States (1820–1990)

Figure 9.10   This is a graph of the number of Irish immigrants who entered the U.S. from 1820 to 1990. The climax of the migration was in 1851 when 221,253 immigrants entered the U.S. This was around the time when the potato famine seized the majority of Ireland.

potato famine was affecting the majority of Ireland. This simple graph could be used in a speech about Irish immigration trends.

Pie graphs show your audience how the parts of an item relate to the whole. It is one of the most popular and effective ways to show how something is divided. The most simple and direct way to demonstrate percentages graphically is with a pie graph. In a budget presentation to the local school board, the chief financial officer might display a series of pie graphs. She might explain that revenue comes from three levels: federal, state, and local. **Figure 9.11** shows that taxes from local communities provide approximately half the revenue generated for the district. The federal government provides only 10 percent, thus illustrating how dependent the school district is on local funding.

No matter what type of two-dimensional aid you choose, clarity is essential. It may happen that you create a two-dimensional aid that makes your audience think, "What does that *mean?*" Any presentational aid you use must clarify rather than confuse. If the aid contains too much information, your audience will be unable to process it easily, and you may lose their attention. If you use graphs, pie charts, maps, or tables, information must be understandable. For example, if you have an x-axis and a y-axis, they should be clearly labeled so your audience knows what you are referring to quickly and easily.

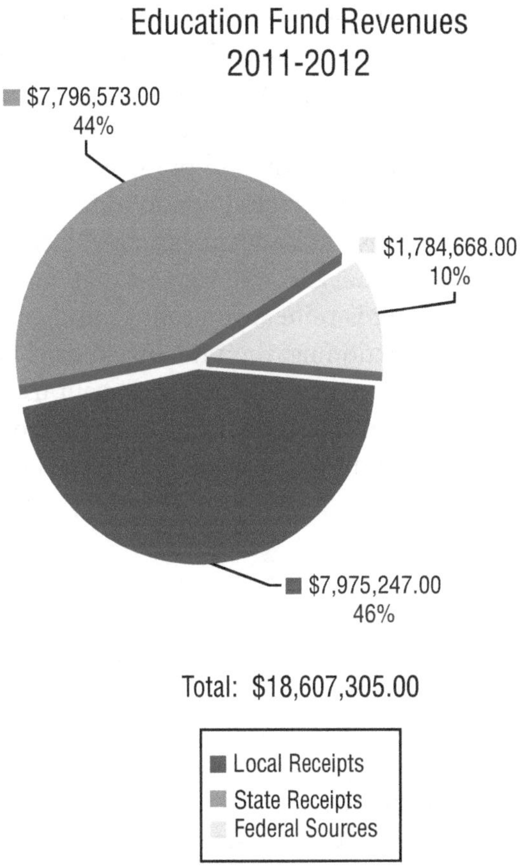

Education Fund Revenues 2011-2012

$7,796,573.00 44%

$1,784,668.00 10%

$7,975,247.00 46%

Total: $18,607,305.00

- Local Receipts
- State Receipts
- Federal Sources

Figure 9.11 The pie chart effectively illustrates how parts of a whole are divided.

Displaying Two-Dimensional Presentational Aids

When you decide to use a line graph to illustrate the volatility of the market place, your next decision involves how to display the graph. Speakers have numerous options for displaying two-dimensional presentational aids. Time and cost alone are not good predictors of the effectiveness of a presentational aid. Sometimes emphasizing important points on a flip chart or using prepared overhead transparencies are acceptable. This next section focuses on how to display two-dimensional aids. In particular, we discuss the benefits and disadvantages of using erasable boards, large Post-its®, posters, and flip charts.

Chalk or Dry Erase Board

It is a rare classroom that does not have some type of erasable board, be it black, green, or white. These serve as the universal presentational aid. Advantages include: It is already in the classroom, you cannot lose or damage it, and it requires no preparation time (other than the day of presentation). Boards are the easiest visual aid to use and involve the least amount of preparation time.

Using a board requires neat, legible handwriting. Seldom is it acceptable to write on the blackboard *during the speech*, but if you must, write as little as possible. Use key terms only. If possible, arrive early and prepare the board in advance. If the board has a screen above it, you might pull the screen down to hide your work until time for your presentation.

In terms of disadvantages, the blackboard is generally viewed as less professional than other presentational aids. We suggest that chalk or eraser boards should serve as your back-up plan. If your poster is ruined, you cannot find an easel for your flip chart, or the computer is unavailable or malfunctioning, then the blackboard is your backup plan.

Your audience may interpret your use of it as lack of preparation. Also, writing on the blackboard requires a speaker to turn away from the audience. Turning your back on your audience is never a good idea, and writing on the board cuts into your valuable speaking time.

Poster Board

A generation ago, the clarity of a poster depended on the art skills of the students since posters were "designed" by hand. If your college has an instructional materials office of some kind, you can make your own posters using die-cuts (generally, Ellison die-cuts). These allow you to cut out letters and shapes to make the poster look more professional. Even better, a computer lab on campus or a photocopying facility will allow access to poster-sized computer-generated graphics. Another option is to use poster-sized foam board in different colors.

Advantages to using a poster board include its low cost and familiarity, and potential use in classrooms where computer-generated technology is not available or difficult to access. Disadvantages include some speaker's lack of time, talent, or patience to create a professional-looking poster, potential difficulty displaying the poster if there is no easel or the chalkboard lacks chalk tray; and posters may get damaged during transportation. Many have abandoned poster boards for computer-generated graphics in the classroom. Where this is not possible, posters are still a viable way to display two-dimensional information.

Flip Chart

Flip charts are still popular way to for displaying two-dimensional information. According to professional speaker and presentation skills expert Lenny Laskowski (2006), since most presentations are delivered before small groups of 35 people or less, the flip chart is the perfect size. Flip charts give speakers the ability to show a sequence of visuals. Studies indicate that listeners are more likely to retain information when the chart is not fully completed ahead of time. Instead, leave out a few key lines or words and fill them in during your speech. This process encourages listeners to perceive the visual as a product of your own expression, and more of an interactive, rather than static presentation.

There are several advantages to using flip charts. The main advantage is that they allow for spontaneity. The speaker may add words or lines based on audience response. A flip chart can be prepared in advance *or* during your speech. Other advantages are that they do not require electricity, they are economical, and one can add color to them easily (Laskowski, 2006).

Disadvantages to using flip charts are they may not be seen by all and they may be distracting. Laskowski (2006) suggests avoiding yellow, pink, or orange markers that are difficult to see, and sticking to one dark color and one lighter color for highlighting. Also, less expensive paper may lead to the marker bleeding through to the following page. Test your markers and paper ahead of time.

Repositional Note Pad

The large repositional note pad, most commonly known as a poster-sized Post-it, is a type of flip chart. These large sticky notes have useful applications in group meetings where members brainstorm and then display the results on multiple pages around the walls. For your speech, you may have some pre-designed Post-its that you stick on the board at different intervals for emphasis. Like posters, these are most useful in rooms lacking more advanced technology.

Two advantages to using poster-sized sticky notes are that you do not have to worry about chalk, tape, push pins, or staples, and you have tremendous flexibility. In addition to being able to stick them just about anywhere, the speaker can write on them before or during the speech. The main disadvantage is that, as they are most likely hand-written, they may not look as professional as some other display techniques. One way to work around it is to use pencil on the pages in advance so the writing is neat and at the same time, so light that only you can see it. Then, during your presentation, go over your work with a marker.

☞ Technology-Based Presentational Aids

Often speakers must clearly communicate statistics, trends, and abstract information. As funds become available and technology costs decrease, more classrooms will be technology-enhanced. This does not mean, however, that older options are now useless. Instances still exist where an audio recording or actual object may make more sense than a computer-generated slide presentation. This next section discusses audio and projected images.

Audio and Projected Images

Rarely is the eraser board your only option for a presentational aid. Depending on the needs of your audience, the content of your speech, the speaking situation, and your own abilities, you may choose a presentational aid requiring the use of other equipment.

Audiotape/CD/iPod

Not all presentational aids are visual, and incorporating some audio clip into your speech is a simple task. If you are trying to describe the messages babies send through their different cries, it would be appropriate and helpful to play an audiotape, CD, iPod, or a smartphone recording of different cries as you explain each. Of course, in a technology-enhanced room, students can access music and many sounds on the computer.

Take care when using an audio clip. Time is an issue, and the clip can overshadow the oral presentation if it consumes too much time. The inexperienced speaker may not have the sound bite or audio clip set up at the right spot or the right volume, and recording quality may be an issue. Getting set up on the computer may take too much time. As always, check the equipment to make sure it is working, the volume is set correctly, and that it is properly queued before the presentation.

Using an overhead projector, object projector, document cameras (for example, ELMO), or smart board allows you to face your listeners and talk as you project images onto a surface. They may be used in normal lighting, which is an important advantage to the speaker. You may face your listeners and use a pointer, just as you would if you were using any other visual. If you choose to remain near the projector instead, you run the risk of talking down to the material you are projecting rather than looking up at your audience. An advantage over PowerPoint is projected images, documents, and transparencies can be altered as you speak, such as underlining a phrase for emphasis or adding a key word.

PowerPoint, Prezi, and Keynote are popular software applications that create visuals to accompany presentations. All have unique features (Prezi lets you create 3-D effects) and common ones (templates, samples, editing, etc.). Using these products as a speech aid is expedient and the finished product looks good and is easy to use, too. For the sake of audiences everywhere, let us offer one plea: Please don't bullet, point, and read us to death. We cannot take it anymore! Keep the presentation centered on you, not the slide show.

Video, DVD, and Online Media Sharing Sites

In certain situations, the most effective way to communicate your message is with a video, DVD, or an online host, such as YouTube. In a speech on tornadoes, showing a video of the damage done by a tornado is likely to be impressive. Showing snippets of a press conference or a movie clip to illustrate or emphasize a particular point can also be interesting and effective.

The novice speaker giving a five-minute speech may not edit the video carefully enough, however. The result may be four minutes of video and one minute of speech. If you choose an audio or video clip, practice with it, plan how to use it, and know how to operate the equipment. Plan for what you will do if the equipment fails.

It is possible to be upstaged by your video clip. Your visual presentation—rather than your speech—may hold center stage. To avoid this, carefully prepare an introduction to support the video clip. Point your listeners to specific parts so they focus on what you want rather than on what happens to catch their interest. After the visual, continue your speech, and build on its content with the impact of your own delivery.

When thinking about using any of the above projected images, allow for sufficient set-up time. Check the equipment to make sure you can operate it and that it is in good working order. Remember also, a darkened room can disrupt your presentation if you need to refer to detailed notes, and if you want people to take notes, the room may be too dark.

Considerations for Technology-Mediated Communication

Speeches have been broadcast via radio and TV for generations. However, these events were coordinated and executed with a team of individuals connected to radio and TV stations.

Now, individuals can create and disseminate their own videos over the Internet, and some self-produced work goes viral on YouTube.

While most speeches you will give will involve a live audience, at times you may be required to record your speech. Technology in this respect is the medium, or the channel through which your speech is presented. In this next section, we provide some suggestions for those specific technology-mediated occasions.

Speaking on Camera

You may find yourself facing traditional cameras, including professional cameras associated with TV stations, video cameras, or less traditional cameras, such as built-in or remote webcams, phone cams, or digital cameras with video capabilities. With an audience present, you still need to follow the basic tenets of public speaking and adapt your speech to the particular audience and situation. Without a live audience, your primary focus becomes creating a message that is conveyed effectively to your intended audience through the camera. Adaptation becomes paramount if you are to succeed.

If you have an audience present, give the speech to them and assume those who record you will do a good job. If you do not have a live audience, you should not "play" to the camera unless directed to do so. Treat the camera as another audience member. President Obama has many positive traits as a speaker, but on occasion, he turns his head to audience members on the left and right, and avoids looking forward toward the camera. The result is the at-home viewer may not feel as connected to Obama's message. Eye contact should be direct and sustained, and strong speakers avoid moving their head, eyes, and hands too quickly.

Posture is important, and the camera may not be as forgiving of imperfections as a live audience. Keep your posture erect. Whether your speech is before a live audience or not, do not forget to gesture naturally. Be sincere and conversational. A recorded speech should be similar to a live audience, but those who are not part of the live audience do not share the same context.

When you know your speech will be recorded, consider how your clothes will look on camera. Professional speaker and speaking coach Tom Antion suggests the following and more on his informative web page (www.public-speaking.org).

* Pastels are the best colors to wear (this applies to men, too!).
* Good clothing colors include beige, gray, green, brown, and blue.
* Avoid white, red, and orange clothing.
* Black, or dark browns and blues are fine alone or combined with pastel colors.
* Avoid fine checks, stripes, herringbone, and similar patterns.
* Avoid very glossy, sequined, or metallic clothing. Also avoid clinging attire, or low-cut necklines.

Radio

A speech on radio may be live or taped, and you may have the option to edit your speech. If it is in front of an audience, you cannot rewind and start again. Audience analysis is a critical element of public speaking. Unlike national and international politicians and dignitaries who may be heard on most radio stations, most speeches you give will be heard locally or regionally. Therefore, it is important to have a basic profile of the listeners within that particular programming market. Establishing common ground is important no matter what the medium.

Once on air, focus on speaking clearly and passionately. Being alone in a room with a microphone may be difficult, but work to energize yourself and deliver your speech enthusiastically. Be aware that pauses are powerful tools, although they may seem longer when the listener can't see you. Since your audience is not present, their awareness of your pacing, articulation, and pronunciation becomes even keener. Work to use pauses strategically and avoid nonfluencies such as um, er, uh, well uh, and so on.

As you craft your message for the radio audience, paying special attention to your main points, transitions, and supporting materials helps ensure effectiveness. Generally, radio also requires us to make key points in shorter sentences. Use effective transitions that help your audience track where you are in your message. Phrases like "Now I will turn to my third point" or "To wrap this talk up" help your listeners understand where you are and where you are headed. Further, anticipate audience questions, and structure your support material in a way that addresses these concerns. For example, if you anticipate many listeners might pose an objection to an idea you present, address the objection yourself and then overcome it with additional support. Often your audience will not have the opportunity to ask for clarification, and lingering questions work against you.

Video Conferencing/Skype/Webinars

Video conferencing can be set up in three ways: computer-based system, desktop system, and studio-based system. A **computer-based system** is often the least expensive method, but its drawback is a lower degree of quality. In essence, computer-based systems often include a webcam and free software like CUseeMe and NetMeeting. A **desktop system** has dedicated software installed on the computer and can improve the audio and video quality. The **studio-based system** offers the best quality, but is also the most expensive and difficult for most to access.

Video conferencing is a "green" technology. By communicating over video, organizations substantially reduce their carbon footprint. With tools that provide a powerful way to enable conferences and other video content to be streamed live or on demand around the world, we can communicate, engage, and interact with others across distances at any time, from wherever they are. The need to hop in a car or jet in, in many cases is now circumvented through these technologies. The effects of videoconferencing are evident within the airline industry. Hewlett Packard, for example, has reduced its global travel by 43 percent (*Travel Weekly*, 2008). Travel management companies predict this trend toward videoconferencing to continue over the next several years.

Yet, because these mediated interactions can be awkward and have the potential for technical problems, sometimes live face-to-face meetings are worth the extra effort, cost, and time. However, *Travel Weekly* notes, "[T]he technology for video and web conferencing has got its act together—no longer does it freeze or crash as soon as you overload the data line, as it did in the early 1990s." Even when all works correctly, as is usually the case, the loss of intimacy, comfort, and ease of communicating as well as the somewhat limited access to immediate nonverbal feedback of those not on camera can impact the effectiveness of the conference.

While videoconferencing is often used for group meetings, the medium is used for public speaking, too. In a video conference speech, we encourage you to look into the camera to create eye contact. Avoid sudden abrupt or sweeping movements to prevent ghosting (motion blur), and in general, move a little more slowly and deliberately than normal to compensate for audio delays.

You may have an occasion to present at a webinar. Generally, a webinar is announced in advance, and people register for it. A date and time for attending via the Web is provided. Depending on the situation, those who miss the webinar may be able to access a recording of it later. The audience participating in the webinar may have the opportunity to speak or type questions or comments for the speaker. These questions can be monitored by a third person or by the speaker. This allows the speaker to clarify points, discuss related information, or respond to the audience in some directed manner.

Podcasts and Streaming Audio

Podcasts most generally are audio presentations. Individuals who produce their own podcasts may not edit their speeches. This leads to mixed success. Podcasts connected to organizations are more likely to have equipment and personnel to create a more polished end result. Podcasts such as "Jimmy's No-Lose Sports Picks of the Week," broadcast live from his parent's garage, on the other hand, can be quite low in production value.

As a speaker, remember that your audience may include people who are listening on their iPods, smartphones, and laptops while working out, sitting at their desk, or driving to work. Listeners may be multitasking. They may choose to skim the podcast, and not catch the whole speech. Since they are not listening in real time, listeners may allow for distractions. Keeping in mind your listeners' attention span limitations, it makes sense to remind listeners who you are and what your central idea is more frequently in your podcast than in a traditional speech.

During an interview with Chris Bjorklund, podcast editor for AllBusiness.com who spent 15 years on radio in the San Francisco Bay Area, several suggestions were offered for creating effective podcasts. She emphasizes that the quality of the audio is of utmost importance. Listeners will tune out if the podcast sounds as though it's coming from a hollow room or a tunnel. A bad connection, a hiss, or some other irritating sound "is a deal breaker." She emphasizes the importance of listening to your surroundings while recording (Is the light buzzing or the air conditioner vent whishing?) as well as the quality of sound after you have finished.

Further, Bjorklund stresses the importance of sounding conversational, and to avoid sounding as though you're lecturing. Communicating energy and enthusiasm is necessary, and she encourages speakers not to "overscript." In other words, the message should not be memorized, and the speaker should focus on creating an effective speaker–audience connection that is less formal than a traditional speech.

Striving for a middle ground between an extemporaneous speech and an informal interpersonal conversation can be difficult to get used to at first, but is usually best received by audiences. Bjorklund encourages individuals who podcast regularly to "brand" themselves by using the same, identifiable theme music to "bookend" the beginning and ending of the program. This helps standardize the podcast, enhances listening enjoyment, and creates a sense of closure at the conclusion. Many radio program talk show hosts use this technique and are identified, in part, by the "bumper" music that has become associated with them.

☞ Effective Use of Presentational Aids

Suppose your speech topic is "College Athletes Don't Graduate." You attend a college that graduates a low percentage of its athletes—a guarded scandal gripping your school. Recent articles in the student newspaper have criticized your school's athletic department for emphasizing winning over education. An editorial in last week's paper asked, "How can student-athletes practice 40 hours a week and still go to class, study, and complete their assignments? The answer is they cannot."

As you collect supporting material for your speech, you find statistics about how much money athletes bring to your university, and you discover that not only do they not get a part of the money, they may not be equipped to go professional or be prepared for anything more than menial work. Making things worse yet, great disparity exists between graduation rates of African American student athletes and their white team members. Here is part of the speech your classmates hear:

> According to a 2010 study by the Institute for Diversity and Ethics (TIDES) at the University of Central Florida, of the 64 colleges and universities with Division 1-A basketball programs, 44 teams, or 69 percent of the total, graduated at least 50 percent of their basketball student–athletes, 37 teams (58 percent) graduated at least 60 percent, and 29 teams (45 percent) graduated at least 70 percent. Only 12 teams (19 percent) graduated less than 40 percent. In terms of equity in graduation rates, 13 of the 67 Division 1-A schools graduated less than 40 percent of their African American players, whereas only four schools graduated less than 60 percent of their white counterparts. Also, eight schools graduated 80 to 100 percent of their African American players, but 39 Division 1-A schools graduated 100 percent of their white basketball players.
>
> The graduation rates for football players of Division 1-A teams is similar. Of the 67 of the 68 teams providing data, 61, or 91 percent, of the total graduated at least 50 percent of their football student athletes, 43 teams (64 percent) graduated at least 60 percent, and 24 teams (36 percent) graduated at least 70 percent. In terms of equity in graduation rates, seven of the 67 Division 1-A schools graduated less than 40 percent of their African American players, whereas no schools graduated less than 40 percent of their white football players. Also, one school graduated 90 percent of its African American players, but 10 schools graduated 90 percent or more of their white counterparts.

Instead of startling your listeners, these statistics numb them. You may see several people yawning, doodling, whispering, and looking out the window. You have no idea why until your classmates comment during the post-speech evaluation. The complaints are all the same: Your "can't miss" speech was boring and difficult to follow. Instead of stimulating your listeners, your long list of statistics put them to sleep.

In this example, an appropriately constructed visual aid could have helped you avoid saying so much in words. Despite the interest your listeners had in your topic before your speech began, the number and complexity of your statistics made it difficult for them to pay attention. By presenting some of your data in visual form, you would communicate the same message more effectively. Consider the difference when the following speech text is substituted for the text above and combined with **Figure 9.12**.

According to a 2010 study by the Institute for Diversity and Ethics (TIDES) at the University of Central Florida, graduation rates for Division 1-A football and basketball

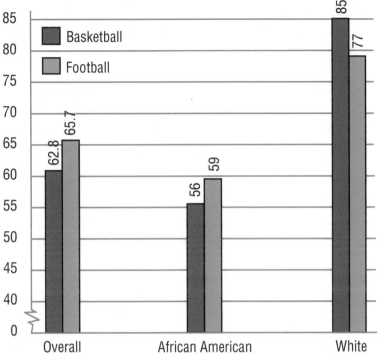

Graduation Success Rates for 2010 Men's Teams in the NCAA Division 1-A Basketball Tournament and Football Bowl Games

Figure 9.12   A visual aid is an effective way to present statistics

players have increased somewhat over previous years. For example, less than half of the basketball teams graduate at least 60 percent of their athletes, and almost two-thirds of the football teams graduate at least 60 percent of their athletes.

The study discovered a disturbing gap between white and African–American student–athletes, however. Eight schools graduated 80–100 percent of their African American basketball players, while 39 schools graduated 100 percent of their white counterparts. In football, one school graduated 90 percent of their African American players whereas 10 schools graduated 100 percent of their white football players. But the worst news is some schools only graduate about a third of their athletes—and our college is one of them.

Numbers are still used, but not as many. With the presentational aid, the audience gets a visual feel for the information and they can process the information awhile longer than if you just stated the numbers.

Criteria for Presentational Aids

Your decision to include an aid should be based on the extent to which it enhances your audience's interest and understanding. The type of aid you choose should relate directly to the specific purpose of your speech and information you intend to convey. Training documents provided by the U.S. Department of Labor remind speakers that presentational aids "enable you to appeal to more than one sense at the same time, thereby increasing the audience's understanding and retention level" (osha.gov, 1996). As you consider using a presentational aid, consider the following four general criteria.

1. **Value to presentation**. Your instructor may require you to use a presentational aid for one or more of your speeches, but it does not mean that *any* aid is better than no aid. First and foremost, the aid must add value to your presentation. If you are considering a presentational aid just to meet assignment requirements, make sure you select something that adds meaning or impact. For example, if a student is giving a speech about "washing your hands to prevent spread of disease" and brings in a half-used bar of soap, there is not much value added to the presentation. We all know what soap looks like. But if the same student gave a speech on "shower sanitation considerations," he might pass around that half-used bar of soap to his listeners as he says:

   Does this bar of soap look clean? Silly question, it's soap, of course it is clean. Let me ask you this: Where is the first part of yourself you wash with a bar like this in the shower? [audience motions towards face and head] That's right, your face. OK, now where is the last place you wash before you get out of the shower? [audience members giggle and indicate buttocks and groin areas] Yes, most people do save the privates for last. Then what do you do? You put the bar of soap back until the next shower when you apply it to your … that's right … face again! As you pick up any bar of soap, including the one I am passing around now, I want you to ask yourself, just where is the last place that bar has been" [those in the audience who handled the bar now frown and look at their hands.

   In this example, the student went on to identify diseases such as hepatitis that can be transmitted by contaminated soap. His attention-grabbing visual aid succeeded in helping make his case more real. Although passing around objects is generally distracting, he decided the impact was worth the added chaos, and we agree. So ask yourself, what is the purpose of the aid? To surprise? To entertain? To illustrate? To make some concept concrete? If you think your presentational aid will improve your speech, then it has value. If you think the audience will benefit from the visual aid, then it has value.

2. **Item safety**. If the item is precious to you, think twice about bringing it to class. It may rain or snow. You might drop it. In the afterglow of your stunning speech, you might leave it behind. Also consider the possible implications of the item not being returned to you if someone in your audience "borrows" it.

3. **Ease of transportation**. Think about what may happen to your object during transportation. Is it a large poster you are trying to carry on a bus or subway? Does it weigh 40 pounds? Do you have to carry it with you all day? Is it bigger than a breadbox? Is it alive? You want to consider how difficult your aid will be to transport, as well as what you are going to do with it before and after your speech.

4. **Size of object and audience**. Imagine spending hours preparing a series of pictures, graphs, and charts for a speech on U.S. immigration reform. However, no one beyond the third row could see them. This violates the cardinal rule of presentational aids: To be valuable, they must be visible. Whether you use a flip-chart or bring in an object of some kind, people in the back of the room need to see it. If they cannot see what is on the table or cannot read a chart clearly, the aid does not serve its purpose.

Consider both object and audience size. Bringing a rare coin, say the 1944 steel penny, to show the class is not helpful because it is too small. And, even if you bring in enough coins for everyone, you take the risk of losing their attention as they examine the penny, drop it, make friendly wagers, or otherwise play with it during your speech. Students are better served by viewing an enlarged picture of the coin on a slide or poster. Showing an 8"x10" picture of the penny would be appropriate in a small class but not in an auditorium where it would need to be projected onto a large screen. Next we examine principles for *using* aids.

Principles for Using Presentational Aids

1. **Do not let your presentational aid distract your audience**. When you pass things around the room, you compete with them as you speak. Your listeners read your handouts, play with foreign coins, eat cookies you baked, and analyze your models instead of listening to you. If handouts are necessary, distribute them at the end of the speech. When appropriate, invite people to take a close look at your displays after your speech. This first suggestion is provided as a general rule, and as noted earlier, exceptions do exist.
2. **Be aware of timing and pauses**. Timing is important. Display each visual only as you talk about it. Do not force people to choose between paying attention to you and paying attention to your aid. If you prepare your flip chart in advance, leave a blank sheet between each page and turn the page when you are finished with the specific point. Cover your models with a sheet. Turn the projector off. Erase your diagram from the blackboard. Turn your poster board around. These actions tell your audience you want them to look at you again.

    Display your presentational aid and then pause two or three seconds before talking. This moment of silence gives your audience time to look at the display. You do not want to compete with your own visual aid. Conversely, try to avoid excessively long pauses as you demonstrate the steps in a process.

    To demonstrate to his class how to truss a turkey, a student brought in everything he needed including a turkey, string, and poultry pins. He began by explaining the procedure but stopped talking for about five minutes while he worked. Although many members of the class paid attention to his technique, several lost interest. He would have benefited from preparing some turkey trivia, stories, or humorous anecdotes that he could slide in while working. Without a verbal presentation to accompany the visual, our attention drifts to other things. Because most audiences need help in maintaining their focus, keep talking.

3. **Make sure the equipment is working but be prepared for failure**. Set up in advance. Make sure equipment is working *before* class, and know how to operate the it. This includes CDs, DVDs, portable music, white board, and the computer/projector. Instructors are frustrated when time is lost, and students become bored when a speaker wastes valuable class time trying to discover how the equipment works. Similarly, find out in advance if the classroom computer is equipped for the Internet, a jump drive or zip disk, and specific programs you are counting on using.

Be prepared for equipment failure. What is Plan B? How much time are you willing to waste before you acknowledge that you cannot use Plan A? Your audience may be sympathetic to your troubles, but we really do not want to hear you complain about it. Your presentation may be acceptable without the high tech. Perhaps bring in a jump drive *and* a CD *and* email the presentation materials to yourself so you have online access to it as well. Maybe you want to use handouts or, as a back-up plan, write on the blackboard. Be prepared. Having multiple ways to get the visuals across may seem redundant until that one really bad day when Plans A, B, and C do not work and you have a Plan D to go to.

4. **Use multimedia presentations only with careful planning and practice**. Multimedia presentations are effective, but they can be challenging. Gracefully moving from a flip chart, to the computer, to a tabletop model requires skill that comes from practice and experience. Mixing media increases your chance that something will go wrong. You can mix media successfully, but careful planning and preparation are essential. Can speakers act with the listener in mind when developing multimedia presentations, just as they do when developing their speeches? Is it possible to have audience-centered advanced technologies accompany a presentation? We believe so, and the following section presents guidelines to help you get there.

Making and Using Computer-Generated Images

You probably learned how to create PowerPoint presentations well before you reached college. By now, you have probably seen hundreds, if not thousands, of PowerPoint presentations. This rise in use is surely because effective computer-generated graphics can have a great impact on listeners. But not always. Too many slides, coupled with a dry, monotonous delivery, spells disaster. "Some of the world's most satisfying naps, deepest day dreams, and most elaborate notebook doodles are inspired by the following phrase, 'I'll just queue up this PowerPoint presentation,'" states Josh Shaffer (2006), staff writer for the Raleigh, North Carolina *News & Observer*.

Some scholars are concerned that when students give speeches with "poorly designed and poorly performed multimedia," they create ineffective presentations; therefore, students must learn to "distinguish ineptitude from eloquence" in accompanying multimedia (Cyphert, 2007, p. 187). In other words, beginning speakers typically lack skill in public speaking *and* creating presentational aids. For this reason, we include guidance for using presentational software. Although aimed primarily at computer-generated graphics, much of the following applies to all presentational aids.

1. **Choose a presentational aid that fits your purpose, the occasion, and your audience**. Develop a clear, specific purpose early in the creative process. If you begin with a specific purpose in mind that fits your goals, the audience's needs, and the requirements of the occasion, you are more likely to find and use relevant technology. Katherine Murray, author of more than 40 computer books, offers the suggestion, "Start with the end in mind" (www.microsoft.com). Knowing what you are trying to accomplish should guide you in designing accompanying multimedia presentations.

    Choose aids appropriate for the occasion. Certain situations are more serious, professional, intimate, or formal than others. Displaying a cartoon during a congressional hearing, for example, may diminish the credibility of the speaker.

    Consider whether the visual support is right for your listeners, analyzing their ages, socioeconomic backgrounds, knowledge, and attitudes toward your subject. Remember that some listeners are offended by visuals that are too graphic. Pictures of abused children, for example, can be offensive to an audience not prepared for what they will see. If you have doubts about the appropriateness of a visual, leave it out of your presentation.

    Presentation specialist Dave Parodi (2004) urges people to "awaken themselves to the power of a well-designed, well-structured, well-delivered presentation, and work as hard as they can to make it happen." These words have great instructional value.

2. **Emphasize only relevant points**. Do not be "PowerPointless," according to Barb Jenkins of the South Australia Department of Education, Training and Employment. Avoid "any fancy transitions, sounds, and other effects that have no discernible purpose, use, or benefit" (www.wordspy.com). The bells and whistles may be fun, but they can be annoying or, worse, distracting.

    In your desire to create an attractive, professional slide presentation, do not forget the message. It is easy to find tips on general design, the number of words per slide, number of slides, images, transitions, color, and so on. After you select the presentational aid that meets your purpose most effectively, decide what information needs to be on each slide. Link only the most important points in your speech with a presentational aid. Focus on your thesis statement and main points, and decide what words or concepts need to be highlighted graphically.

    Our suggestion: Keep your visuals simple: Convey one idea. You may want to use a second visual rather than include more information than your listeners can process. Animations, sound, and visual effects tend to be overused, distracting, and time consuming both in creation and display. Eliminate extraneous material.

3. **Implement the "Rule of Six."** Use no more than six words per line, and no more than six lines per slide. Avoid using full sentences. This is an outline, not an essay. Make the text easy to read. Words need to be large enough, and do not think that using CAPITALIZED words will help. In addition to being a symbol for yelling when instant messaging, it actually takes more effort to read words that are all capitalized. Try using 24-point type or larger.

Figure 9.13A What features make this an ineffective PowerPoint slide?

Tips on Traveling Abroad:
Before you go

- Apply for passport
- Copy important documents
- Visit pharmacy
- Email itinerary
- Contact neighbor
- Pack; Re-pack

Figure 9.13B What features make this an effective PowerPoint slide?

If the audience cannot read your slide, the message is lost.

Compare **Figure 9.13A** with **Figure 9.13B**. Similarities include the title, points covered, and organization. However, Figure 9.13A violates many rules of effective PowerPoint, including too many icons (too busy), full sentences, and small font size. Figure 9.13B is clear, simple, and professional. The template used would be appropriate for all slides used for a presentation on traveling abroad.

4. **Select appropriate design features**. Decisions need to be made regarding template, type of font, and color. The template, which provides color, style, and decorative accents may be distracting to your audience if you change it regularly. Use one template consistently. In general, select a simple font. While font types may look fun, cute, or dramatic, they may be hard to read and distracting. Keep your audience focused on the message; they may be distracted from the text if you have moving animation and slides filled with special effects.

Make sure the font type and font color complement the template. Rely on strong, bold colors that make your message stand out even in a large auditorium. In their article "About Choosing Fonts for Presentations," Microsoft Office Online suggests, "To ensure readability, choose font colors that stand out sharply against the background" (Microsoft Office PowerPoint, 2003). The words you place on the slide should not melt into the background color. Aim for contrast but keep in mind that the contrast you see on your computer screen may not exist on the projected screen.

Research on college students shows that color aids students' ability to organize and recall information and to solve problems (Kraus, 2008). The color wheel in **Figure 9.14** will help you choose contrasting colors. You will achieve the strongest contrasts by using colors opposite one another. Blue and orange make an effective visual combination, as do red and green, and so on. Colors opposite each other on this wheel provide the most striking contrasts for visual displays.

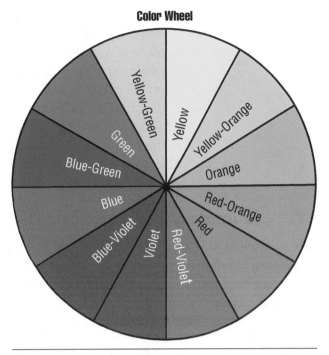

Figure 9.14 Colors opposite each other on this wheel provide the most striking contrast for visual displays. Using an overhead projector during your speech gives you greater flexibility than many other visual aids.

5. **Avoid allowing your presentational aid to upstage you**. Keep in mind that your audience has come to hear you, not to see your presentational aids. If you create a situation in which the visual support is more important than the speaker or the purpose of the speech, you will have defeated your purpose and disappointed your audience.

Be protective of the beginning and end of your presentation. It is usually prudent to avoid using any presentational aid for the first few moments. After you set the tone of your speech and introduce your main idea, turn to your first aid. Likewise, do not use a presentational aid to end your speech. Doing this risks the person-to-person contact you have built to that point by shifting the focus away from you. These are merely guidelines. Some speakers have both begun and ended speeches effectively with well-selected media.

6. **Preview and practice**. An inability to navigate smoothly through your slides limits your effectiveness (Howell, 2008). After creating your slides, run through them. Make sure slides are in the correct order, and that font type, font color, and font size are consistent. Proofread and run spell check. Make printouts of your slides. Then practice the speech using your slides. According to a 2009 survey, the most annoying aspect of the PowerPoint presentation is "the speaker read the slides to us" (Paradi, 2009).

One way to avoid sounding as though you are reading to the audience is through practice. Adding some type of presentational aid makes practicing even more important because you do not want to disrupt the flow of your speech. A reflective pause after displaying a slide can be powerful (Howell, 2008).

During your practice session, focus on your audience, not your presentational aid. Many speakers turn their backs on the audience. They talk to the projection screen or poster instead of looking at the audience. To avoid this tendency, become familiar with your aid so that you have little need to look at it during your talk. Use a remote control, if possible, so you can move more freely.

☛ Summary

Presentational aids serve many functions in a speech. For public speakers, choosing a presentational aid that fits the purpose, occasion, and above all, is audience-centered is paramount. Advantages of using aids in a speech include making the message more memorable, available, clear, persuasive, and entertaining. On the other hand, they can be impersonal, time consuming, serve as a smoke screen for ineffective speakers, result in reductionism, and be too predictable.

Presentational aids fall into four general categories, including actual objects, three-dimensional models, two-dimensional reproductions, and technology-based visual aids. Two-dimensional reproductions include photographs, diagrams and drawings, maps, tables, and charts. Two-dimensional visual aids can be mounted on poster board and displayed on an easel or displayed on a flip chart, or on repositional note pads. Technology-based visual aids include slides, videotape and audiotape, projections, and computer-generated images.

To present effective aids, choose the points in your speech that need visual support; set up your presentation in advance; never let your presentational aids upstage you. Use multimedia presentations only if they are well planned and rehearsed. Avoid repeating what your audience sees in the visual and learn to display each aid only when you are talking about it. Focus on your audience, not your visual. Display your visual, then pause before talking, although you need to avoid long pauses during demonstrations. Do not circulate your presentational aids around the room. Presentational technology should be used when it emphasizes relevant points, adheres to the "Rule of Six," offers appropriate design features, does not upstage, and is used comfortably because it has been well rehearsed.

Typically we give a speech before live audiences, but we may also record that speech for later playback. A speech may be given over the radio, during a video conference, or presented as part of a webinar or podcast. Speakers using technology as a medium for their speeches make important adjustments when an audience is not "live" and face-to-face. These include dressing appropriately for the camera, if present, communicating energy, articulating clearly, avoiding meaningless pauses and verbal fillers, and maintaining acceptable audio quality and sound levels.

References

Alley, M., & Neeley, K. A. (2005). Rethinking the Design of Presentation Slides: A Case for Sentence Headlines and Visual Evidence. *Technical Communication, 52*(4), 417–426.

Carey, R. (1999). Spice it up. *Successful Meetings, October,* 47–50.

CTIA Semi-Annual Wireless Industry Survey. Retrieved May 17, 2011 from ctia.org/research.

Cyphert, D. (2007). Presentation Technology in the Age of Electronic Eloquence: From Visual Aid to Visual Rhetoric. *Communication Education, 56*(2), 168–192.

Foresman, C. *Wireless Survey: 91% of Americans Use Cell Phones.* Retrieved May 17, 2011 from arstechnica.com.

German Twenty-Somethings Prefer Internet to Partner. Retrieved March 2, 2009 from reuters.com.

Hickey, A. R. (2010, August 2). *Social Networking Dominates U.S. Web Use; Facebook Leads the Way.* Retrieved from www.crn.com.

Howell, D. D. (2008). Four Key Keys to Powerful Presentations in PowerPoint: Take Your Presentation to the Next Level. *TechTrends, 52*(6).

Internet Usage Statistics for the Americas. Retrieved June 30, 2010 from internetworldstats.com.

Kalyuga, P., Chandler, P., & Sweller, J. (1991). When Redundant On-Screen Text in Multimedia Technical Instruction Can Interfere with Learning. *Human Factors, 46*(3), 567–581.

Kraus, R. (2008). Presentation Software: Strong Medicine or Tasty Placebo? *Canadian Journal of Science, Mathematics and Technology Education, 8*(1), 70–81.

Lapchick, R. E., Harrison, K., & Hill, F. *Keeping Score When It Counts: Academic Rates for Teams in the 2009–2010 NCAA Division Bowl Games.* Retrieved from www.tidessports.com.

Lapchick, R. E., Harrison, K., & Hill, F. *Keeping Score When It Counts: Academic Rates for Teams in the 2011 NCAA Division I Men's Basketball Study.* Retrieved from www.tidessports.com.

Mayer, R. E. (2001). *Multimedia Learning.* New York: Cambridge University Press.

Morales, X. Y. Z. G. (2010). *Networks to the Rescue: Tweeting Relief and Aid During Typhoon Ondoy.* Thesis abstract. Retrieved from www.firstsearch.oclc.org.

Nicholson, D. T. (2002, Summer). Lecture Delivery Using MSPowerPoint: Staff and Student Perspectives at MMU. *Learning and Teaching in Action.* Retrieved from www.celt.mmu.ac.uk.

Paradi, D. (2009). *Results from the 2009 Annoying PowerPoint Survey.* Retrieved from thinkoutsidetheslide.com.

A Polycom Fact Sheet. *The Top Five Benefits of Video Conferencing.* Retrieved from polycom.com/telepresence.

Purcell, K., Rainie, L., Rosenstiel, T., & Mitchell, A. (2011, March 14). *How Mobile Devices Are Changing Community Information Environments.* Retrieved from pewinternet.org.

Smith, A. (2011, March 17). *The Internet and Campaign 2010.* Retrieved from pewinternet.org.

Travel Weekly. (2008, October 16). Business Travel: The Rise of Video-Conferencing. Retrieved from travelweekly.com.

Tufte, E. R. (1997). *Visual Explanations: Images and Quantities, Evidence and Narrative.* Cheshire, CT: Graphics Press.

Tufte, E. R. (2006). *The Cognitive Style of PowerPoint: Pitching Out Corrupts Within,* 2nd Ed. Graphics Press: Cheshire CT.

U.S. Department of Education, National Center for Education Statistics. (2008). *Distance Education at Degree-Granting Postsecondary Institutions: 2006–07.* Retrieved May 16, 2011 from nces.ed.gov/fastfacts.

Wazlawick, P., Bevelas, J. B., & Jackson, D. D. (1967). *Pragmatics of Human Communication: A Study of Interactional Patterns, Pathologies, and Paradoxes.* New York: Norton.

Wright, J. (2009). The Role of Computer Software in Presenting Information. *Nursing Management, 16*(4).

Zetter, K. (2011). TED 2011: Wael Ghonim—Voice of Egypt's Revolution. *Wired,* March 5. Retrieved from www.wired.com.

Chapter 10

Informative Speaking

"Perhaps hell is nothing more than an enormous conference of those who, with little or nothing to say, take an eternity to say it."

Dudley C. Stone

SPEECH: Franklin Delano Roosevelt — First Fireside Chat (1933)

Franklin Delano Roosevelt (1882–1945) became the 32nd President of the United States at the depth of the Great Depression. Roosevelt's most pressing concern upon assuming office was to resolve the banking system crisis. He declared a "bank holiday," which served a two-fold purpose of (a) giving him time to prepare a proposal for Congress without bank conditions further deteriorating and (b) preventing withdrawals from banks, which sent a message of hope to the American public that perhaps the Depression had bottomed out. The House and Senate approved Roosevelt's bill in record time, which was a testament to the deep sense of crisis felt by the nation and the legislative bodies. The banks reopened after the bill was signed. President Roosevelt spoke to the nation in a radio address to explain what he had done to restore confidence and to dispel fear.

Source: Andrews, J., & Zarefsky, D. (1989). *American Voices: Significant Speeches in American History, 1640–1945.* White Plains, NY: Longman, pp. 440–441.

Franklin Delano Roosevelt

The Banking Crisis (First Fireside Chat)

Delivered 12 March 1933, Washington D.C.
    AUTHENTICITY CERTIFIED: Text version below transcribed directly from audio

My friends:

I want to talk for a few minutes with the people of the United States about banking to talk with the comparatively few who understand the mechanics of banking, but more particularly with the overwhelming majority of you who use banks for the making of deposits and the drawing of checks.

I want to tell you what has been done in the last few days, and why it was done, and what the next steps are going to be. I recognize that the many proclamations from State capitols and from Washington, the legislation, the Treasury regulations, and so forth, couched for the most part in banking and legal terms, ought to be explained for the benefit of the average citizen. I owe this, in particular, because of the fortitude and the good temper with which everybody has accepted the inconvenience and hardships of the banking holiday. And I know that when you understand what we in Washington have been about, I shall continue to have your cooperation as fully as I have had your sympathy and your help during the past week.

First of all, let me state the simple fact that when you deposit money in a bank, the bank does not put the money into a safe deposit vault. It invests your money in many different forms of credit in bonds, in commercial paper, in mortgages and in many other kinds of loans. In other words, the bank puts your money to work to keep the wheels of industry and of agriculture turning around. A comparatively small part of the money that you put into the bank is kept in currency an amount which in normal times is wholly sufficient to cover the cash needs of the average citizen. In other words, the total amount of all the currency in the country is only a comparatively small proportion of the total deposits in all the banks of the country.

What, then, happened during the last few days of February and the first few days of March? Because of undermined confidence on the part of the public, there was a general rush by a large portion of our population to turn bank deposits into currency or gold a rush so great that the soundest banks couldn't get enough currency to meet the demand. The reason for this was that on the spur of the moment it was, of course, impossible to sell perfectly sound assets of a bank and convert them into cash, except at panic prices far below their real value. By the afternoon of March third, a week ago last Friday, scarcely a bank in the country was open to do business. Proclamations closing them, in whole or in part, had been issued by the Governors in almost all the states. It was then that I issued the proclamation providing for the national bank holiday, and this was the first step in the Government's reconstruction of our financial and economic fabric.

The second step, last Thursday, was the legislation promptly and patriotically passed by the Congress confirming my proclamation and broadening my powers so that it became possible in view of the requirement of time to extend the holiday and lift the ban of that holiday gradually in the days to come. This law also gave authority to develop a program of rehabilitation of our banking facilities. And I want to tell our citizens in every part of the Nation that the national Congress Republicans and Democrats alike showed by this action a devotion to public welfare and a realization of the emergency and the necessity for speed that it is difficult to match in all our history.

The third stage has been the series of regulations permitting the banks to continue their functions to take care of the distribution of food and household necessities and the payment of payrolls.

This bank holiday, while resulting in many cases in great inconvenience, is affording us the opportunity to supply the currency necessary to meet the situation. Remember that no sound bank is a dollar worse off than it was when it closed its doors last week. Neither is any bank which may turn out not to be in a position for immediate opening. The new law allows the twelve Federal Reserve Banks to issue additional currency on good assets and thus the banks that reopen will be able to meet every legitimate call. The new currency is being sent out by the Bureau of Engraving and Printing in large volume to every part of the country. It is sound currency because it is backed by actual, good assets.

Another question you will ask is this: Why are all the banks not to be reopened at the same time? The answer is simple and I know you will understand it: Your Government does not intend that the history of the past few years shall be repeated. We do not want and will not have another epidemic of bank failures.

As a result, we start tomorrow, Monday, with the opening of banks in the twelve Federal Reserve Bank cities those banks, which on first examination by the Treasury, have already been found to be all right. That will be followed on Tuesday by the resumption of all other functions by banks already found to be sound in cities where there are recognized clearing houses. That means about two hundred and fifty cities of the United States. In other words, we are moving as fast as the mechanics of the situation will allow us.

On Wednesday and succeeding days, banks in smaller places all through the country will resume business, subject, of course, to the Government's physical ability to complete its survey. It is necessary that the reopening of banks be extended over a period in order to permit the banks to make applications for the necessary loans, to obtain currency needed to meet their requirements, and to enable the Government to make common sense checkups.

Please let me make it clear to you that if your bank does not open the first day you are by no means justified in believing that it will not open. A bank that opens on one of the subsequent days is in exactly the same status as the bank that opens tomorrow.

I know that many people are worrying about State banks that are not members of the Federal Reserve System. There is no occasion for that worry. These banks can and will receive assistance from member banks and from the Reconstruction Finance Corporation. And, of course, they are under the immediate control of the State banking authorities. These State banks are following the same course as the National banks except that they get their licenses to resume business from the State authorities, and these authorities have been asked by the Secretary of the Treasury to permit their good banks to open up on the same schedule as the national banks. And so I am confident that the State Banking Departments will be as careful as the national Government in the policy relating to the opening of banks and will follow the same broad theory.

It is possible that when the banks resume a very few people who have not recovered from their fear may again begin withdrawals. Let me make it clear to you that the banks will take care of all needs, except, of course, the hysterical demands of hoarders, and it is my belief that hoarding during the past week has become an exceedingly unfashionable pastime in every part of our nation. It needs no prophet to tell you that when the people find that they can get their money that they can get it when they want it for all legitimate purposes the phantom of fear will soon be laid. People will again be glad to have their money where it will be safely taken care of and where they can use it conveniently at any time. I can assure you, my friends, that it is safer to keep your money in a reopened bank than it is to keep it under the mattress.

The success of our whole national program depends, of course, on the cooperation of the public on its intelligent support and its use of a reliable system.

Remember that the essential accomplishment of the new legislation is that it makes it possible for banks more readily to convert their assets into cash than was the case before. More liberal provision has been made for banks to borrow on these assets at the Reserve Banks and more liberal provision has also been made for issuing currency on the security of these good assets. This currency is not fiat currency. It is issued only on adequate security, and every good bank has an abundance of such security.

One more point before I close. There will be, of course, some banks unable to reopen without being reorganized. The new law allows the Government to assist in making these reorganizations quickly and effectively and even allows the Government to subscribe to at least a part of any new capital that may be required.

I hope you can see, my friends, from this essential recital of what your Government is doing that there is nothing complex, nothing radical in the process.

We have had a bad banking situation. Some of our bankers had shown themselves either incompetent or dishonest in their handling of the people's funds. They had used the money entrusted to them in speculations and unwise loans. This was, of course, not true in the vast majority of our banks, but it was true in enough of them to shock the people of the United States, for a time, into a sense of insecurity and to put them into a frame of mind where they did not differentiate, but seemed to assume that the acts of a comparative few had tainted them all. And so it became the Government's job to straighten out this situation and do it as quickly as possible. And that job is being performed.

I do not promise you that every bank will be reopened or that individual losses will not be suffered, but there will be no losses that possibly could be avoided; and there would have been more and greater losses had we continued to drift. I can even promise you salvation for some, at least, of the sorely presses banks. We shall be engaged not merely in reopening sound banks but in the creation of more sound banks through reorganization.

It has been wonderful to me to catch the note of confidence from all over the country. I can never be sufficiently grateful to the people for the loyal support that they have given me in their acceptance of the judgment that has dictated our course, even though all our processes may not have seemed clear to them.

After all, there is an element in the readjustment of our financial system more important than currency, more important than gold, and that is the confidence of the people themselves. Confidence and courage are the essentials of success in carrying out our plan. You people must have faith; you must not be stampeded by rumors or guesses. Let us unite in banishing fear. We have provided the machinery to restore our financial system, and it is up to you to support and make it work.

It is your problem, my friends, your problem no less than it is mine. Together we cannot fail.

http://www.presidency.ucsb.edu/ws/index.php?pid=14540

Whether you are a nurse conducting CPR training for new parents at the local community center, a museum curator delivering a speech on Impressionist art, or an auto repair shop manager lecturing to workers about the implications of a recent manufacturer's recall notice, your **informative speech** goal is to communicate information and ideas in a way that your audience will understand and remember. In your job, community activities, and in this public speaking class, remember that the audience should hear *new* knowledge, not facts they already know. For example, the nurse conducting CPR training for new parents would approach the topic differently if the audience comprised individuals from various fields working on their yearly recertification. New parents most likely are also new to CPR training, whereas professionals receive training at least once a year.

In this chapter, we first distinguish informative speaking from persuasive or commemorative speaking. We identify different types of informative speeches, and guidelines for informative speaking are presented. Last, the issue of ethics and informative speaking is examined.

Differentiating Informative, Persuasive, and Entertaining Purposes

The situation or context often suggests what type of speech that is expected. Commencement speeches are motivational, as are keynote speeches at conventions. Speakers deliver commemorative speeches on Veteran's Day, presidents' birthdays, and other occasions that recognize individuals or groups of individuals. Speeches can be classified into three major categories—informative, persuasive, and entertaining (commemorative or inspirational). The next few paragraphs distinguish among these categories.

When you deliver an informative speech, your intent is to enlighten your audience—to increase understanding or awareness and, perhaps, to create a new perspective. In contrast, when you deliver a persuasive speech, your intent is to influence your audience to agree with your point of view—to change attitudes or beliefs or to bring about a specific, desired action. And when you deliver a speech as part of some special occasion, your intent is to entertain, commemorate, inspire, or humor your listeners. In theory, these three forms are different. In practice, these distinctions are much less obvious.

For example, if you developed an informative speech on the consequences of calling off a marriage, your main points might include relationship damage (friends and family), emotional trauma, and financial difficulties. These are acceptable informative topic areas. If, however, you go beyond identifying these issues to suggesting that the engaged couples in your audience implement safeguards to prevent emotional or financial damage, you are being implicitly persuasive. When you tell the men in your audience that they should obtain a written statement from their fiancées pledging the return of the engagement ring if the relationship ends, you are asking for explicit action, and you have blurred the line between information and persuasion. Similarly, if you devote large portions of your speech to a humorous rant about the institution of marriage and why no one should be institutionalized, you have crossed the line toward entertainment.

The key to informative speaking is *intent*. If your goal is to expand understanding, your speech is informational. If, in the process, you want your audience to share or agree with your point of view, you may also be persuasive. And if you want them to pay attention and recall key points later, a little humor and entertaining storytelling always help. After a speech describing the types of assault rifles available to criminals, some of your audience may be moved to write to Congress in support of stricter gun control while others may send contributions to lobbying organizations that promote stricter gun control legislation. Although your speech brought about these actions, it is still informational because your intent was educational. Objective facts can be persuasive even when presented with an informational intent.

A critical place where we often see the intent lines blur is in the conclusion of an informative speech. Take care to avoid providing them with an action plan. Avoid ending a speech with something like "So now that I've explained the history and sociopsychological benefits and drawbacks of tattoos, I hope that you will consider getting one." This final "tag" line changes the nature of the speech from informative to persuasive.

To make sure your speech is informational rather than persuasive or entertaining, start with a clear, specific purpose signifying your intent. Compare the following specific purpose statements:

Specific purpose statement #1 (SPS#1). To inform my listeners how the military has responded historically to minorities in the military, including Japanese Americans, African Americans, women, and gays, bisexuals, transgendered individuals, and lesbians

Specific purpose statement #2 (SPS#2). To inform my listeners how the military has responded poorly and in an untimely fashion to minorities in the military, including Japanese

Americans, African Americans, women, and gays, bisexuals, transgendered individuals, and lesbians

Specific purpose statement #3 (SPS#3). To pay tribute to my listeners from minority groups who have suffered under Don't Ask, Don't Tell policies simply to provide invaluable service to our country

While the intent of the first statement is informational, the intent of the second is persuasive, and the third, entertaining. The speaker in SPS#1 is likely to discuss how and where Japanese Americans and African Americans served during WWII, the evolution of women from support positions to combat positions, and the development of the Don't Ask, Don't Tell policy. The speaker in SPS#2 uses subjective words such as "poorly and in an untimely fashion." Most likely this speech would focus more on the negative impact military policy had on minority groups, including being victims of segregation, being placed in high-risk combat situations, and allowing the harassment of women and homosexuals. SPS#3 clearly sets out to commemorate a group of people at a special event, perhaps honoring fallen minority soldiers at a Memorial Day celebration.

Types of Informative Speaking

Although all informative speeches seek to help audiences understand, there are three distinct types of informative speeches. A **speech of description** helps an audience understand *what* something is. When the speaker wants to help us understand *why* something is so, they are offering a **speech of explanation**. Finally, when the focus is on *how* something is done, it is a **speech of demonstration**. Each of these is discussed in detail.

Speeches of Description

Describing the safety features of a typical nuclear power plant, describing the effects of an earthquake, and describing the buying habits of teenagers are all examples of informative speeches of description. These speeches paint a clear picture of an event, person, object, place, situation, or concept. The goal is to create images in the minds of listeners about your topic or to describe a concept in concrete detail. Here, for example, is a section of a speech describing a poetry slam. We begin with a brief, specific purpose and thesis statement:

> **General purpose**: To inform
> **Specific purpose**: To describe to my audience how poetry slams moved the performance of poetry to a competitive event
> **Thesis statement**: To understand the poetry slam, one must understand its history, the performance, and the judging process.

Imagine reading a piece of poetry in a quaint bookstore with bongo drums playing in the background as a mellow audience snaps their fingers in appreciation. This is how some perceive the traditional poetry reading. Imagine instead, a smoke-filled bar, filled with rowdy individuals, many inebriated, anticipating being entertained in three-minute intervals by young poets yearning for the adrenaline rush found in fierce competition. This is how poetry reading becomes the poetry slam.

According to slampapi.com, slam poetry is a competitive event founded by Chicago author Marc Smith in 1987. Individuals perform original poetry designed to elicit an emotional response, and then are judged by experts in the poetry community. Venues across the U.S. include the Bowery Street Poetry Club in New York, Green Mill in Chicago, and the national slam competition hosted in a different city each year.

In this excerpt, the speaker describes a competitive outlet for poets. Audience members learn that this event takes place in bars and clubs, and audience members respond fully. One gets a feeling for the setting through vivid language use. Following is a short list of some possible speech topics for the informative speech of description:

* To describe the important aspects of the Cinco de Mayo celebration
* To describe the life and philosophy of Franz Kafka
* To describe the causes and symptoms of Chronic Fatigue Syndrome (CFT)

Speeches of Explanation

Speeches of explanation deal with more **abstract topics** (ideas, theories, principles, and beliefs) than speeches of description or demonstration. They also involve attempts to simplify complex topics. The goal of these speeches is audience understanding, such as a psychologist addressing parents about the moral development of children or a cabinet official explaining U.S. farm policy.

To be effective, speeches of explanation must be designed specifically to achieve audience understanding of the theory or principle. Avoid abstractions, too much jargon, or technical terms by using verbal pictures that define and explain. Here, for example, a speaker demonstrates the error of using unfamiliar terms to define spiritualism:

> **General purpose:** To inform
> **Specific purpose**: To explain to my audience how the connection between physical and spiritual elements is a basic foundation of Spiritualism
> **Thesis statement**: Spiritualism is a belief system grounded in the idea that each being has both physical and spiritual elements.

According to the National Spiritualist Association of Churches (2011), spiritualism consists of Prophecy, Clairvoyance, Clairaudience, Laying on of Hands, Healing, Visions, Trance, Apports, Levitation, Raps, and Automatic and Independent Writings and Paintings, Voice, Materialization, Photography, Psychometry, and any other manifestation proving the continuity of life as demonstrated through the Physical and Spiritual senses and faculties of man.

While the previous description identifies phenomena associated with spiritualism, too many terms are used to process at one time, and some are not familiar terms. Imagine the speaker saying the following, instead:

> According to Alan Kaslev, developer of the website Kheper.net (meaning transformation), the philosophy known as Spiritualism is based on the premise that man is a dual being; consisting of a physical and spiritual component. The physical element (the body) disintegrates at death, but the spiritual (the "soul") continues exactly as it was, only in another form of existence, the "Spirit-world" or heaven. Spiritualists further claim that communication between the living and those in the spirit-world is possible through a medium.

If the first description is presented alone, listeners are limited in their ability to anchor the concept to something they understand. The second explanation is more effective, and listeners have a clearer idea where the speaker will lead them.

Speeches of explanation may involve policies; statements of intent or purpose that guide or drive future decisions. The president may announce a new arms control policy. A school superintendent may implement a new inclusion policy. The director of human resources of a major corporation may discuss the firm's new flextime policy.

A speech that explains a policy should focus on the questions likely to arise from an audience. For example, prior to a speech to teachers and parents before school starts, the superintendent of a school district implementing a new inclusion policy should anticipate what the listeners will probably want to know—when the policy change will be implemented, to what extent it will be implemented, when it will be evaluated, and how problems will be monitored, among other issues. When organized logically, these and other questions form the basis of the presentation. As in all informative speeches, your purpose is not to persuade your listeners to support the policy, but to inform them about the policy.

To reiterate, strive to keep focused on the informative intent. For example, a group of university employees gathered to hear about the changes in insurance benefits. One particular insurance plan would cost the state less but cost employees more. The speaker, who represented the state, described each option, but made several references to the plan that cost employees more and the state less. After several such references, audience members started making side comments about how the speaker was trying to persuade individuals into the state's preferred plan. The intent was advertised as an informative one, but the speaker's message had strong persuasive undertones.

Following are some sample topics that could be developed into speeches of explanation:

* To explain the five principles of Hinduism
* To explain the effect of colonization on African cultures
* To explain popular superstitions in American culture
* To explain how different cultures perceive beauty
* To explain why Japanese internment occurred in the United States during World War II

Speeches of Demonstration

Speeches of demonstration focus on a process by describing the gradual changes that lead to a particular result. These speeches often involve two approaches, one is "how" and the other is a "how to" approach. Here are examples of specific purposes for speeches of demonstration:

* To inform my audience *how* college admissions committees choose the most qualified applicants
* To inform my audience *how* diabetes threatens health
* To inform my audience *how to* sell an item on eBay
* To inform my audience *how to* play the Facebook game FarmVille by Zygna

Speeches that take a "how" approach have audience understanding as their goal. They create understanding by explaining how a process functions without teaching the specific skills needed to complete a task. After listening to a speech on college admissions, for example, you may understand the process but may not be prepared to take a seat on an admissions committee.

Let's look more closely at a small section of a "how" speech about election judges.

"You're going to be one of those old ladies at the polling place?" was my daughter's response when I told her I would be an election judge for midterm elections. When she followed up with, "What *is* an election judge?" I realized that many people don't know how election judges are selected. Voters should be aware that the people who check off your name and give you a ballot on election day represent both parties and complete training so that a fair voting procedure exists and is executed in accordance to the law. According to a brochure published by the Illinois government, election judges are selected by the board of elections commissioners, based on lists furnished by the chairs of the county central committees.

Although this excerpt begins to explain how election judges are selected, its primary goal is understanding, not application. In contrast, "how to" speeches communicate specific skills, such as selling an item on eBay, changing a tire, or making a lemon shake-up. Compare the previous "how" example discussing election judges with the following "how to" presentation, How to Buy a New Home.

According to the U.S. Department of Housing and Urban Development, when it comes time to buying a home, there are seven steps to follow. Given the housing market crisis that exists, the very first step is to figure out how much you can afford. What you can afford depends on your income, credit rating, current monthly expenses, down payment, and the interest rate. Your monthly expenses are not only what it costs to live in an apartment or a rental home, but how much you pay each month for a car as well as any ongoing loan payments. Will you need a newer car soon? Is your job secure? Will you have money left over after paying housing expenses? Do you want to be mortgage free in 15 years? 30 years? All of these are questions you need to answer before you determine how much you can spend on a new home.

The second step in buying a new home is to know your rights. There are several legal documents you must sign. You have rights as a borrower, and you should also be aware of predatory lending.

Notice that the "how to" speech has several steps. These are generally in chronological order, and once learned, should result in "mastery" of a particular ability or skill. In the above example, one should know how to engage in the house-buying process.

One clear difference between the speech of demonstration and speeches of presentation and explanation is that the *speech of demonstration benefits from presentational aids*. When your goal is to demonstrate a process, you may choose to complete the entire process—or a part of it—in front of your audience. The nature of your demonstration and time constraints determine your choice. If you are giving CPR training, a partial demonstration will not give your listeners the information they need to save a life. If you are demonstrating how to cook a stew, however, your audience does not need to watch you chop onions; prepare in advance to maintain audience interest and save time.

Following are several topics that could be developed into demonstration speeches:

* How to make flower arrangements
* How grapes are processed into wine
* How to pick a bottle of wine
* How to swing a golf club
* How to make a website
* How to organize a closet
* How to find cheap airline tickets
* How to determine if you have sleep apnea

☞ Five Goals of Informative Speaking

Although the overarching goal of an informative speech is to communicate information and ideas so the audience will understand, there are other goals as well. Whether you are giving a speech to explain, describe, or demonstrate, the following five goals are relevant: be accurate, objective, clear, meaningful, and memorable. After each goal, we present two specific strategies for achieving that goal.

1. Accurate

Informative speakers strive to present the truth. They understand the importance of careful research for verifying information they present. Facts must be correct and current. Research is crucial. Do not rely solely on your own opinion; find support from other sources. For example, in a speech talking about financing college, you may want to discuss how much debt college students have. After talking with your friends, you may believe that students are deeply in debt. After doing research, you find a source from the Huffington Post in February 2010 that states recent college graduates are carrying an average of $23,200 of debt. This provides specific support.

However, if you looked at a publication from the National Center for Education Statistics in 2000, you would find that in 1997, 46 percent of undergraduates had no debt from college, and the average loan debt was $10,100. Information that is not current may be inaccurate or misleading. Offering an incorrect fact may hurt speaker credibility and cause people to stop listening. The following two strategies will help you present accurate information.

Question the source of information

Is the source a nationally recognized magazine or reputable newspaper, or is it from someone's post on a random blog? Source verification is important. Virtually anyone can post to the Internet. Check to see if your source has appropriate credentials, such as education, work experience, or verifiable personal experience. For example, how valid do you think information is from the Huffington Post?

Consider the timeliness of the information

Information becomes dated. If you want to inform the class about the heart transplant process, relying on sources more than a few years old would mislead your audience because science and technology change rapidly. Your instructor may require sources within a five- or 10-year span. If not, check the date your source was published (online or print), and determine whether it will be helpful or harmful to the overall effectiveness of your speech.

2. Objective

Present information fairly and in an unbiased manner. Purposely leaving out critical information or "stacking the facts" to create a misleading picture violates the rule of objectivity. The following two strategies should help you maintain objectivity.

Take into account all perspectives

Combining perspectives creates a more complete picture. Avoiding other perspectives creates bias, and may turn an informative speech into a persuasive one. The chief negotiator for a union may have a completely different perspective than the administration's chief negotiator on how current contract negotiations are proceeding. They may use the same facts and statistics, but interpret them differently. An impartial third party trying to determine how the process is progressing needs to speak with both sides and attempt to remove obvious bias.

Show trends

Trends put individual facts in perspective as they clarify ideas within a larger context. The whole—the connection among ideas—gives each detail greater meaning. If a speaker tries to explain how the stock market works, it makes sense to talk about the stock market in relation to what it was a year ago, five years ago, 10 years ago, or even longer, rather than focus on today or last week. Trends also suggest what the future will look like.

3. Clear

To be successful, your informative speech must communicate your ideas without confusion. When a message is not organized clearly, audiences become frustrated and confused and, ultimately, they miss your ideas. Conducting careful audience analysis helps you understand what your audience already knows about your topic and allows you to offer a distinct, targeted message at their level of understanding. Choosing the best organizational pattern will also help your listeners understand your message. The following two strategies are designed to increase the clarity of your speech.

Define unfamiliar words and concepts

Unfamiliar words, especially technical jargon, can defeat your informative purpose. When introducing a new word, define it in a way your listeners can understand. Because you are so close to your material, knowing what to define can be one of your hardest tasks. Put yourself in the position of a listener who knows less about your topic than you do or ask a friend or colleague's opinion.

In addition to explaining the dictionary definition of a concept or term, a speaker may rely on two common forms of definitions: operational and through example.

Operational definitions specify procedures for observing and measuring concepts. For example, in the United States an IQ test (Intelligence Quotient) is used to define how "smart" we are. According to Gregory (2004), someone who scores 95–100 is of average intelligence, a score of 120 or higher is above average, and a score of 155 or higher is considered "genius." The government tells us who is "poor" based on a specified income level, and communication researchers can determine if a person has high communication apprehension based on his or her score on McCroskey's Personal Report of Communication Apprehension.

Definition through example helps the audience understand a complex concept by giving the audience a "for instance." In an effort to explain what is meant by the term "white-collar criminal," a speaker could provide several examples, such as Jeff Skilling (former Enron executive convicted on federal felony charges relating to the company's financial collapse), Rod Blagojevich (former Illinois governor found guilty of several charges related to his trying to sell President Obama's Illinois Senate seat), and Wesley Snipes (actor convicted of tax evasion and jailed for three years in December 2010).

Carefully organize your message

Find an organizational pattern that makes the most sense for your specific purpose. Descriptive speeches, speeches of demonstration, and speeches of explanation have different goals. Therefore, you must consider the most effective way to organize your message. *Descriptive speeches* are often arranged in spatial, topical, and chronological patterns. For example, if a speaker chose to talk about Oktoberfest in Munich, a topical speech might talk about the beer tents, food possibilities, entertainment, and tourist activities. A speech following a chronological pattern might talk about when to start planning for the festival, when the festival begins, and what events occur on particular days. The topic is still Oktoberfest, but based on the organizational pattern, the speech focuses differently and contains different information.

Speeches of demonstration often use spatial, chronological, and cause-and-effect or problem–solution patterns. For example, in a speech on how to buy a home, a few organizational patterns are possible, depending on what aspect of the topic you chose as your focus. It would make sense to organize spatially if your focus is on what to examine as you search for homes. You might want to start with the roof and work down toward the basement (or vice versa) or you might look at the lot and outside features and then move inside. The lot could be divided into small parts, such as how big the lot is, how close neighbors are, what the view is all around the house, how much maintenance is needed on the lot, and so on. As you move inside, you could talk about the number of rooms, electricity, plumbing, access (stairs, attic, or crawl space), and so on.

A chronological pattern for how to buy a house would be more appropriate when talking about getting a real estate agent, finding a house, setting up financing, getting an appraisal, making an offer, getting the house appraised, and accepting an offer. As you can see, the speech that is set up to follow a spatial pattern is significantly different than the speech that uses a chronological pattern.

Speeches of explanation are frequently arranged chronologically, or topically, or according to cause-and-effect or problem–solution. For example, for several years, the Asian carp has made headlines in the Great Lakes area because of its potential to harm the habitat of the Great Lakes. Using the Asian carp as a topic, a speech arranged chronologically could discuss how this threat has developed over the last decade, and what the future projection is. A problem–solution speech, on the other hand, could talk about the dangers related to the fish invasion of the Great Lakes and possible solutions to the problem. Important with the second organizational pattern is that the speech be kept as informative as possible, and not identify the "best" solution.

4. Meaningful

A meaningful, informative message focuses on what matters to the audience as well as to the speaker. Relate your material to the interests, needs, and concerns of your audience. A speech explaining the differences between public and private schools delivered to the parents of students in elementary and secondary schools would not be as meaningful in a small town where no choice exists. Here are two strategies to help you develop a meaningful speech:

Consider the setting

The setting may tell you about audience goals. Informative speeches are given in many places, including classrooms, community seminars, and business forums. Audiences may attend these speeches because of an interest in the topic or because attendance is required. Settings tell you the specific reasons your audience has gathered. A group of middle-aged women attending a lifesaving lecture at a local YMCA may be concerned about saving their husbands' lives in the event of a heart attack, while a group of nursing students listening to the same lecture in a college classroom may be fulfilling a graduation requirement.

Avoid information overload

When you are excited about your subject and you want your audience to know about it, you can find yourself trying to say too much in too short a time. You throw fact after fact at your listeners until you literally force them to stop listening. Saying too much is like touring London in a day—it cannot be done if you expect to remember anything.

Information overload can be frustrating and annoying because the listener experiences difficulty in processing so much information. Your job as an informative speaker is to know how much to say and, just as important, what to say. Long lists of statistics are mind-numbing. Be conscious of the relationship among time, purpose, and your audience's ability to absorb information. Tie key points to stories, examples, anecdotes, and humor. Your goal is not to get it all in but to communicate your message as effectively as possible.

5. Memorable

Speakers who are enthusiastic, genuine, and creative and who can communicate their excitement to their listeners deliver memorable speeches. Engaging examples, dramatic stories, and tasteful humor applied to your key ideas in a genuine manner will make a long-lasting impact.

Use examples and humor

Nothing elicits interest more than a good example, and humorous stories are effective in helping the audience remember the material. When Sarah Weddington, winning attorney in the Roe v. Wade Supreme Court case, talks about the history of discriminatory practices in this country, she provides a personal example of how a bank required her husband's signature on a loan even though she was working and he was in school. She also mentions playing "girls" basketball in school and being limited to three dribbles (boys could dribble the ball as many times as they wanted). While these stories stimulate interest and make the audience laugh, they also communicate the message that sex discrimination was pervasive when Weddington was younger (Reaves, 2003).

Physically involve your audience

Many occasions lend themselves to some type of audience participation. Consider asking for audience response to a observation: "Raise your hand if you have ever seen a tornado." Seek help with your demonstration. If you are demonstrating how to make a cake, for example, you could ask someone to stir the batter. Ask some audience members to take part in an experiment that you conduct to prove a point. For example, hand out several headsets to volunteers and ask them to set the volume level where they usually listen to music. Then show how volume can affect hearing.

Guidelines for Effective Informative Speeches

Regardless of the type of informative speech you plan to give, characteristics of effective informative speeches cross all categories. As you research, develop, and present your speech, keep the following 10 guidelines in mind.

Consider Your Audience's Needs and Goals

Concern for your audience is the theme of the book and applies here. The best informative speakers know what their listeners want to learn from their speech. A group of Weight Watchers members may be motivated to attend a lecture on dieting to learn how to lose weight, while nutritionists drawn to the same speech may need the information to help clients. Audience goals are also linked to knowledge. Those who lack knowledge about a topic may be more motivated to listen and learn than those who feel they already know the topic. However, it is possible that technology has changed, new information has surfaced, or new ways to think about or do something have emerged. The speaker needs to find a way to engage those who are less motivated.

Make connections between your subject and your audience's daily needs, desires, and interests. For example, some audience members might have no interest in a speech on the effectiveness of halfway houses until you tell them how much money is being spent on prisons locally, or better yet, how much each listener is spending per year. Now the topic is more relevant. People care about money, safety, prestige, family and friends, community, and their own growth and progress, among other things. Show how your topic influences one or more of these and you will have an audience motivated to listen.

Consider Your Audience's Knowledge Level

If you want to describe how to use eSnipe when participating in eBay auctions, you may be speaking to students who have never heard of it. To be safe, however, you might develop a brief pre-speech questionnaire to pass out to your class. Or you can select several individuals at random and ask what they know. You do not want to bore the class with mundane minutia, but you do not want to confuse them with information that is too advanced for their knowledge level. Consider this golf example:

> As the golf champion of your district, you decide to give your informative speech on the game. You begin by holding up a golf club and saying, "This is a golf club. They come in many sizes and styles." Then you hold up a golf ball. "This is a golf ball. Golf balls are all the same size, but they come in many colors. Most golf balls are white. When you first start playing golf, you need a lot of golf balls. So, you need a golf club and a golf ball to play golf."

Expect your listeners to yawn in this situation. They do not want to hear what they already know. Although your presentation may be effective for an audience of children who have never seen a golf club or ball, your presentation is too simplistic for adults.

Capture Attention and Interest Immediately

As an informative speaker, your goal is to communicate information about a specific topic in a way that is understandable to your listeners. In your introduction, you must first convince your audience that your topic is interesting and relevant. For example, if you are delivering a speech on white-collar crime, you might begin like this:

> Imagine taking part of your paycheck and handing it to a criminal. In an indirect way, that's what we all do to pay for white-collar crime. Part of the tax dollars you give the federal government goes into the hands of unscrupulous business executives who pad their expenses and overcharge the government by millions of dollars. For example, General Dynamics, the third-largest military supplier, tacked on at least $75 million to the government's bill for such "overhead" expenses as country-club fees and personal travel for corporate executives.

This approach is more likely to capture audience attention than a list of white-collar crimes or criminals.

Sustain Audience Attention and Interest by Being Creative, Vivid, and Enthusiastic

Try something different. Change your pace to bring attention or emphasis to a point. Aloud, say the following phrase at a regular rate, and then slow down and emphasize each word: "We must work together!" Slowing down to emphasize each word gives the sentence greater impact. Varying rate of speech is an effective way to sustain audience attention.

Show some excitement! Talking about accounting principles, water filters, or changes in planet designations with spirit and energy may keep people listening. Delivery can make a difference. Enthusiasm is infectious, even to those who have no particular interest in your subject. It is no accident that advertising campaigns are built around slogans, jingles, and other memorable language that people are likely to remember after a commercial is over. We are more likely to remember vivid language than dull language.

Cite Your Oral Sources Accurately

Citing sources accurately means putting in the work ahead of time to understand the source. Anytime you offer facts, statistics, opinions, and ideas that you found in research, you should provide your audience with the source. In doing this, you enhance your own credibility. Your audience appreciates your depth of research on the topic, and you avoid accusations of plagiarism.

Accurate source representation comes from having a well-rounded understanding of the source. Critical thinking is necessary when assessing the source you intend to use. Among other information, it makes sense to check out who the author is or what the source is, what bias, if any exists, what the intention of the author or source is, and what its intended use was.

Your audience needs enough information to judge the credibility of your sources. If you are describing how the HBO show *True Blood* became HBO's most popular show in recent years, it is not sufficient to say, "Jessica Gelt states ..." because Jessica Gelt's qualification to comment on this show may be based on the fact that she watches television regularly. However, by adding, "Jessica Gelt, reporter for the *LA Times*, states ...," we know she has more credibility.

Signpost Main Ideas

Your audience may need help keeping track of the information in your speech. Separating one idea from another may be difficult for listeners when trying to learn all the information at once. You can help your audience understand the structure of your speech by creating oral lists. Simple "First, second, third, fourth ..." or "one, two, three, four ..." helps the audience focus on your sequence of points. Here is an example of signposting:

> Having a motorized scooter in college instead of a car is preferred for two reasons. The first reason is financial. A scooter gets at least 80 miles per gallon. Over a period of four years, significant savings occur. The second reason a scooter is preferred in college is convenience. Parking problems are virtually eliminated. No longer do you have to worry about being late to class, because you can park in the motorcycle parking area. They're all around us.

Signposting at the beginning of a speech tells the audience how many points you have or how many ideas you intend to support. Signposting during the speech acts as a transition because it keeps the audience informed as to where you are in the speech.

Relate the New with the Familiar

Informative speeches should introduce new information in terms of what the audience already knows. Using metaphors, analogies, similes, and other forms of speech is useful. Here is an example of an analogy:

> A cooling-off period in labor–management negotiations is like a parentally imposed time-out. When we were children, our parents would send us to our rooms to think over what we had done. We were forbidden to come out for some time in the hope that by the time we were released, our tempers had cooled. Similarly, by law, the President can impose an 80-day cooling-off period if a strike threatens to imperil the nation's health or safety.

Most of us can relate to the "time-out" concept referred to in this example, so providing the analogy helps us understand the cooling-off period if a strike is possible. References to the familiar help listeners assimilate new information. Following is a metaphor for the recent economic crisis.

> The economy is a train wreck. The conductor saw the other train coming toward it, and thought the switchman would set the oncoming train onto the sidetrack and save the day. It didn't happen. The train completely derailed, leaving total destruction in its path.

This metaphor is a way to express visually the idea that banks hoped the regulators would cover their losses and stabilize the economy. Everyone is familiar with the concept of a train wreck, but understanding an economic crisis is not so easy. Using various language devices can help with the explanation.

Use Repetition

Repetition is important when presenting new facts and ideas. You help your listeners by reinforcing your main points through summaries and paraphrasing. For example, if you were trying to persuade your classmates to purchase a scooter instead of a car, you might have three points: (1) a scooter is cheaper than a car; (2) a scooter gets better gas mileage than a car; and (3) you can always find a nearby parking spot for your scooter. For your first point, you mention purchase price, insurance, and maintenance costs. As you finish your first point, you could say, "So a scooter is cheaper than a car in at least three ways, purchase price, insurance, and maintenance." You have already mentioned these three subpoints, but noting them as an internal summary before your second main point helps reinforce the idea that scooters are cheaper than cars.

Offer Interesting Visuals

As Cyphert (2007) states, "There is no doubt that good visual design can make information clearer and more interesting" (p. 170). He elaborates:

> Audience expectations have changed, not merely in terms of technical bells and whistles available in the creation of visual aids, but with respect to the culture's understanding of what it means to deliver an eloquent public address (p. 170).

Your audience expects you to put effort into your presentation. This means more than practicing. Using pictures, charts, models, PowerPoint slides, and other presentational aids helps maintain audience interest. Use humorous visuals to display statistics, if appropriate. Demonstrate the physics of air travel by throwing paper airplanes across the room. With ever-increasing computer accessibility and Wi-Fi in the classroom, using computer-generated graphics to enhance and underscore your main points and illustrations is a convenient and valuable way to inform your audience effectively.

Consider How to Respond to Audience Questions and Distractions

In an informative speech, your audience may have the opportunity to ask questions. Before you give your speech, decide whether you want questions during your presentation or at the end. If you prefer they wait, tell your audience early in your speech or at the first hand raised. Perhaps try, "I ask that you hold all questions to the end of this presentation, where I have built in some time for them."

When fielding questions, develop the habit of doing four things in this order: *thank* the questioner, *paraphrase* the question (put it in your own words), *answer* the question briefly, and then *ask* the questioner if you answered his/her question. Paraphrasing allows the speaker to stay in control of the situation by pointing questions in desirable directions or away from areas you are not willing to address.

For any question, you have five options: (1) answer it (Remember, "I do not know" is an answer), (2) bounce it back to the questioner ("Well, that is interesting. How might you answer that question?"), (3) bounce it to the audience ("I see, does anyone have any helpful thoughts about this?"), (4) defer the question until later ("Now you and I would find this interesting, but it is outside the scope of my message today. I'd love to chat with you individually about this in a moment"), and (5) promise more answers later ("I would really like to look further into that. May I get back to you later?"). Effective speakers know and use all five as strategies to keep their question-and-answer period productive and on track.

While questions may be expected, distractions are not. When random interruptions occur, do not ignore them. Call attention to the distraction. This allows your audience to get it out and then return their attention to you. One speaker was interrupted when a window washer suspended outside the building dropped into view, ropes and all. The speaker paused, looked at the dangling distraction and announced, "Spiderman!" Everyone laughed, and he then returned to his speech. At a banquet, a speaker was interrupted by the crash of shattering dishes from the direction of the kitchen. She quipped, "Sounds like someone lost a contact lens." Whether humorous or not, calling attention to distractions is key to maintaining control.

☞ Ethics of Informative Speaking

Think about the advertising you see on TV and the warning labels on certain products you purchase. After listening to a commercial about a new weight-loss tablet, you believe you have found a solution to get rid of those extra 20 pounds you carry with you. Several happy people testify about how wonderful the drug is, and how it worked miracles for them. At the end of the commercial, you hear a speaker say, "This drug is not for children under 16. It may cause diarrhea, restlessness, sleeplessness, nausea, and stomach cramps. It can lead to strokes and heart attacks. Those with high blood pressure, epilepsy, diabetes, or heart disease should not take this medicine ..." After listening to the warnings, the drug may not sound so miraculous. We have government regulations to make sure consumers make informed choices.

As an individual speaker, *you regulate yourself*. A speaker has ethical responsibilities, no matter what type of speech he or she prepares and delivers. The informative speeches you deliver in class and those you listen to on campus are not nearly as likely to affect the course of history as those delivered by high-ranking public officials in a time of war or national political campaigns. Even so, *the principles of ethical responsibility are similar for every speaker*.

The president of the United States, the president of your school, and the president of any organization to which you belong all have an obligation to inform their constituencies (audiences) in nonmanipulative ways and to provide them with information they need and have a right to know. Professors, doctors, police officers, and others engaged in informative speaking ought to tell the truth as they know it, and not withhold information to serve personal gain. You, like others, should always rely on credible sources and avoid what political scientists label as "calculated ambiguity." **Calculated ambiguity** is a speaker's planned effort to be vague, sketchy, and considerably abstract.

You have many choices to make as you prepare for an informative speech. Applying reasonable ethical standards will help with your decision-making. An informative speech requires you to assemble accurate, sound, and pertinent information that will enable you to tell your audience what you believe to be the truth. Relying on outdated information, not giving the audience enough information about your sources, omitting relevant information, being vague intentionally, and taking information out of context are all violations of ethical principles.

☞ Summary

A blurry line exists between informative, persuasive, and special-occasion speaking. Remember that in an informative speech your goal is to communicate information and ideas in a way that your audience will understand and remember. In a persuasive speech, your intent is to influence your audience in some way—to change attitudes or beliefs or to bring about a specific, desired action. In a special occasion speech, your goal is to entertain or commemorate. The key determinant in whether a speech is informative, persuasive, or entertaining is speaker intent.

Informative speeches fall into three categories. Speeches of description paint a picture of an event, person, object, place, situation, or concept; speeches of explanation deal with such abstractions as ideas, theories, principles, and beliefs; and speeches of demonstration focus on a process, describing the gradual changes that lead to a particular result.

Informative speakers should strive to be accurate, objective, clear, meaningful, and memorable. Preparing and delivering an effective informative speech involves applying the strategies identified in this chapter. To increase accuracy, make sure you question the source of information, consider the timeliness, and accurately cite your sources orally. Being objective includes taking into account all perspectives and showing trends. Crucial to any speech is clarity. To aid your audience, carefully organize your message, define unfamiliar words and concepts, signpost main ideas, relate the new with the familiar, and use repetition.

Audiences gather for different reasons. You want your speech to be meaningful to all listeners. In doing so, consider the setting, your audience's needs, goals and knowledge level, and avoid information overload. An informative speaker wants people to remember his or her speech. To meet that goal, capture attention and interest immediately, sustain audience attention and interest by being creative, vivid, and enthusiastic, use examples and humor, offer interesting visuals, and physically involve your audience.

As you prepare your informative speech, make sure the choices you make are based on a reasonable ethical standard. You have an obligation to be truthful as you prepare your speech and when you deliver it.

References

Cyphert, D. (2007). Presentation Technology in the Age of Electronic Eloquence: From Visual Aid to Visual Rhetoric. *Communication Education*, 56(2), 168–192.

Gregory, R. J. (2004). *Psychological Testing: History, Principles, and Application*. Needham, MA: Allyn & Bacon.

National Spiritualist Association of Churches. (2011). *Spiritualism. Definitions*. Retrieved June 16, 2011 from www.nsac.org/Definitions.aspx?id=3.0.

Official Slam Poetry History and Beliefs. Retrieved June 16, 2011 from slampapi.com.

Reaves, J. (2003). Interview: Sarah Weddington. *Time* (January 16). Retrieved September 1, 2011 from www.time.com/time/nation/article/0,8599,409103,00.html.

Rockoff, H. (1995). The 'Wizard of Oz' as a Monetary Allegory. In R. Whaples & D. C. Betts (Eds.), *Historical Perspective on the American Economy*. New York: Cambridge University Press.

Spiritualism. Retrieved June 16, 2011 from Kheper.net.

U.S. Department of Housing and Urban Development. *Buying a Home*. Retrieved June 17, 2011 from portal.hud.org.

Chapter 11

Persuasive Speaking

In a republican nation, whose citizens are to be led by reason and persuasion and not by force, the art of reasoning becomes of first importance.

– Thomas Jefferson

SPEECH: Teddy Roosevelt — Man with the Muck-Rake

President William McKinley was assassinated on September 14, 1901. Vice President Theodore Roosevelt (1858–1919) completed McKinley's second term. Roosevelt was then elected President of the United States in 1904. Roosevelt believed in the concept of a strong president; he spoke directly to the public in hopes of influencing Congress. He initiated presidential press conferences, which were then private and infrequent meetings with select members of the press. In the time leading up to the speech presented below, there were several media accounts of wide-ranging corruption — in politics, in the insurance industry, in the exploitation of African Americans, and in the unsanitary conditions in slaughterhouses. While pleased that these accounts encouraged the public to support government regulations, Roosevelt was increasingly concerned by the sensational nature of the reports. Roosevelt took the occasion of the laying of the cornerstone of the new congressional office building to address his concerns — an event that was of sufficient magnitude to garner considerable press coverage.

Source: Reid, Ronald F. (1995). *American Rhetorical Discourse* (2nd ed.). Prospect Heights, IL: Waveland Press, pp. 673–675.

Theodore Roosevelt
The Man with the Muck-rake

delivered 14 April 1906

Over a century ago Washington laid the corner stone of the Capitol in what was then little more than a tract of wooded wilderness here beside the Potomac. We now find it necessary to provide by great additional buildings for the business of the government.

This growth in the need for the housing of the government is but a proof and example of the way in which the nation has grown and the sphere of action of the national government has grown. We now administer the affairs of a nation in which the extraordinary growth of population has been outstripped by the growth of wealth in complex interests. The material problems that face us today are not such as they were in Washington's time, but the underlying facts of human nature are the same now as they were then. Under altered external form we war with the same tendencies toward evil that were evident in Washington's time, and are helped by the same tendencies for good. It is about some of these that I wish to say a word today.

In Bunyan's "Pilgrim's Progress" you may recall the description of the Man with the Muck Rake, the man who could look no way but downward, with the muck rake in his hand; who was offered a celestial crown for his muck rake, but who would neither look up nor regard the crown he was offered, but continued to rake to himself the filth of the floor.

In "Pilgrim's Progressy" the Man with the Muck Rake is set forth as the example of him whose vision is fixed on carnal instead of spiritual things. Yet he also typifies the man who in this life consistently refuses to see aught that is lofty, and fixes his eyes with solemn intentness only on that which is vile and debasing.

Now, it is very necessary that we should not flinch from seeing what is vile and debasing. There is filth on the floor, and it must be scraped up with the muck rake; and there are times and places where this service is the most needed of all the services that can be performed. But the man who never does anything else, who never thinks or speaks or writes, save of his feats with the muck rake, speedily becomes, not a help but one of the most potent forces for evil.

There are in the body politic, economic and social, many and grave evils, and there is urgent necessity for the sternest war upon them. There should be relentless exposure of and attack upon every evil man, whether politician or business man, every evil practice, whether in politics, business, or social life. I hail as a benefactor every writer or speaker, every man who, on the platform or in a book, magazine, or newspaper, with merciless severity makes such attack, provided always that he in his turn remembers that the attack is of use only if it is absolutely truthful.

The liar is no whit better than the thief, and if his mendacity takes the form of slander he may be worse than most thieves. It puts a premium upon knavery untruthfully to attack an honest man, or even with hysterical exaggeration to assail a bad man with untruth.

An epidemic of indiscriminate assault upon character does no good, but very great harm. The soul of every scoundrel is gladdened whenever an honest man is assailed, or even when a scoundrel is untruthfully assailed.

Now, it is easy to twist out of shape what I have just said, easy to affect to misunderstand it, and if it is slurred over in repetition not difficult really to misunderstand it. Some persons are sincerely incapable of understanding that to denounce mud slinging does not mean the endorsement of whitewashing; and both the interested individuals who need whitewashing and those others who practice mud slinging like to encourage such confusion of ideas.

One of the chief counts against those who make indiscriminate assault upon men in business or men in public life is that they invite a reaction which is sure to tell powerfully in favor of the unscrupulous scoundrel who really ought to be attacked, who ought to be exposed, who ought, if possible, to be put in the penitentiary. If Aristides is praised

As a matter of personal conviction, and without pretending to discuss the details or formulate the system, I feel that we shall ultimately have to consider the adoption of some such scheme as that of a progressive tax on all fortunes, beyond a certain amount, either given in life or devised or bequeathed upon death to any individual-a tax so framed as to put it out of the power of the owner of one of these enormous fortunes to hand on more than a certain amount to any one individual; the tax of course, to be imposed by the national and not the state government. Such taxation should, of course, be aimed merely at the inheritance or transmission in their entirety of those fortunes swollen beyond all healthy limits. Again, the national government must in some form exercise supervision over corporations engaged in interstate business-and all large corporations engaged in interstate business-whether by license or otherwise, so as to permit us to deal with the far reaching evils of overcapitalization.

This year we are making a beginning in the direction of serious effort to settle some of these economic problems by the railway rate legislation. Such legislation, if so framed, as I am sure it will be, as to secure definite and tangible results, will amount to something of itself; and it will amount to a great deal more in so far as it is taken as a first step in the direction of a policy of superintendence and control over corporate wealth engaged in interstate commerce; this superintendence and control not to be exercised in a spirit of malevolence toward the men who have created the wealth, but with the firm purpose both to do justice to them and to see that they in their turn do justice to the public at large.

The first requisite in the public servants who are to deal in this shape with corporations, whether as legislators or as executives, is honesty. This honesty can be no respecter of persons. There can be no such thing as unilateral honesty. The danger is not really from corrupt corporations; it springs from the corruption itself, whether exercised for or against corporations.

The eighth commandment reads, "Thou shalt not steal." It does not read, "Thou shalt not steal from the rich man." It does not read, "Thou shalt not steal from the poor man." It reads simply and plainly, "Thou shalt not steal."

No good whatever will come from that warped and mock morality which denounces the misdeeds of men of wealth and forgets the misdeeds practiced at their expense; which denounces bribery, but blinds itself to blackmail; which foams with rage if a corporation secures favors by improper methods, and merely leers with hideous mirth if the corporation is itself wronged.

The only public servant who can be trusted honestly to protect the rights of the public against the misdeeds of a corporation is that public man who will just as surely protect the corporation itself from wrongful aggression.

If a public man is willing to yield to popular clamor and do wrong to the men of wealth or to rich corporations, it may be set down as certain that if the opportunity comes he will secretly and furtively do wrong to the public in the interest of a corporation.

But in addition to honesty, we need sanity. No honesty will make a public man useful if that man is timid or foolish, if he is a hot-headed zealot or an impracticable visionary. As we strive for reform we find that it is not at all merely the case of a long uphill pull. On the contrary, there is almost as much of breeching work as of collar work. To depend only on traces means that there will soon be a runaway and an upset.

The men of wealth who today are trying to prevent the regulation and control of their business in the interest of the public by the proper government authorities will not succeed, in my judgment, in checking the progress of the movement. But if they did succeed they would find that they had sown the wind and would surely reap the whirlwind, for they would ultimately provoke the violent excesses which accompany a reform coming by convulsion instead of by steady and natural growth.

On the other hand, the wild preachers of unrest and discontent, the wild agitators against the entire existing order, the men who act crookedly, whether because of sinister design or from mere puzzle headedness, the men who preach destruction without proposing any substitute for what they intend to destroy, or who propose a substitute which would be far worse than the existing evils-all these men are the most dangerous opponents of real reform. If they get their way they will lead the people into a deeper pit than any into which they could fall under the present system. If they fail to get their way they will still do incalculable harm by provoking the kind of reaction which in its revolt against the senseless evil of their teaching would enthrone more securely than ever the evils which their misguided followers believe they are attacking.

More important than aught else is the development of the broadest sympathy of man for man. The welfare of the wage worker, the welfare of the tiller of the soil, upon these depend the welfare of the entire country; their good is not to be sought in pulling down others; but their good must be the prime object of all our statesmanship.

Materially we must strive to secure a broader economic opportunity for all men, so that each shall have a better chance to show the stuff of which he is made. Spiritually and ethically we must strive to bring about clean living and right thinking. We appreciate that the things of the body are important; but we appreciate also that the things of the soul are immeasurably more important.

The foundation stone of national life is, and ever must be, the high individual character of the average citizen.

You cannot escape attempts at persuasion. Either you are the one trying to convince someone of something, or you are the target of the persuasive act. Without consciously thinking about it, much of your communication is persuasive. Through persuasion, you try to make your life better by influencing those around you. On an *interpersonal level*, you attempt to:

* Convince your friend to go to dinner with you; thus enjoying time with a friend.
* Persuade someone to share an apartment with you; thus giving you companionship and saving you money on rent.

On a *professional level*, persuasion can enhance your life. Perhaps you try to:

* Persuade your supervisor to recommend you for promotion; thus giving you money and/ or, perhaps, prestige.
* Convince your employer to fund your trip to a conference; thus allowing you to make professional contacts and gain more knowledge of your profession.

On the *societal level*, persuasion is used to get people to change attitudes or change behaviors so society can improve. Perhaps you to try to:

* Convince your legislator to vote in favor of a health bill that will reduce health care costs for all citizens.
* Persuade your local city council to enact curbside recycling so less household waste goes to the local landfill.

Many times throughout the day, we try to convince people to agree with us about small things ("Xbox is better than Wii") and significant things ("We shouldn't have children"). The reverse is also true. Through emails, IMs, advertisements, commercials, infomercials, and conversations, others attempt to influence you. Persuasion permeates your life, all day, every day. The ability to influence is the cornerstone of our democratic republic.

Learning the tools of persuasion helps you become a stronger advocate for what matters in your life. Everything from your daily interactions and friendships to your career advancements is linked to your persuasive abilities. Those who study persuasion gain a competitive edge.

The Audience in Persuasive Speaking

Imagine the following situations:

* You speak before your church's congregation to persuade them to vote to withdraw from your church's national organization because of the church's stance on gay clergy.
* You talk to a student group on campus about the benefits of spending a semester with the Disney College Program in Orlando, Florida.
* You speak before your city council, urging them to implement a curbside recycling program.
* You speak before a group of parents of the high school musical cast to get them to volunteer to help make tickets, sell tickets, sell concessions, monitor students during rehearsal, work on the set, work backstage, sell advertisements, work with costume rental, and design and sell T-shirts.

Your success or failure to get your audience to act in the situations above is determined by a number of factors. Knowing who your listeners are is important, as we discussed in an earlier chapter. But, in a persuasive speech, knowing *the attitude of your audience* is crucial, and trying to *determine the needs* of the audience is important to your success.

In general, we can classify audience attitudes into three categories: (1) they agree, (2) they don't agree, (3) they are undecided. When you are clear on which category your audience rests in, you will be able to craft a more targeted, effective message. Here is a closer examination of each category.

The **supportive audience**, the audience that agrees with you, poses the least difficulty. This type of audience is friendly; its members like you, and they are interested in hearing what you have to say. Your main objective is to reinforce what they already accept. You want to strengthen their resolve or use it to encourage behavioral change. You also want to keep them enthused about your point of view or action plan. A candidate for state's attorney who has invited a group of friends and colleagues to an ice cream social will use that time to restate his/her strengths and urge attendees to help him/her with the campaign.

The audience that agrees with you will welcome *new* information, but does not need a re-hashing of information already known and accepted. The speaker should work to strengthen the audience's resistance to counterpersuasion. For example, the candidate for state's attorney who is running against an incumbent can talk about how change is necessary, and how his/her experience or background will bring a fresh perspective to the office.

With the **opposed audience**, the speaker runs the risk of having members in the audience who may be hostile. This audience does not agree with you, it is not friendly or sympathetic, and most likely, will search for flaws in your argument. Your objective in this case is to get a fair hearing. A persuasive speaker facing a group that does not agree with him/her needs to set reasonable goals. Also, developing arguments carefully by using fair and respected evidence may help persuade an audience that disagrees with you.

One thing to consider when facing an audience opposed to you is the nature of their opposition. Is it to you? Your cause? A specific statement you made or information made available to them? If you can determine why they are opposed, your effort can be spent on addressing the nature of the opposition.

Seeking common ground is a good strategy when people do not agree with you. Find a place where you and your audience can stand without disagreeing. For example, hospital employees who smoke may not be willing to quit, but they may recognize the need to have smoking banned on hospital property, so they may still smoke on break if they go off-site.

Acknowledging differences is also a helpful strategy for the opposed audience. Making sure you do not set your attitudes, beliefs, or values to be "right" and the audience's to be "wrong" is essential if any movement toward your point of view is likely. Avoid needless confrontation.

Speaking before an **uncommitted audience** can be difficult because you don't know whether they are uninformed, indifferent, or are adamantly neutral. This audience is neither friendly nor hostile, but most likely, they are not sympathetic.

The uninformed audience is the easiest to persuade, because they need information. A scholarship committee trying to determine which of the five candidates will receive $2,000 needs sufficient information about the candidates to make an informed choice.

The indifferent audience member doesn't really care about the issue or topic. These audience members can be found in most "mandatory" meetings held at work, school, and sometimes training. In this case, it is important that the speaker gets the attention of the audience members and gives them a reason to care. Making the message relate to their lives is important, and providing audience members with relevant, persuasive material helps move audience members out of the uncommitted category. However, it may be difficult to sway most or all audience members.

Maslow's Hierarchy of Needs

Knowing the audience's disposition toward you helps you structure a more effective persuasive speech. Speakers should also consider the needs of the audience. The persuader can develop lines of reasoning that relate to pertinent needs. Human needs can be described in terms of logic or what makes sense to a listener, but needs are immersed in emotions of the individual as well.

Psychologist Abraham Maslow (1943) classified human needs according to the hierarchy pictured in **Figure 11.1**. Maslow believed that our most basic needs—those at the foundation of the hierarchy—must be satisfied before we can consider those on the next levels. In effect, these higher-level needs are put on "hold," and have little effect on our actions until the lower-level needs are met. Maslow's hierarchy provides a catalog of targets for emotional appeals, including:

Physiological needs At the foundation of the hierarchy are our biological needs for food, water, oxygen, procreation, and rest. If you were delivering a speech in favor of a proposed new reservoir to a community experiencing problems with its water supply, it would be appropriate to appeal to our very basic need for safe and abundant water, without which, our lives would be in danger.

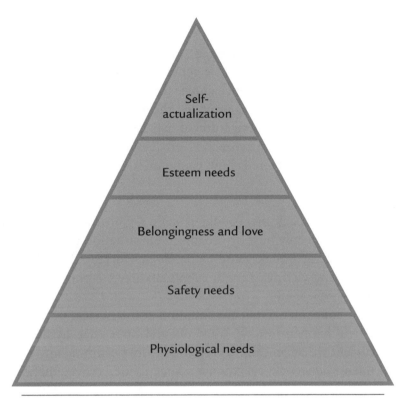

FIGURE 11.1   Maslow's Hierarchy of Needs

Safety needs. Safety needs include the need for security, freedom from fear and attack, a home that offers tranquility and comfort, and a means of earning a living. If you are delivering the same speech to a group of unemployed construction workers, you might link the reservoir project to safe, well-paying jobs and a steady family income.

Belongingness and love needs. These needs refer to our drive for affiliation, friendship, and love. When appealing to the need for social belonging, you may choose to emphasize the unity and cohesiveness that will emerge from the community effort to bring the reservoir to completion.

Esteem needs. Esteem needs include the need to be seen as worthy and competent and to have the respect of others. In this case, an effective approach would be to praise community members for their initiative in helping to make the reservoir project a reality.

Self-actualization needs. People who reach the top of the hierarchy seek to fulfill their highest potential through personal growth, creativity, self-awareness and knowledge, social responsibility, and responsiveness to challenge. Addressing this audience, you might emphasize the long-range environmental and ecological implications of the reservoir. Your appeal to your audience's sense of social responsibility would stress the need to safeguard the water supply for future generations.

Maslow's Hierarchy of Needs can guide you in preparing a persuasive speech. Think about the needs of your audience and how you can reach them. Understanding the basis for Maslow's hierarchy is helpful when developing a persuasive speech, for if you approach your listeners at an inappropriate level of need, you will find them unable or unwilling to respond.

👉 Elements of Persuasion

We define persuasion as attempting to influence others through communication. Critical building blocks of persuasion have been studied by generations of rhetorical scholars, starting with Aristotle. Persuasion is intended to influence choice through what Aristotle termed *ethos*, *pathos*, and *logos*. More recent scholarly work has provided the addition of *mythos*. These four elements provide the underpinnings of our modern study of persuasion.

To illustrate these, let's consider the speech given days after the deadly earthquake, tsunami, nd nuclear disaster struck Japan. Here is how Emperor Akihito addressed a stunned nation on 1arch 16, 2011:

> The 9.0 earthquake that struck the Tohoku-Pacific region was an extraordinarily large earthquake. I have been deeply hurt by the miserable situation in the affected areas. The number of deaths from earthquakes and tsunamis has increased day by day, and we do not know yet how many victims we will eventually have. I pray for the survival of as nany people as possible.
>
> I am also deeply concerned about the situation at the nuclear power plant, as no one an predict what will happen next. It is my deepest hope that, by the effort of people concerned, the current situation can be prevented from becoming any worse.
>
> Currently, a nationwide rescue operation is taking place … (www.americanrhetoric.com)

Emperor Akihito relied heavily on ethos in his speech, as we will see later with other excerpts.

Ethos and the Power of the Speaker's Credibility

As speaker, you must decide not only what to tell your audience, but also what you should avoid saying. In a persuasive speech, you ask listeners to think or act in ways needed to achieve a desired response. Aristotle believed that **ethos**, which refers to speaker credibility, makes speakers worthy of belief. Audiences trust speakers they perceive as honest. Ethics provide standards for conduct that guide us. Persuasive speaking requires asking others to accept and act on ideas we believe to be accurate and true.

We see the Japanese emperor standing on the firm ground of the credibility of his office. In Japanese culture, the emperor has typically been recognized as both statesman-ruler and messenger from God. When the emperor spoke, everyone listened, due in large part to his inherent credibility. Let's take a closer look at what makes up an impression of ethos or speaker credibility.

Dimensions of Speaker Credibility

What your audience knows about you before you speak and what they learn about your position during your speech may influence your ability to persuade them. Credibility can be measured according to three dimensions: competence, trustworthiness, and dynamism.

Competence. In many cases, your audience will decide your message's value based on perceived speaker competence. Your listeners will first ask themselves whether you have the background to speak. If the topic is crime, an audience is more likely to be persuaded by the Atlanta chief of police than by a postal worker delivering her personal opinions. Second, your audience will consider whether the content of your speech has firm support. When it is clear that speakers have not researched their topic, their ability to persuade diminishes. Finally, audiences will determine whether you communicate confidence and control of your subject matter through your delivery.

In our example above, Emperor Akihito makes clear that he is abreast of all the relevant information. He relays the strength of the earthquake, the results of the tsunami, and the seriousness of the nuclear disaster. Listeners quickly understood that he was well informed in this emergency. His display of competence by demonstrating an understanding of the facts increases his credibility even further.

Trustworthiness. When someone is trying to persuade us to think or act a certain way, trusting that person is important. And although competence is important, research has shown that the trustworthy communicator is more influential than the untrustworthy one, regardless of his/her level of expertise (Pornpitakpan, 2004).

Audience perceptions of trustworthiness are based largely on your perceived respect for them, your ethical standards, and your ability to establish common ground. Audiences gauge a speaker's *respect* for them by analyzing the actions a speaker has taken before the speech. If a group is listening to a political candidate running for office in their community, they will have more respect for someone who has demonstrated concern for their community through past actions.

Trustworthiness is also influenced by the audience's perception of your *ethical standards*. Telling the truth is paramount for the persuasive speaker. If your message is biased and you make little attempt to be fair or to concede the strength of your opponent's point of view, your listeners may question your integrity.

Your credibility and your ability to persuade increase if you convince your audience that you share "common ground." In the popular movie *300*, Queen Gorgo addresses a reluctant Spartan Council, pleading with them to send the Spartan army into battle. Rather than appealing to the council as queen, she is made to appeal to common ground in the opening: "Councilmen, I stand before you today not only as your Queen: I come to you as a mother; I come to you as a wife; I come to you as a Spartan woman; I come to you with great humility" (www.americanrhetoric.com).

While few can identify with being a queen, most feel a sense of identification with a humble mother, wife, woman, or citizen. With this common ground appeal in place, the stage is set for the queen to persuade the council to side with her. In this instance, Queen Gorgo establishes common ground by identifying with her audience and provoking them to identify with her.

Dynamism. Your credibility and, therefore, your ability to persuade are influenced by the audience's perception of you as a dynamic spokesperson. Dynamic speakers tend to be vibrant, confident, vigorous, attractive, and skilled in public speaking. Your listeners will make critical decisions about how dynamic you are as they form a first impression. This impression will be reinforced or altered as they listen for an energetic style that communicates commitment to your point of view, and for ideas that build on one another in a convincing, logical way. While charisma plays a part in being dynamic, it is not enough. Dynamic public speakers tend to be well-practiced presenters.

Does credibility make a difference in your ability to persuade? Pornitakpan (2004), who examined five decades of research on the persuasiveness of speaker credibility, found that "a high-credibility source is more persuasive than is a low-credibility source in both changing attitudes and gaining behavioral compliance" (p. 266). Lifelong learning in the art of persuasion involves building and enhancing your speaker competence, trustworthiness, and dynamism.

Pathos and the Power of Emotion

Aristotle argued that **pathos**, which is the "consideration of the emotions of people in the audience" is an integral part of persuasion (Kennedy, 2007, p. 15). Aristotle explained:

> The emotions are those things through which, by undergoing change, people come to differ in their judgments and which are accompanied by pain and pleasure, for example, anger, pity, fear, and other such things and their opposites" (Aristotle, 2007).

Emperor Akihito makes use of emotion in his message. Although stoic by American standards, he acknowledges the suffering of victims:

> [U]nder the severe cold weather, many evacuees have been placed in an unavoidable situation where they are subject to extreme suffering due to the lack of food, drinking water, fuel, and so on. I truly hope that, by making the greatest effort possible to rescue the victims promptly, we can improve their lives as much as possible" (www .americanrhetoric.com).

Akihito's reference to extreme suffering adds an emotional appeal to support the need for continued rescue efforts.

Emotional appeals have the power to elicit happiness, joy, pride, patriotism, fear, hate, anger, guilt, despair, hope, hopelessness, bitterness, and other feelings. Some subjects are more emotionally powerful than others and lend themselves to emotional appeals. Look at the list of topics that follow:

* The homeless
* Abused children
* Cruelty to animals
* Death penalty
* Sex education in school
* Teaching evolution in school
* Gun control
* Terrorist attacks

Many of these topics cause listeners to have emotional responses. Emotional appeals are often the most persuasive type of appeal because they provide the motivation listeners need to change their minds or take action. For example, instead of simply listing the reasons high fat foods are unhealthy, a more effective approach is to tie these foods to frightening consequences:

> Jim thought nothing could ever happen to him. He was healthy as an ox—or so he thought. His world fell apart one sunny May morning when he suffered a massive heart attack. He survived, but his doctors told him that his coronary arteries were blocked and that he needed bypass surgery. "Why me?" he asked. "I'm only 42 years old." The answer, he was told, had a lot to do with the high-fat diet he had eaten since childhood.

This illustration appeals to the listener's emotional state, and is ultimately more persuasive than a list of facts.

We must not forget that emotional appeals are powerful, and as such, can be tools of manipulation in the hands of unscrupulous speakers who attempt to arouse audiences through emotion rather than logic. For example, in an effort to lose weight, individuals may buy pills or exercise equipment that may be useless, or worse, a true health risk. Those selling the products accept the emotional message ("lose weight, look beautiful, gain friends, have a great life").

The speaker has an ethical responsibility when using emotional appeals. The ethically responsible speaker does not distort, delete, or exaggerate information for the sole purpose of emotionally charging an audience to manipulate their feelings for self-centered ends.

Logos and the Power of Logical Appeals and Arguments

Logos, or logical appeals and arguments, refer to the "rational, factual basis that supports the speaker's position" (Walker, 2005, p. 3). For example, if a friend tried to convince you *not* to buy a new car by pointing out that you are in college, have no savings account, and are currently unemployed, that friend would be making a logical argument.

Anatomy of an Argument: Claim, Data, Warrant

Logical, critical thinking increases your ability to *assess*, *analyze*, and *advocate* ideas. Decades ago, Stephen Toulmin (1958), a British philosopher, developed a model of practical reasoning that consists of three basic elements: claim, data, and warrant. To construct a sound, reasonable argument, you need to use three essential parts:

1. The **claim** is a statement or contention the audience is urged to accept. The claim answers the question, "So what is your point?

    Example: It's your turn to do the dishes; I did them last time.
    Example: You need to call your sister this week; She called you last week.

2. The **data** are evidence in support of an idea you advocate. Data provide the answer to "So what is your proof?" or "Why?"

    Example: It looks like rain. Dark clouds are forming.
    Example: When I stop at McDonald's on the road, they seem to have clean bathrooms.

3. The **warrant** is an inference that links the evidence with the claim. It answers the question, "Why does that data mean your claim is true?"

Example: Augie is running a fever. I bet he has an ear infection.
Example: Sarah will be on time. There isn't any traffic right now.

To put the three elements of an argument together, let's consider another example. At a restaurant, u take a bite of a steak sandwich and say, "This is the worst sandwich I have ever tried." With this announcement you are making a *claim* that you *infer* from tasting the meat.

The evidence (*data*) is the food before you. The *warrant* is the link between data and claim is the inference, which may be an *unstated belief* that the food is spoiled, old, or poorly prepared, and will taste bad.

When you reason with your audience it is important to craft claims, warrants, and data your audience will understand and accept. Sound reasoning is especially important when your audience is skeptical. Faced with the task of trying to convince people to change their minds or do something they might not otherwise be inclined to do, your arguments must be impressive.

We persuade others that a claim or conclusion is highly probable by **inductive** and **deductive reasoning**. Strong evidence shows that you have carefully analyzed the support of your points. Only when strong probability is established can you ask your listeners to make *the inductive leap* from specific cases to a general conclusion, or to take the *deductive* move from statements as premises to a conclusion you want them to accept. We now look more closely at inductive and deductive reasoning.

Inductive Reasoning

Through inductive reasoning, we generalize from specific examples to draw conclusions from what we observe. Inductive reasoning moves us from the specific to the general in an orderly, logical fashion. The inference step in the argument holds that what is true of specific cases can be generalized to other cases of the same class, or of the class as a whole. Suppose you are trying to persuade your audience that the decline of downtown merchants in your town is a problem that can be solved with an effective plan you are about to present. You may infer that what has worked to solve a similar problem in a number of similar towns is likely to work in this case as well.

One problem with inductive reasoning is that individual cases do not always add up to a correct conclusion. Sometimes a speaker's list of examples is too small, leading to an incorrect conclusion based on limited information. With inductive reasoning, you can never be sure that your conclusions are absolutely accurate. Because you are only looking at a sample of all the possible cases, you must persuade your audience to accept a conclusion that is probable, or maybe even just possible. The three most common strategies for inductive reasoning involve analogy, cause, and sign.

Reasoning by Analogy

Analogies establish common links between similar and not-so-similar concepts. They are effective tools of persuasion when your audience is convinced that the characteristics of one case are similar enough to the characteristics of the second case that your argument about the first also applies to the second.

As noted in the chapter on language, a *figurative analogy* draws a comparison between things that are distinctly different, such as "Eating fresh marshmallows is like floating on a cloud." Figurative analogies can be used to persuade, but they must be supported with relevant facts, statistics, and testimony that link the dissimilar concepts you are comparing.

Whereas a figurative analogy compares things that are distinctly different and supplies useful illustrations, a *literal analogy* compares things with similar characteristics and, therefore, requires less explanatory support. One speaker compared the addictive power of tobacco products, especially cigarettes, with the power of alcoholic beverages consumed on a regular basis. His line of reasoning was that both are consumed for pleasure, relaxation, and often as relief for stress. While his use of logical argument was obvious, the listener ultimately assesses whether or not these two things—alcohol and tobacco are sufficiently similar.

The distinction between literal and figurative analogies is important because only literal analogies are sufficient to establish logical proof. Your analogy should meet the following characteristics:

* There are significant points of similarity.
* Similarities are tied to critical points of the comparison.
* Differences need to be relatively small.
* You have a better chance of convincing people if you can point to other successful cases (Freely, 1993, pp. 119–120).

Reasoning from Cause

When you reason from cause, you infer that an event of one kind contributes to or brings about an event of another kind. The presence of a cat in a room when you are allergic to cats is likely to bring about a series of sneezes until the cat is removed. As the following example demonstrates, causal reasoning focuses on the cause-and-effect relationship between ideas.

> **Cause:** An inaccurate and low census count of the homeless in Detroit
> **Effect:** Fewer federal dollars will be sent to Detroit to aid the homeless

An advocate for the homeless delivered the following message to a group of supporters:

> We all know that money is allocated by the federal government, in part, according to the numbers of people in need. The census, conducted every 10 years, is supposed to tell us how many farmers we have, how many urban dwellers, and how many homeless.
>
> Unfortunately, in the 2010 census, many of the homeless were not counted in Detroit. The government told us census takers would go into the streets, into bus and train station waiting rooms, and into the shelters to count every homeless person. As advocates for the homeless, people in my organization know this was not done. Shelters were never visited. Hundreds and maybe thousands of homeless were ignored in this city alone.

A serious undercount is inevitable. This undercount will cause fewer federal dollars to be spent aiding those who need our help the most.

When used correctly, causal reasoning can be an effective persuasive tool. You must be sure that the cause-and-effect relationship is sound enough to stand up to scrutiny and criticism. To be valid, your reasoning should exhibit the following characteristics:

* The cause and effect you describe should be connected.
* The cause should be acting alone.
* The effect should not be the effect of another cause.
* The claim and evidence must be accurate (Sprague & Stuart, 1988, pp. 165–166).

To be effective, causal reasoning should never overstate. By using phrases like "This is one of several causes" or "The evidence suggests there is a cause-and-effect link," you are giving your audience a reasonable picture of a complex situation. More often than not, researchers indicate that cause-and-effect relationships are not always clear, and links may not be as simple as they seem.

Reasoning from Sign

With the argument from sign, the inference step is that the presence of an attribute can be taken as the presence of some larger condition or situation of which the attribute is a part. As you step outside in the early morning to begin jogging, the gray clouds and moist air can be interpreted as signs that the weather conditions are likely to result in a rainy day.

Argumentation professor David Vancil (1993) tells us that "arguments from sign are based on our understanding of the way things are associated or related to each other in the world with them, [so] we conclude that the thing is present if its signs are present. The claim of a sign argument is invariably a statement that something is or is not the case" (p. 149).

The public speaker who reasons from sign must do so with caution. Certainly there are signs all around us to interpret in making sense of the world, but signs are easy to misinterpret. For example, saying, "Where there's fire, there's smoke" is a strong sign relationship, but saying, "Where there's smoke, there's fire," is not so strong. Therefore, the responsible speaker must carefully test an argument before using it to persuade an audience.

Deductive Reasoning

Through deductive reasoning, we draw conclusions based on the connections between statements that serve as premises. Rather than introducing new facts, deductions enable us to rearrange the facts we already know, putting them in a form that will make our point. Deductive reasoning is the basis of police work and scientific research, enabling investigators to draw relationships between seemingly unrelated pieces of information.

At the heart of deductive reasoning is the *syllogism*, a pattern of reasoning involving a major premise, a minor premise, and a conclusion. When deductive reasoning is explicitly stated as a complete syllogism, it leads us down an inescapable logical path. The interrelationships in a syllogism can be established in a series of deductive steps:

Step 1: Define the relationship between two terms.
Major premise: Plagiarism is a form of ethical abuse.

Step 2: Define a condition or special characteristic of one of the terms.
Minor premise: Plagiarism involves using the words of another without quotations or footnotes as well as improper footnoting.

Step 3: Show how a conclusion about the other term necessarily follows (Sprague & Stuart, 1988, p. 160).
Conclusion: Students who use the words of another, but fail to use quotations or footnotes to indicate this or who intentionally use incorrect footnotes are guilty of an ethical abuse.

Your ability to convince your listeners depends on their acceptance of your original premises and the conclusion you draw from them. The burden of proof rests with your evidence. You must convince listeners through the strength of your supporting material to accept your premises and, by extension, your conclusion.

Sound and reasonable statements that employ inductive and deductive reasoning are the foundation for effective persuasion. More recently, scholars have recognized the story or narrative as a powerful persuasive appeal they call *mythos*.

Mythos and the Power of Narratives

Humans are storytellers by nature. Long before the written word people used narratives to capture, preserve, and pass on their cultural identity. Within the last several decades, scholars have begun to recognize the power of stories, folklore, anecdotes, legends, and myths to persuade (Osborn, 1990). **Mythos** is the term given when content supports a claim by reminding an audience how the claim is consistent with cultural identity.

The strength of the mythos depends on how accurately it ties into preexisting attitudes, values, histories, norms, and behaviors for a cultural, national, familial, or other collective. For example, when you were a child, you may have been told stories of the boy who cried wolf. Every culture has similar myths and stories that define what is unique and important to that culture. In the case of the boy who cried wolf, the cultural value is honesty and the intent is to teach children that bad things happen when we lie.

When speakers use mythos effectively, they create common ground with their listeners. If you were addressing an American audience and chided them to not listen to "that little boy who cries wolf" when refuting claims of an impending economic crises, your audience will likely be receptive to your position because of the common ground you invoked through their understanding of the myth.

Mythos may not work as well when the argument is inconsistent with other, stronger cultural myths, however. So, if you offered the same retort of the boy crying wolf in response to allegations that you have engaged in illegal, illicit activities, including collusion, embezzlement, and racketeering, the audience will be less likely to agree with your claim of innocence. They are more likely instead to reject the comparison you are drawing to the myth of the boy crying wolf, and instead decide "sometimes cries are warranted, you crook."

Recall the example of Japan's emperor addressing his people following their calamity. Notice how mythos is employed in the following statement that ties the perceived virtues of a disciplined, collectivist orientation to the need for order and calm solidarity:

> I have been informed that there are many people abroad discussing how calm the Japanese have remained—helping one another, and showing disciplined conduct, even though they are in deep grief. I hope from the bottom of my heart that we can continue getting together and helping and being considerate of one another to overcome this unfortunate time.

The extent to which Emperor Akihito's audience embraces these collectivist ideals reflects a cultural value that becomes a reason for pride in their actions that are consistent with these values.

Aristotle offers the advice of employing all available means when crafting persuasive messages. Availing yourself of ethos, pathos, logos, and mythos brings a balanced, well-received message much of the time. Critical thinking is essential for both persuasive speakers and effective listeners if strong, reasonable arguments are the goal. Recognizing fallacies is an important aspect of critical thinking and can prevent poor arguments from leading us astray.

Argument Fallacies

Sometimes speakers develop arguments either intentionally or unintentionally that contain faulty logic of some kind. A *fallacy* is traditionally regarded as an argument that seems plausible but turns out on close examination to be misleading (Hample et al., 2009). So whether the speaker intended to misuse evidence or reasoning to complete his/her persuasive goal, the result is that the audience is led to believe something that is not true. Following are six oft-used fallacies.

Attacking the person. Also known as *ad hominem* ("to the man"), this occurs when a speaker attacks the person rather than the substance of the person's argument. A personal attack is often a cover-up for lack of evidence or solid reasoning. Name calling and labeling are common with this fallacy, and the public is exposed to the ad hominem fallacy regularly through political shenanigans. While fallacies do not meet ethical standards, politicians been elected based on attacks on their opponents rather than refuting stances on issues.

Tina Fey, who won an Emmy award for her spoof of then–vice presidential candidate Sarah Palin, notes that those who dislike her do not identify evidence that she is not funny or original. Instead, she says, "Let's face it, ... there is a certain 50 percent of the population who think we are pinko Commie monsters" (Hirsen, 2011).

Red herring. A **red herring** occurs when a speaker attempts to divert the attention of the audience from the matter at hand. Going off on a tangent, changing the focus of the argument, engaging in personal attacks, or appealing to popular prejudice are all examples of the red herring fallacy.

The red herring fallacy appears regularly in interpersonal communication. A son might be told to "take your shoes off the table," and retort with, "these are boots, not shoes," thus changing the focus of the argument from the issue to the object. In a public speaking environment, red herrings are relatively common. For example, suppose an audience member asks a candidate at a political debate the following: "Do you realize your proposal to bring in a new megastore will result in the loss of livelihood for owners of smaller businesses in town who are active, contributing members to this community? A red herring response might be: "I think everyone likes to shop for bargains!"

Hasty generalization. A **hasty generalization** is a fallacy based on quantity of data. A faulty argument occurs because the sample chosen is too small or is in some way not representative. Therefore, any conclusion based on this information is flawed. Stereotypes about people are common examples of this fallacy. Imagine getting a B on a test, and asking the students on your right and left what grade they received. Finding out they also received a B on the test, you tell your roommates that "everybody received a B on the test."

Suppose you're in a public speaking class that you think is easy. You talk to two friends who share your view. You conclude this class is easy. The problem is, many people find public speaking time-consuming and difficult. Also, it is possible that various public speaking teachers differ in their expectations for students as well as in their grading standards.

False cause. A **false cause** is also known as *post hoc ergo propter hoc* ("after this, therefore, because of this"). The speaker using this fallacy points out that because one event happened before another event, the first event caused the second event. For example, a speaker might say that the reason students are doing better on standardized tests is because teachers are helping them cheat. The school district is facing a budget crisis because teachers are greedy. Or the reason college students leave town on the weekend is because there aren't enough restaurants.

Superstitions are popular examples of false cause. You have bad luck because you broke a mirror. You get in a wreck because your friend said, "Make sure you don't get in a wreck" before you left. A theatre production is not successful because its actors were wished good luck instead of being told "Break a leg." It is important to recognize that an event is seldom the result of a single cause (such as those provided in the above examples).

False analogy. A **false analogy** compares two things that are not really comparable. You may have heard someone say, "You're comparing apples and oranges," or worse, "You're comparing apples to footballs." In the first case, you may be making a faulty comparison because apples and oranges, while both fruits, are different. In the second case, the listener believes you are comparing two things with nothing in common.

For example, you may argue that online dating is like learning to ride a bicycle. If you fall off (or have a bad dating experience), you get up and try again (date some more). However, when you get on a bicycle, you know whether it is a 10-speed or a one-speed, whether it is built for racing or for rough terrain. Your risk is getting physically hurt. In an online dating situation, you may be deceived by that person, you may be hurt psychologically, and if a face-to-face meeting goes badly, the physical risks are different. Overall, the bicycle–online dating analogy is not appropriate.

Some arguments clearly involve the use of a false analogy, but other arguments may rest on the perspectives or values of the listeners. For example, in the argument about abortion, pro-life individuals generally argue that an adult human being and a fetus are similar, and as such, we cannot violate their human rights. Those who do not see an adult human being and a fetus as being similar do not share that perspective. In this case, the strength or weakness of the analogy is based on values held by the individuals involved in the discussion.

Slippery slope. A speaker using this fallacy claims that if we take even one step onto the **slippery slope**, we will end up sliding all the way to the bottom; that we can't stop. In other words, there will be a chain reaction that will end in some dire consequence.

For example, a booster club ran a concession stand near the gymnasium and the auditorium at the local high school. At a meeting, the president tried to convince the group to maintain control of the room by allowing certain booster club members to have keys to the room, even though many school functions took place in the auditorium, and other groups could raise money through the concession stand.

She suggested that if they give keys to the choir director for the musical, then they'll probably have to give a key to the band director, the speech teacher, and to any groups that meet or perform in the auditorium. She argued that their inventory would be stolen, they'd lose money, their equipment would get vandalized, and the popcorn machine might start a fire that could burn down the whole school. In other words, giving a key to the musical director may lead to the school burning down! Speakers use the slippery slope argument to play on audience's fears, even though the arguments frequently lack specific evidence.

☞   Focusing Persuasive Messages: Goals, Aims, and Claims

Since Aristotle, some researchers have emphasized the outcomes or the results of persuasion. Researcher Herbert Simons (2001) explains: "Persuasion is a form of attempted influence in the sense that it seeks to alter the way others think, feel or act, but it differs from other forms of influence" (p. 7). We are not talking about coercion, bribes, or pressure to conform. Persuasion is accomplished through ethical communication. Careful consideration of the goals of persuasion, the aims of your speech, and the type of proposition you are making helps focus your persuasive message.

Goals of Persuasion

Critical to the success of any persuasive effort is a clear sense of what you are trying to accomplish. As a speaker, you must define for yourself your overall persuasive goal and the narrower persuasive aim. The two overall goals of persuasion are *to address attitudes* and *to move an audience to action.*

Speeches that focus on attitudes. In this type of speech, your goal is to convince an audience to share your views on a topic (e.g., "The tuition at this college is too high" or "Too few Americans bother to vote"). The way you approach your goal depends on the nature of your audience.

When dealing with a negative audience, you face the challenge of trying to change your listeners' opinions. The more change you hope to achieve, the harder your persuasive task. In other words, asking listeners to agree that U.S. automakers need the support of U.S. consumers to survive in the world market is easier than asking the same audience to agree that every American who buys a foreign car should be penalized through a special tax.

By contrast, when you address an audience that shares your point of view, your job is to reinforce existing attitudes (e.g., "U.S. automakers deserve our support"). When your audience has not yet formed an opinion, your message must be geared to presenting persuasive evidence. You may want to explain to your audience, for example, the economic necessity of buying U.S. products.

Speeches that require action. Here your goal is to bring about actual change. You ask your listeners to make a purchase, sign a petition, attend a rally, write to Congress, attend a lecture, and so on. The effectiveness of your message is defined by the actions your audience takes.

Motivating your listeners to act is perhaps the hardest goal you face as a speaker, since it requires attention to the connection between attitudes and behavior. Studies have shown that what people feel is not necessarily what they do. Ahmad may be favorably inclined to purchase a BMW, but still not buy it. Jill may have a negative attitude toward birth control pills, but still use them.

According to Simons (2001), "some people are highly influenced by what other people they value would have them do; others are more self-reliant" (p. 34). Even if you convince your audience that you are the best candidate for student body president, they may not bother to vote. Similarly, even if you persuade them of the dangers of smoking, confirmed smokers will probably continue to smoke. Researchers have found several explanations for this seeming inconsistency.

First, attitude is likely to predict behavior when the attitude involves a specific intention to change behavior, when specific attitudes and behaviors are involved, and when the listener's attitude is influenced by firsthand experience (Zimbardo, 1988, pp. 618–619). Firsthand experience is a powerful motivator. If you know a sun worshipper dying from melanoma, you are more likely to heed the speaker's advice to wear sun block than if you have no such acquaintance. An experiment by Regan and Fazio (1977) proves the point:

A field study on the Cornell University campus was conducted after a housing shortage had forced some of the incoming freshmen to sleep on cots in the dorm lounges. All freshmen were asked about their attitudes toward the housing crisis and were then given an opportunity to take some related actions (such as signing a petition or joining a committee of dorm residents). While all of the respondents expressed the same attitude about the crisis, those who had had more direct experience with it (were actually sleeping in a lounge) showed a greater consistency between their expressed attitudes and their subsequent behavioral attempts to alleviate the problem (pp. 28–45).

Therefore, if you were a leader on this campus trying to persuade freshmen to sign a petition or join a protest march, you would have had greater persuasive success with listeners who had been forced to sleep in the dorm lounges. Once you establish your overall persuasive goals you must then decide on your persuasive aim.

Persuasive Aims

Determining your persuasive goal is a critical first step. Next, you must define the narrower persuasive aim or the type and direction of the change you seek. Four persuasive aims define the nature of your overall persuasive goal.

Adoption. When you want your audience to start doing something, your persuasive aim is to urge the audience to adopt a particular idea or plan. As a spokesperson for the American Cancer Society, you may deliver the following message: "I urge every woman over the age of 40 to get a regular mammogram."

Continuance. Sometimes your listeners are already doing the thing you want them to do. In this case, your goal is to reinforce this action. For example, the same spokesperson might say:

> I am delighted to be speaking to this organization because of the commitment of every member to stop smoking. I urge all of you to maintain your commitment to be smoke free for the rest of your life.

Speeches that urge continuance are necessary when the group is under pressure to change. In this case, the spokesperson realized that many reformed smokers constantly fight the urge to begin smoking again.

Discontinuance. You attempt to persuade your listeners to stop doing something you disagree with.

> I can tell by looking around that many people in this room spend hours sitting in the sun. I want to share with you a grim fact. The evidence is unmistakable that there is a direct connection between exposure to the sun and the deadliest of all skin cancers—malignant melanoma.

Deterrence. In this case, your goal is avoidance. You want to convince your listeners not to start something, as in the following example:

> We have found that exposure to asbestos can cause cancer 20 or 30 years later. If you have flaking asbestos insulation in your home, don't remove it yourself. Call in experts who have the knowledge and equipment to remove the insulation, protecting themselves as well as you and your family. Be sure you are not going to deal with an unscrupulous contractor who will probably send in unqualified and unprotected workers likely to do a shoddy job.

Speeches that focus on deterrence respond to problems that can be avoided. These messages are delivered when a persuasive speaker determines something is highly threatening or likely to result in disaster. The speaker may try to bring about some sort of effective block or barrier to minimize, if not eliminate, the threat or danger. New homeowners, for example, may find themselves listening to persuasive presentations about the purchase of a home security system. The thrust of such a persuasive speech is the need to prevent burglary through use of an effective and economical security system.

☞ Types of Persuasive Claims

Within the context of these persuasive goals and aims, you must decide the type of persuasive message you want to deliver. Are you dealing with an issue of fact, value, or policy? To decide, look at your thesis statement. In persuasive speeches, the thesis statement is phrased as a proposition that must be proved.

For example, if your thesis statement was "All college students should be required to take a one-credit physical education course each year," you would be working with a proposition of policy. If instead, your thesis statement was "Taking a physical education course each year will improve the college experience," this would be a proposition of value.

Propositions are necessary because persuasion always involves more than one point of view. If yours were the only way of thinking, persuasion would be unnecessary. Because your audience is faced with differing opinions, your goal is to present your opinion in the most effective way. The three major types of propositions are those of *fact*, *value*, and *policy*.

Proposition of fact. A proposition of fact suggests the existence of something. You try to prove or disprove some statement. Because facts, like beauty, are often in the eye of the beholder, you may have to persuade your listeners that your interpretation of a situation, event, or concept is accurate. Like a lawyer in a courtroom, you have to convince people to accept your version of the truth. Here are four examples of facts that would require proof:

1. Water fluoridation can lead to health problems.
2. College is not the place for all students.
3. Hunting is a way to control the deer population.
4. American corporations are not paying enough in income taxes.

When dealing with propositions of fact, you must convince your audience that your evaluation is based on widely accepted standards. For example, if you are trying to prove that water fluoridation leads to health problems, you might point to a research article that cites the Environmental Protection Agency (EPA) warning that long-term exposure to excessive fluoridation can lead to joint stiffness, pain, and weak bones. You may also support your proposition by citing another research study that reports that children who are exposed to too much fluoridation may end up having teeth that are pitted and/or permanently stained.

Informative speakers become persuasive speakers when they cross the line from presenting facts to presenting facts within the context of a point of view. The informative speaker lets listeners decide on a position based on their own analysis of the facts. By contrast, the persuasive speaker draws the conclusion for them.

Proposition of value. Values are deep-seated ideals that determine what we consider good or bad, moral or immoral, satisfying or unsatisfying, proper or improper, wise or foolish, valuable or invaluable, and so on. Persuasive speeches that deal with propositions of value are assertions rooted in judgments based on these ideals. The speaker's goal is to prove the worth of an evaluative statement, as in the following examples:

1. It is *wrong* to criminalize recreational or medicinal use of marijuana.
2. Violence in professional sports is *unjustified*.
3. Plagiarizing to complete an assignment is *dishonest*.

When you use words that can be considered judgments or evaluations, such as those italicized above, you are making a proposition of value. When designing a persuasive speech based on a proposition of value, it is important to present facts, statistics, or examples to support your points. Also, using expert opinion and testimony will provide credible support.

Proposition of policy. Propositions of policy propose a course of action. Usually, the speaker is arguing that something should or should not be done. Propositions of policy are easily recognizable by their use of "should," "ought to," "have to," or "must":

1. Campus safety should be reevaluated by the college administration.
2. The same general student academic standards ought to apply to student-athletes, too.
3. Collegiate athletes should be paid.
4. Animals must not be used for product testing in scientific laboratories.

In a policy speech, speakers convince listeners of both the need for change and what that change should be. They also give people reasons to continue listening and, in the end, to agree with their position and, sometimes, to take action.

Propositions of policy have both fact and value aspects to them. Facts need to support the need for the course of action, and values are inherently part of the policy statement. For example, in a speech about using animals for product testing, the person giving the speech against it most likely values animals, and believes in the humane and ethical treatment of animals.

A speaker's persuasive appeal, in summary, derives from the audience's sense of the speaker's credibility as well as from appeals to an audience's emotion and logic. At times, one persuasive element may be more important to one audience than others. Many speakers try to convince audiences based on logical appeals, emotional appeals, myth appeals, and their image and credibility as a speaker. The most effective speakers consider their audience expectations and intended outcomes. Now we turn our attention to common techniques used to organize persuasive messages.

☞ Organizing Persuasive Speeches

Earlier in this text, we presented different ways to organize your speech. Certain organizational patterns are unique to the persuasive speech pattern. In the chapter on organizing and outlining, we presented the **problem–solution pattern**, which involves presenting an audience with a problem and then examining one or more likely solutions. For a persuasive speech, the speaker persuades the audience to accept one particular solution. We also noted the **cause-and-effect pattern**, which entails arranging main points into causes and effects. The persuasive speaker constructs a case for the audience that persuades them to accept the cause–effect connection.

In the following we present three more possible organizational patterns: comparative advantage, criteria satisfaction, and Monroe's Motivated Sequence. Our primary focus is on the latter, since this pattern follows the normal process of human reasoning as it presents a clear way to move through the problem-solving process.

Comparative Advantages

A **comparative-advantages organizational pattern** is useful when the audience already agrees there is a problem that needs a solution. The problem may not be grave, but it is one that may have several potentially acceptable solutions. As a speaker using this pattern, try to convince the audience that your plan is the best. You place alternative solutions or plans side-by-side and discuss the advantages and disadvantages of each. To some extent, this organizational pattern can be viewed as a structured process of elimination.

For example, Lauren, a high school senior, is trying to decide which college to attend. She has prior approval from her parents to look at both in-state and out-of-state schools. Lauren, a minority student who wants to pursue international study and work possibilities, decides that she wants to attend an out-of-state school, and chooses the comparative-advantages approach when persuading her parents to accept her choice.

College 1: Instate U
Advantages: Less expensive, close to home, friends are also attending, small to medium-sized college
Disadvantages: Too close to home (might go home too often), school's reputation is OK, but not great, might not make new friends, lack of diversity
College 2: Outstate U
Advantages: Within four hours of home, diverse population, large university that offers wide range of diverse majors (can major in Folklore), large study abroad program; ability to live in international dorm, many cultural and entertainment possibilities; good scholarship possibilities
Disadvantages: Significantly more expensive, campus is large, possible safety concern

Since Lauren's parents were prepared to pay out-of-state tuition, Lauren can construct a persuasive argument making the comparison between these schools. Although this example is an interpersonal one (persuading her parents, not a large audience), if we switched the scenario to Lauren being a college student at Outstate U speaking to a group of students at her high school, the same pattern could be applied.

Using a comparative-advantages pattern, you can compare two possibilities, or you can compare several possibilities. For example, if you were talking about how to solve the energy crisis, you could compare solar, wind, and nuclear power to convince your audience that one method is superior to the others.

Criteria-Satisfaction

When using the **criteria-satisfaction pattern**, you demonstrate how your idea has the features your audience needs. It is a clear pattern that is useful when you have an audience opposed to your idea. You can help establish a "yes" response from your audience through identification of criteria they find acceptable. You indicate the necessary criteria and show how your solution meets or exceeds the criteria.

Consider a "calendar committee" trying to convince the local school board to change the dates for beginning and ending the school year. The committee might argue that any solution should meet the following criteria:

1. acceptable to teachers
2. acceptable to parents
3. cost effective (not have to turn on air conditioning too soon)
4. enhances education or at least does not interfere with learning environment
5. includes appropriate start and ending dates for each term
6. balances mandatory and optional vacation and teacher institute dates

Based on these criteria, the committee could present the solution to the school board that meets all these criteria. With the criteria-solution pattern, it is important that you find criteria your audience will accept. For example, if the committee identified one of the criteria as "starts as late as possible and ends as early as possible," that might not have been viewed as an acceptable criterion by the school board. Similarly, criteria may differ, depending on circumstances. In a small college town, having spring break and holiday breaks at the same time the college has them may be an appropriate criterion, but in a large city that has several colleges and universities, this may not be as important.

Monroe's Motivated Sequence

As emphasized throughout this text, effective communication requires connecting with your audience. Audience awareness is particularly important in speeches to persuade, for without taking into account the mental stages your audience passes through, your persuasion may not succeed. The *motivated sequence*, a widely used method for organizing persuasive speeches developed by Monroe (1965), is rooted in traditional rhetoric and shaped by modern psychology.

Monroe's motivated sequence focuses on five steps to motivate your audience that follows the normal pattern of human thought from attention to action. If you want only to persuade the audience there is a problem, then only the first two steps are necessary. If the audience is keenly aware of a problem, then a speaker may focus only on the last three steps. Most of the time, however, all five steps are necessary, and they should be followed in order.

Step 1: Attention Persuasion is impossible without attention. Your first step is to capture the minds of your listeners and convince them that you have something important to say. Many possibilities were discussed in the chapter on introductions and conclusions. For example, addressing the United Nations regarding prospects for peace in the Middle East, Israeli Prime Minister Benyamin Netanyahu (2009) began his speech by saying:

…Netanyahu (2009) began his speech by saying that he was speaking on behalf of the Jewish state. He lashed out against the President of Iran, whom he said was insisting that the Holocaust was a lie.

The prime minister's keen use of irony and strong language surely engaged all listening. His opening also establishes his credibility and introduces his topic. In your attention step, you must catch your audience's attention, introduce and make your topic relevant, and establish your credibility.

Step 2: Need In the need step, you describe the problem you will address in your speech. You hint at or suggest a need in your introduction, then state it in a way that accurately reflects your specific purpose. You motivate listeners to care about the problem by making clear a problem exists, it is significant, and it affects them. You illustrate need by using examples, intensifying it through the use of carefully selected additional supporting material, and *linking* it directly to the audience. Too often the inexperienced speaker who uses the motivated sequence will pass through the need step in haste to get to the third step, the satisfaction step.

The need step has four parts: (1) it establishes there is a problem, (2) explains the problem, (3) proves that the problem is serious, and (4) connects the problem to specific needs the audience holds dear.

Step 3: Satisfaction The satisfaction step presents a solution to the problem you have just described. You offer a proposition you want your audience to adopt and act on. A clear explanation as well as statistics, testimony, examples, and other types of support ensure that your audience understands what you propose. Show your audience how your proposal meets the needs you presented earlier in your speech. You may use several forms of support accompanied by visuals or audiovisual aids.

An audience is usually impressed if you can show where and how a similar proposal has worked elsewhere. Before you move to the fourth step, meet objections that you predict some listeners may hold. We are all familiar with the persuader who attempts to sell us a product or service and wants us to believe it is well worth the price and within our budget. In fact, a considerable amount of sales appeal today aims at selling us a payment we can afford as a means to purchasing the product, whether it is an automobile, a vacation, or some other attractive item. If we can afford the monthly payment, a major objection has been met.

In sum, a strong satisfaction step involves clearly stating an acceptable solution, offering strong evidence supporting the solution, demonstrating how the solution solves the problem, proving that it is a workable solution, and clarifying how the solution will satisfy the audience's unresolved needs.

Step 4: Visualization The visualization step compels listeners to picture themselves either benefiting or suffering from adopting or rejecting your proposal. It focuses on powerful imagery to create a vision of the future if your proposal is adopted or, just as important, if it is rejected. It may also contrast these two visions, strengthening the attractiveness of your proposal by showing what will happen if no action is taken.

Positive visualization is specific and concrete. Your goal is to help listeners see themselves under the conditions you describe. You want them to experience enjoyment and satisfaction. In contrast, negative visualization focuses on what will happen without your plan. Here you describe the discomfort with conditions that would exist. Whichever method you choose, make your listeners feel part of the future.

The visualization step can be enhanced with powerful visuals. Movie clips, sound tracks, interviews, and memorable photos have all been used successfully to help listeners fully engage their imagination in the future scenario.

Step 5: Action The action step acts as the conclusion of your speech. Here you tell your listeners what you want them to do or, if action is unnecessary, the point of view you want them to share. You may have to explain the specific actions you want and the timing for these actions. This step is most effective when immediate action is sought.

Many students find the call to action a difficult part of the persuasive speech. They are reluctant to make an explicit request for action. Can you imagine a politician failing to ask people for their vote? Such a candidate would surely lose an election. When sales representatives have difficulty in closing a deal because they are unable to ask consumers to buy their products, they do not last long in sales. Persuasion is more likely to result when direction is clear and action is the goal.

In review, remember the five-step sequence if you want to lead your audience from attention to action. The motivated sequence is effective but like all tools of persuasion, can be misused. The line between use and abuse of persuasive tools warrants further examination.

Ethics and Persuasive Speaking

The importance of ethics is stressed both implicitly and explicitly throughout this textbook. Ethics provide standards of conduct that guide us. The ethics of persuasion call for honesty, care, thoroughness, openness, and a concern for the audience without manipulative intent. The end does *not* justify the means at all costs. In a world as complex as ours, one marked in part by unethical as well as ethical persuaders, the moral imperative is to speak ethically.

> Ethical communication is fundamental to responsible thinking, decision making, and the development of relationships and communities within and across contexts, cultures, channels, and media. Moreover, ethical communication enhances human worth and dignity by fostering truthfulness, fairness, responsibility, personal integrity, and respect for self and others (Pearson et al., 2006, p. 521).

The choice between right and wrong is not simple. Informing people on a particular topic assumes providing knowledge to an audience that, in turn, learns more about the topic. In a persuasive speech, however, you are asking listeners to think or act in ways called for to achieve your specific purpose.

As members of an audience, many of the choices we make are inconsequential, such as which soft drink to buy at a convenience store or which magazine to read in a doctor's waiting room. Far more important however, is the decision to reject our religious, social, or political beliefs in order to embrace new ones. Even the purchase of an expensive automobile is a considerable decision for us when weighed against the selection of a soft drink.

As a speaker, you must decide not only what to tell your audience but what you should avoid saying. Be mindful of your audience's needs and values, and weigh benefits of successful persuasion against possible risks or harms. If a doctor, for example, prescribes a medication for a patient that results in the patient having to fight addiction to the medication, was that an appropriate act on the part of the doctor? Unless the patient was terminally ill, it was probably unethical.

As you prepare for any persuasive speech, respect your audience. Be informed, truthful, and clear about your motives, use various appeals ethically, avoid misleading your audience through faulty argument, and work to create your most effective, honest persuasive message.

Summary

In a persuasive speaking situation, the audience may be supportive, opposed, or uncommitted. The effective speaker develops strategies related to the type of audience as well as the needs of the audience. Understanding Maslow's hierarchy of human needs is helpful to persuasive speakers. The five levels of Maslow's hierarchy form a pyramid; from bottom to top, these needs are physiological, safety, belongingness and love, esteem, and self-actualization. If you approach your listeners at an appropriate level of need, you will find them more able or willing to respond.

Your credibility as a speaker is determined by the way the audience perceives you. Credibility is measured in terms of trustworthiness, competence, and dynamism. A persuasive speaker constructs arguments that have emotional, logical, ethical, or mythic appeal. Emotional appeals (pathos) can be powerful because they provide the motivation for action and attitude change. As a persuasive speaker, you should be conscious of ethical standards (ethos), and what the implications are of the choice you are asking your audience to make. The audience needs to be treated to the truth, without manipulative intent. The newest form of appeal, mythos, recognizes the persuasive power of stories, folklore, and myths.

When making logical arguments (logos), one can take an inductive or deductive approach. Inductive reasoning enables you to generalize from specific instances and draw a conclusion from your observations. Deductive reasoning draws a conclusion based on the connections between statements. Depending on your purpose for persuasion, you may choose to reason from examples, analogies, causal relations, or with enthymemes. Choose the right amount of support, the most persuasive kind of evidence, and then reason carefully.

Arguments that have faulty reasoning are considered fallacies. Fallacies can distract and mislead listeners as well as pose ethical problems. Fallacies discussed in this chapter are attack on the person, hasty generalization, false cause, slippery slope, and red herring.

The two overall persuasive goals are to address audience attitudes and to move an audience to action. Four specific persuasive aims define the focus of your speech. These aims include adoption, continuance, discontinuance, and deterrence. Your point of view, or thesis statement, is expressed in the form of a proposition that must be proved. Propositions take three basic forms: fact, value, and policy.

Three organizational patterns were discussed: comparative-advantages, criteria-satisfaction, and Monroe's motivated sequence. Monroe's motivated sequence includes five steps designed to motivate the audience to action: attention, need, satisfaction, visualization, and action. The motivated sequence is a widely used method for organizing persuasive speeches that follows the normal pattern of human thought from attention to action.

References

300. American Rhetoric Movie Speeches. Retrieved July 8, 2011 from www.americanrhetoric.com/MovieSpeeches/moviespeech300queengorgo.html.

Emperor Akihito. (2011, March 16). *Speech to the Nation on Disaster Relief and Hope*. Retrieved July 8, 2011 from www.americanrhetoric.com/speeches/emperorakitodisasterspeech.htm.

Freeley, A. J. (1993). *Argumentation and Debate: Critical Thinking for Reasonable Decision-Making*, 8th Ed. Belmont, CA: Wadsworth Publishing.

Hample, D., Sells, A., & Valazquez, A. L. I. (2009). The Effects of Topic Type and Personalization of Conflict on Assessments of Fallacies. *Communication Reports*, *22*(2), 74–88.

Hirsen, J. (2011, April 13). Tina Fey Voices Palin Parody Pangs; 'Idol' Voting Needs Reboot. Retrieved July 8, 2011 from www.newsmax.com/Hirsen/Tina-Fay-Palin-Parody/2011/04/13/id/392760.

Kennedy, G. A. (2007). Aristotle's 'On Rhetoric': A Theory of Civic Discourse, 2nd Ed. (G. A. Kennedy, Trans.). New York: Oxford University Press. (Original work published 350 BCE.)

Maslow, A. H. (1943). A Theory of Human Motivation, *Psychological Review*, *50*(4), 370–396.

Monroe, A. H. (1965). *The Psychology of Speech* (Seminar). Purdue University.

Netanyahu, Benjamin. (2009, September 24). *Speech Delivered Before the United Nations*. Retrieved July 8, 2011 from www.washingtontimes.com/news/2009/sep/transcript-Israeli-Prime-Minister-Benjamin-Netanya.

Osborn, M. (1990). In Defense of Broad Mythic Criticism—A Reply to Rowland. *Communication Studies*, *41*, 121–127.

Pearson, J. C., Child, J. T., Mattern, J. L., & Kahl, D. H., Jr. (2006). What Are Students Being Taught About Ethics in Public Speaking Textbooks? *Communication Quarterly*, *54*(4), 507–521.

Pornpitakpan, C. (2004). The Persuasiveness of Source Credibility: A Critical Review of Five Decades' Evidence. *Journal of Applied Social Psychology*, *34*(2), 243–281.

Regan, D. T., & Fazio, R. (1977). On the Consistency Between Attitudes and Behavior: Look to the Method of Attitude Formation. *Journal of Experimental Social Psychology*, *13*, 28–45 (Cited in Zimbardo, p. 618.)

Simons, H. (2001). *Persuasion in Society*. Thousand Oaks, CA: Sage Publications.

Sprague, J., & Stuart, D. (1988). *Speaker's Handbook*, 2nd Ed. San Diego: Harcourt Brace Jovanovich.

Spurling, C. (1992). Batter up-Batter down. *Winning orations of the interstate oratorical association*. Mankato State University: The Interstate Oratorical Association.

Toulmin, S. (1958). *The Uses of Argument*. Cambridge, UK: Cambridge University Press.

Vancil, D. L. (1993). *Rhetoric and Argumentation*. Boston: Allyn and Bacon.

Wicker, A. W. (1969). Attitudes versus Actions. The Relationship of Verbal and Overt Behavioral Responses to Attitude Objects. *Journal of Social Sciences*, *25*(4), 41–78.

Walker, F. R. (2005). The Rhetoric of Mock Trial Debate: Using Logos, Pathos and Ethos in Undergraduate Competition. *College Student Journal*, *39*(2), 277–286.

Zimbardo, P. G. (1988). *Psychology and Life*, 12th Ed. Glenview, IL: Scott, Foresman and Company.

Chapter 12

Special-Occasion Speaking

At a backyard barbeque toast: "If I could just say a few words ... I'd be a better speaker."

Homer Simpson (Matt Groening)

SPEECH: Mary Fisher—1992 RNC Address—Whisper of AIDS

Mary Fisher delivered this speech at the Republican National Convention in Houston, Texas on 19 August 1992. Ms. Fisher had worked in President Ford's Administration. As a person living with AIDS, she called on her party for empathy and awareness of a disease that was seen as a death sentence and a taboo subject. Ms. Fisher is a global AIDS activist.

Source: Shaw, Dan (22 August 2012) Defined by Words, Not by a Disease. New York Times

Mary Fisher

1992 Republican National Convention Address

delivered 19 August 1992, Houston, TX

[AUTHENTICITY CERTIFIED: Text version below transcribed directly from audio.]

Less than three months ago at platform hearings in Salt Lake City, I asked the Republican Party to lift the shroud of silence which has been draped over the issue of HIV and AIDS. I have come tonight to bring our silence to an end. I bear a message of challenge, not self-congratulation. I want your attention, not your applause.

I would never have asked to be HIV positive, but I believe that in all things there is a purpose; and I stand before you and before the nation gladly. The reality of AIDS is brutally clear. Two hundred thousand Americans are dead or dying. A million more are infected. Worldwide, forty million, sixty million, or a hundred million infections will be counted in the coming few years. But despite science and research, White House meetings, and congressional hearings, despite good intentions and bold initiatives, campaign slogans, and hopeful promises, it is—despite it all—the epidemic which is winning tonight.

In the context of an election year, I ask you, here in this great hall, or listening in the quiet of your home, to recognize that AIDS virus is not a political creature. It does not care whether you are Democrat or Republican; it does not ask whether you are black or white, male or female, gay or straight, young or old.

Tonight, I represent an AIDS community whose members have been reluctantly drafted from every segment of American society. Though I am white and a mother, I am one with a black infant struggling with tubes in a Philadelphia hospital. Though I am female and contracted this disease in marriage and enjoy the warm support of my family, I am one with the lonely gay man sheltering a flickering candle from the cold wind of his family's rejection.

This is not a distant threat. It is a present danger. The rate of infection is increasing fastest among women and children. Largely unknown a decade ago, AIDS is the third leading killer of young adult Americans today. But it won't be third for long, because unlike other diseases, this one travels. Adolescents don't give each other cancer or heart disease because they believe they are in love, but HIV is different; and we have helped it along. We have killed each other with our ignorance, our prejudice, and our silence.

We may take refuge in our stereotypes, but we cannot hide there long, because HIV asks only one thing of those it attacks. Are you human? And this is the right question. Are you human? Because people with HIV have not entered some alien state of being. They are human. They have not earned cruelty, and they do not deserve meanness. They don't benefit from being isolated or treated as outcasts. Each of them is exactly what God made: a person; not evil, deserving of our judgment; not victims, longing for our pity—people, ready for support and worthy of compassion.

My call to you, my Party, is to take a public stand, no less compassionate than that of the President and Mrs. Bush. They have embraced me and my family in memorable ways. In the place of judgment, they have shown affection. In difficult moments, they have raised our spirits. In the darkest hours, I have seen them reaching not only to me, but also to my parents, armed with that stunning grief and special grace that comes only to parents who have themselves leaned too long over the bedside of a dying child.

With the President's leadership, much good has been done. Much of the good has gone unheralded, and as the President has insisted, much remains to be done. But we do the President's cause no good if we praise the American family but ignore a virus that destroys it.

We must be consistent if we are to be believed. We cannot love justice and ignore prejudice, love our children and fear to teach them. Whatever our role as parent or policymaker, we must act as eloquently as we speak—else we have no integrity. My call to the nation is a plea for awareness. If you believe you are safe, you are in danger. Because I was not hemophiliac, I was not at risk. Because I was not gay, I was not at risk. Because I did not inject drugs, I was not at risk.

My father has devoted much of his lifetime guarding against another holocaust. He is part of the generation who heard Pastor Nemoellor come out of the Nazi death camps to say,

They came after the Jews, and I was not a Jew, so, I did not protest. They came after the trade unionists, and I was not a trade unionist, so, I did not protest. Then they came after the Roman Catholics, and I was not a Roman Catholic, so, I did not protest. Then they came after me, and there was no one left to protest.

The—The lesson history teaches is this: If you believe you are safe, you are at risk. If you do not see this killer stalking your children, look again. There is no family or community, no race or religion, no place left in America that is safe. Until we genuinely embrace this message, we are a nation at risk.

Tonight, HIV marches resolutely toward AIDS in more than a million American homes, littering its pathway with the bodies of the young—young men, young women, young parents, and young children. One of the families is mine. If it is true that HIV inevitably turns to AIDS, then my children will inevitably turn to orphans. My family has been a rock of support.

My 84-year-old father, who has pursued the healing of the nations, will not accept the premise that he cannot heal his daughter. My mother refuses to be broken. She still calls at midnight to tell wonderful jokes that make me laugh. Sisters and friends, and my brother Phillip, whose birthday is today, all have helped carry me over the hardest places. I am blessed, richly and deeply blessed, to have such a family.

But not all of you—But not all of you have been so blessed. You are HIV positive, but dare not say it. You have lost loved ones, but you dare not whisper the word AIDS. You weep silently. You grieve alone. I have a message for you. It is not you who should feel shame. It is we—we who tolerate ignorance and practice prejudice, we who have taught you to fear. We must lift our shroud of silence, making it safe for you to reach out for compassion. It is our task to seek safety for our children, not in quiet denial, but in effective action.

Someday our children will be grown. My son Max, now four, will take the measure of his mother. My son Zachary, now two, will sort through his memories. I may not be here to hear their judgments, but I know already what I hope they are. I want my children to know that their mother was not a victim. She was a messenger. I do not want them to think, as I once did, that courage is the absence of fear. I want them to know that courage is the strength to act wisely when most we are afraid. I want them to have the courage to step forward when called by their nation or their Party and give leadership, no matter what the personal cost.

I ask no more of you than I ask of myself or of my children. To the millions of you who are grieving, who are frightened, who have suffered the ravages of AIDS firsthand: Have courage, and you will find support. To the millions who are strong, I issue the plea: Set aside prejudice and politics to make room for compassion and sound policy.

To my children, I make this pledge: I will not give in, Zachary, because I draw my courage from you. Your silly giggle gives me hope; your gentle prayers give me strength; and you, my child, give me the reason to say to America, "You are at risk." And I will not rest, Max, until I have done all I can to make your world safe. I will seek a place where intimacy is not the prelude to suffering. I will not hurry to leave you, my children, but when I go, I pray that you will not suffer shame on my account.

To all within the sound of my voice, I appeal: Learn with me the lessons of history and of grace, so my children will not be afraid to say the word "AIDS" when I am gone. Then, their children and yours may not need to whisper it at all.

God bless the children, and God bless us all.

Good night.

☞ Special-Occasion Speeches

As with other forms of public speaking, a speech delivered on a special occasion can rise to the level of the extraordinary. Certainly as a college student, few ceremonies are likely to be more important than your commencement ceremony. In the following excerpt from his 2010 commencement address at Syracuse University, CEO of JPMorgan Chase Jamie Dimon acknowledged the mixed feelings individuals have about Wall Street executives by setting up the speech in the following manner:

> Graduating today means you are through with final exams, through with submitting term papers, all that nervousness, the cold sweat of sleepless nights preparing to answer seemingly impossible questions. Well, that's a feeling we banking executives know pretty well these days—we call it "testifying before Congress."
>
> I am honored to be here today, but I also know that some of your fellow students have raised questions about me being your commencement speaker … Today I will talk about what it takes to be accountable, in the hope that it might be valuable to you in years to come.

Like all good ceremonial speeches, Dimon expressed sincere feelings about the event and his audience. As his method for setting the tone, he chose humor—but only briefly. He quickly moved on to address the banking controversy head-on, and his interest in accountability is relevant to an audience of college graduates.

To parents and students alike, commencement is, indeed, a special occasion. Other special occasions, to name a few, include marriages, anniversaries, deaths, retirements, award ceremonies, special events, and important dates in history. Some speeches may include a little humor or even a great deal of humor; others do not. An overriding principle to remember is that, no matter how short or long, a special-occasion speech has a specific purpose; it should be designed to achieve some objective.

Seven General Guidelines for Special-Occasion Speeches

Most likely, you will be called on to give a special-occasion speech at least once in your lifetime. Many occur within the high school environment. Perhaps you were chosen to speak at your high school graduation ceremony. Maybe you were asked to respond briefly after receiving an award such as "Athlete of the Year." Or maybe, as president of a high school organization, you introduced a featured speaker or an award winner.

Special-occasion speeches, while aptly named, are given every day. To prepare you to provide an impromptu toast or say a few words of praise or thanks, this chapter provides some general suggestions for the special-occasion presentation, and then offers guidelines for several of the most common speaking situations.

Whether you are introducing a guest speaker at your church, presenting an award honoring the volunteer of the year, or toasting the marriage of your sister, the following seven guidelines will help you decide what to say and how best to say it. Although differences exist among the types of special-occasion speeches, as addressed later in this chapter, these guidelines apply in most cases.

1. Make Sure Your Speech Meets Expectations

Ceremonies and the speeches that mark them are surrounded by sets of expectations. Mourners listening to a eulogy, graduates listening to a commencement address, and members of a wedding party toasting the new couple expect certain words, gestures, and acts. Do not disappoint them. The words you choose to mark the occasion should remind people of the event they are commemorating. Even if you are sure everyone realizes the reason for your speech, explain it anyway. Following are a few brief examples of special-occasion speeches and some corresponding expectations:

* **Presenting an award.** Audiences expect the speaker to mention the background and purpose of the award and reasons the recipient was chosen.
* **A speech of acceptance.** Audiences expect the speaker to acknowledge the people who deliberated on the award, and to say thank you to individuals who bestowed the award and people who helped the recipient reach this level.
* **A eulogy.** Audiences expect to hear some background information on the deceased, a few stories about the person's life, and acknowledgment of the mourners' grief.
* **Toast.** Audiences expect the speech to be brief, to identify the purpose of the toast, and to provide some memorable comment that reflects well on the occasion or individuals involved.

2. Tailor Your Remarks to the Audience/Occasion

Saying what people expect is not the same as delivering a generic speech that could be given before any audience on a similar occasion. It is not enough to change a few facts here and there and give the same speech of introduction no matter who the audience is. For example, introducing a candidate at a fundraiser comprised of close friends and colleagues is different than introducing that same candidate before a group of citizens gathered for a candidates' forum. In the first situation, the audience knows the candidate and supports his or her positions on issues. In the second situation, the audience may not know the candidate, and may be unclear as to his or her stance on various positions.

3. Use Personal Anecdotes and Appropriate Humor

The more you say about the people gathered and the occasion, the more intimate and fitting your speech becomes. Personal anecdotes—especially sentimental or humorous ones—create the feeling that the speech was written for that event and no other.

Actress Lisa Kudrow gave the 2010 commencement address at Vassar College, her alma mater. She begins the speech by saying:

> Thank you, President Hill, for inviting me to speak, and thank you to the Class of 2010 for not protesting ... seriously. I was wondering what I should say to you—there are so many possibilities, you know? So I asked some of you—and by "some" I mean two—who I happened to see in passing (It was convenient for me). Well I couldn't ask every one of you. It's not like there's some kind of social network wherein I could communicate with such a large number of people at once ...

After including some humor in her introductory remarks, Kudrow connects with the audience further by describing her graduation from Vassar in 1985. She provides a personal anecdote, with humor, that describes the quick transformation from biology major to actress.

Not every occasion is one in which humor is anticipated or expected, but as Lisa Kudrow illustrates, it can draw the audience in, and personal anecdotes keep listeners interested.

4. Avoid Clichés

Although speeches for special occasions should follow a predictable form, they should not be trite. To avoid delivering yet another tired introductory, presentation, acceptance, or commemorative speech, dodge the clichés that seem to be part of every speaker's vocabulary. The fact that clichés are overused makes them fairly meaningless, and certainly shows a lack of creativity. These include:

"And now ladies and gentlemen …"

Use this line only if you are introducing Conan O'Brien or David Letterman. Simply avoid saying "ladies and gentlemen." Try saying something like, "And now I am honored to introduce … ," or make reference to the occasion. Other meaningless, annoying, and overworked phrases to avoid include:

"Without further ado …"

How many times have you heard this expression in ordinary conversation? We do not use the word "ado," so try "Finally" or "And now."

"I don't know what to say."

An alternative might be to express a statement of feeling, such as "I'm stunned!" or "How *wonderful* this is."

"My friends, we are truly honored tonight."

Is the audience filled with personal friends? Instead, it makes more sense to say, "I'm very honored tonight …"

"Ladies and gentlemen, here is a speaker who needs no introduction."

Then why bother speaking? Just eliminate the phrase. Everyone needs an introduction. Find something else to say about the speaker, occasion, or award. Try "Our speaker is well known for …"

5. Be Aware That You Are Speaking for Others as Well

Whether you are presenting a gold watch to commemorate a vice-president's 25th year of employment or toasting the conference championship of your college football team, you are speaking as a representative of the group. Although your words are your own, your purpose is to echo the sentiments of those who have asked you to speak. In this capacity, you are the group spokesperson. It is acceptable to make "we" statements when you are referencing events and experiences shared by the audience and honoree. Remember, for the most part, it is not about you.

6. Be Sincere but Humble

You cannot fake sincerity. If you have been asked to give an award or to introduce a person you have never met, do not pretend an intimate relationship. You can make reference to the person's accomplishments that are well known, or you can ask others about the person you will introduce and use that information. Instead of saying "I've seen what Jim can do when he puts his mind to it," tell your listeners "I've spoken to the people who know Jim best—his supervisors and coworkers. They told me how, single-handedly, he helped two dozen of his coworkers escape a fire-filled office and how he refused medical attention until he was certain everyone was safe. I'm proud to honor Jim as our Employee of the Year." Generally speaking, using real information from people the speaker knows creates greater impact.

Being humble is also important. Even when you are accepting an award or being honored as Person of the Year, resist the temptation to tell everyone how great you are. It is in poor taste. Be appropriately humble, remembering that your audience is aware of your accomplishments. When Philip Seymour Hoffman won Best Actor in a Leading Role for his portrayal of Truman Capote in *Capote* at the March 2005 Academy Awards, he started his acceptance speech with these words:

> Wow, I'm in a category with some great, great, great actors. Fantastic actors, and I'm overwhelmed. I'm really overwhelmed. I'd like to thank Bill Vince and Caroline Baron. And Danny Rosett. The film wouldn't have happened without them. I'd like to thank Sarah Fargo, I'd like to thank Sara Murphy. I'd like to thank Emily Ziff, my friends, my friends, my friends. I'd like to thank Bennett Miller and Danny Futterman, who I love, I love, I love, I love. You know, the Van Morrison song, I love, I love, I love, and he keeps repeating it like that. And I'd like to thank Tom Bernard and Michael Barker. Thank you so much. And my mom's name is Marilyn O'Connor, and she's here tonight. And I'd like if you see her tonight to congratulate her, because she brought up four kids alone, and she deserves a congratulations for that.

It was not necessary to attend the ceremony to experience Seymour Hoffman's enthusiasm and gratitude. It may not be the most eloquent acceptance speech, but he avoids bragging, and even requests that his mother be congratulated.

7. Be Accurate

Avoid embarrassing yourself with factual mistakes. If you are introducing a guest speaker, find out everything you need to know before the presentation by talking with the person or reading his or her résumé. If you are giving a commencement address, learn the names of the people who must be acknowledged at the start of your talk as well as the correct pronunciation of the names. If you are toasting an employee for years of dedicated service, make sure you get the number of years right! You do not want to give people higher or lower rank (captain/lieutenant, CEO/CFO), or state incorrect marital status (Ms./Mrs./Miss), or give incorrect information about children, current and past employment, or education.

The guidelines we provided above fit almost any special-occasion speech. As we have mentioned throughout the book, the speech should be audience centered. While all special-occasion speeches should follow general guidelines, we now turn to some of the specific types of special-occasion speeches to see how these general guidelines apply and how other, more specific rules define these speech forms. Several types of special-occasion speeches are not covered here. At the end of the chapter we identify other special-occasion speeches and provide brief outlines to help you plan for most occasions you may encounter.

Speeches of Introduction

The purpose of a speech of introduction is to introduce the person who will give an important address. Keynote speakers are introduced, as are commencement speakers and speakers delivering inaugural remarks. When you deliver this type of speech, think of yourself as the conduit through which the audience learns something about the speaker. This speech is important because it has the potential to enhance the introduced speaker's credibility.

A **speech of introduction** can be viewed as a creative minispeech. Even the speech of introduction has an introduction, body, and conclusion. It is your job to heighten anticipation and prepare your audience for a positive experience. You can accomplish these goals by describing the speaker's accomplishments appropriately. Tell your listeners about the speaker's background and why he or she was invited to address the gathering. This can be accomplished briefly but effectively, as is demonstrated in the following speech of introduction found at Buzzle.com:

> Eight years in office, businessman, environmental activist, Nobel Prize winner, recipient of a Grammy and an Emmy, and runner up for *Time*'s Person of the Year; a pretty mean task for one person to achieve. But our chief guest for today is no ordinary person. A politician and a keen environmentalist, what most people do not know about him is that he has politics in his genes; his father was also the senator of Tennessee for 18 years. He studied at Harvard, graduating in 1969. He volunteered to go to Vietnam as reporter for the Army, after deciding not to find a way to dodge the draft, and forcing someone with lesser privileges to go to war.
>
> After the war, he attended Vanderbilt University but won a seat in Congress before he got a degree. This started his political life, which we are all familiar with. Without delay, here he is, former vice president of the United States, Mr. Al Gore.

Specific Guidelines for Speeches of Introduction

The following four guidelines will help you prepare appropriate introductory remarks:

Set the Tone and Be Brief but Personal

The tone for the speech of introduction should match the tone of the speech to follow. If a comedian is going to do his/her act following the speech of introduction, then a humorous tone is warranted. If the main speaker will discuss something serious, then the speech of introduction should set that tone.

If you are going to err in an introductory speech, err on the side of brevity and personalization. In other words, an introductory speech should be relatively short, set the appropriate tone, and be specifically designed for the individual being introduced.

Recently, we heard a speech introducing a member of congress at a U.S. Naval retirement ceremony. The speaker went into great detail introducing the man, detailing his education, military service, activities in community service organizations, campaigns for Congress, and so on. This introductory speech was too long, it was not personal, and the speaker failed to set the appropriate tone for the featured speaker. As a result of this information overload, members of the audience shifted restlessly, coughed, yawned, and may have even dozed off. The main speaker began his speech at a big disadvantage.

As part of your preparation, it is helpful to talk with the featured speaker. Doing so may give you important information for the speech as well as some indication of the person's expectations for the introduction. Oftentimes, professional or experienced speakers will have prepared a short introduction for you to weave into your remarks.

Create Realistic Expectations

By telling the audience, "This is the funniest speech you'll ever hear" or "This woman is known as a brilliant communicator," you are making it difficult for the speaker to succeed. Few speakers can match these expectations. Instead, the audience may "appreciate the wisdom" of someone's remarks, or "be inspired" or "be entertained fully" by the speaker. Identify what you hope the audience will experience without creating a bar too high for anyone to clear.

When you read the "A" and then the "B" statements that follow; reflect on how the audience might feel if the speaker did not achieve what is indicated in the "A" statement.

At a gathering of salespeople who are about to listen to a motivational speaker:

A: "Starting tonight, he will change how you think forever."
B: "He will challenge you to think in ways you haven't considered before."

In an auditorium where individuals are gathered who are experiencing significant credit card and loan debt:

A: "Her understanding of personal finance is truly amazing. She will solve all your financial problems."
B: "Her background and experience give her insight into many aspects of personal finance. She will give you the tools to begin your climb to financial success."

Avoid Summarizing the Speaker's Intended Remarks

Your job is to provide an enticement to listen, not a summary of the remarks to follow. You might tell an audience of college students that you brought a well-known financial advisor to your college to help you make wise financial decisions. Avoid saying, "This speaker will tell you to reduce your spending, save a little money each month, distinguish between wants and needs, and pay your credit card balance on time." This is clearly interfering with the speaker's plan.

Teasing a message means providing your audience with a hint of what is to come by mentioning something specific they will want to learn from the speaker. If you have any questions about how much to include in the introduction, share your proposed comments with the main speaker before your presentation.

Recognize the Potential for Spontaneity

Spontaneous introductions are sometimes appropriate. An unexpected guest whom you want to acknowledge may be in the audience. Something may have happened to the speaker, to the audience, or in the world just before the introductory speech, making the planned introduction less effective. For example, when actor Dustin Hoffman was taking his curtain calls after completing a performance of a Shakespeare play on Broadway, he noticed that Arthur Miller, well-known playwright, was seated in the audience. Hoffman raised his hands, asked for quiet, and said:

> When we were doing the play in London, we had the pleasure of playing one night to an audience that included Dame Peggy Ashcroft, who was introduced from the stage. We do not have knights in America, but there is someone special in the audience tonight. He is one of the greatest voices and influences in the American theater—Mr. Arthur Miller (Heller Anderson, 1990).

Hoffman's impromptu introduction demonstrated that brevity and grace are the hallmarks of an effective introduction.

☞ Speeches of Presentation

The presentation speech is delivered as part of a ceremony to recognize an individual or group chosen for special honors. Our personal and professional lives are marked, in part, by attendance and participation in award ceremonies to recognize personal achievement. Some occasions for presentation speeches include commencements (high school, college, and graduate school), where special presentations are made to students with exceptional academic and community service records, and corporate awards ceremonies, where employees are honored for their years of service or exemplary performance. Televised ceremonies involve award presentations such as the Academy Awards, the Emmy Awards, and Country Music Awards. Other ceremonies recognize achievement in a sport, such as the Heisman Memorial Trophy, presented each year to the nation's most outstanding college football player. Each of these ceremonies includes one or more presentation speeches.

Specific Guidelines for Speeches of Presentation

Every **speech of presentation** should accomplish several goals. Using an example of a speech marking the presentation of the "Reporter of the Year" award for a student newspaper we will illustrate our four guidelines for speeches of presentation.

State the Importance of the Award

Many departmental scholarships and awards are available in college to qualified students. A scholarship may be significant because the selection criteria include finding the individual with the most outstanding academic achievement. Other scholarships may have been established to help single mothers, residents of the town, or students who engage in significant community service. Some awards are established in the names of people living and deceased or companies and organizations.

The award may be worth $100 or it may be $5,000. Regardless of the monetary value, the audience wishes to understand why the award is important. You may need to describe the achievements of the individual or individuals for whom the award has been established.

Here is the beginning of a speech of presentation, as Tom speaks about his fellow reporter, Kathryn Remm.

> I am pleased to have been asked by our editorial staff to present the Reporter of the Year award—the college's highest journalistic honor. This award was established six years ago by a group of alumni who place great value on maintaining our newspaper's high standard of journalism.

In this example, Tom clearly states the importance of the award when he mentions that it is the college's highest journalistic honor. Further, he clarifies how the award came to be by mentioning who began the award and why.

Explain the Selection Process

The selection process may involve peers, students, teachers, or a standard committee. The audience needs to know that the award was not given arbitrarily or based on random criteria. Explaining the criteria and selection process helps establish the significance of the award. If the award is competitive, you might mention the nature of the competition, but do not overemphasize the struggle for victory at the expense of the other candidates.

The following passage illustrates how this guideline can be followed effectively. Tom continues:

> The award selection process is long and arduous. It starts when the paper's editorial staff calls for nominations and then reviews and evaluates dozens of writing samples. The staff sends its recommendations to a selection committee made up of two alumni sponsors and two local journalists. It is this group of four who determines the winner.

Note the Honoree's Qualifications

Many organizations honor their members and employees for specific accomplishments. For example, the Midas Auto Service "South Central Regional Dealer of the Year" award honors an employee for excellence in regional retail sales, overall retail image, and customer satisfaction. The Edward Jones Investing firm chooses employees for the "Partner's Award" based on sales and service efforts over the past year. The nature of the award suggests what to say about the honoree. The following example shows why the reporter is being recognized.

> This year's honoree is Kathryn Remm, the community affairs reporter for the paper. Almost single-handedly, Kathryn reached out to noncollege community residents and established channels of communication that have never been open. In a series of articles, she told students about the need for literacy volunteers at the community library and for Big Brothers/Big Sisters at our local youth club.

Be Brief

Like speeches of introduction, the key to a successful presentation speech is brevity. Choose your words with care so that the power of your message is not diminished by unnecessary detail. Within this limited context, try to humanize the award recipient through a personal—perhaps humorous—anecdote.

As a final note about speeches of presentation, occasionally it is appropriate to ask past recipients of the award to stand up and receive applause. This decision should be based, in part, on your conviction that this acknowledgment will magnify the value of the award to the current recipient as well as to the audience.

Here is how Tom finishes his speech:

> Kathryn was a bit surprised when she learned that student volunteerism for Big Brothers/ Big Sisters rose 150 percent after her outreach and articles. This makes her the biggest sister in our community. Please help me acknowledge Kathryn Remm as our reporter of the year.

☞   Speeches of Acceptance

The main purpose of an **acceptance speech** is to express gratitude for an award. It is personal, gracious, and sincere. Most speakers begin with something like "I am genuinely grateful for this award, and I want to express my sincere thanks to everyone here."

Most acceptance speeches are brief. In many instances, such as an awards night in high school and departmental recognition in college, several individuals are honored for their achievements. If acceptance speeches are long, the event will seem interminable. However, in some cases, such as the Nobel Peace Prize ceremony, recipients are asked to do more than express gratitude. These speeches fit within the category of "keynote speeches," which are discussed later in this chapter. Following are four guidelines for the successful speech of acceptance.

Specific Guidelines for Speeches of Acceptance

Restate Importance of the Award

Restating the importance of the award shows the audience as well as those involved in the award that the recipient values and acknowledges the importance of the award. For example, scholarships are generally established by an individual, an organization, or a group of individuals who have contributed financially. Representatives of the scholarship, along with the scholarship committee, appreciate hearing that the scholarship is viewed as important. Along with this, communicate to your audience what receiving the award means to you.

Be Sincere

An acceptance speech is built around the theme of "thank you." You thank the person, group, or organization bestowing the award. You recognize the people who helped you gain it. Your acceptance should be sincere and heartfelt. The audience wants to feel that the individuals bestowing the award have made the right choice.

So if you know you will be asked to give a brief acceptance speech, think about who deserves recognition. It is not necessary to give a long list of all the individuals who have influenced you in your lifetime, but you want to acknowledge those who have had an impact on you in some way that relates to your accomplishing this goal. A well-developed and appropriately-delivered acceptance speech allows the listeners to be part of the moment and share the recipient's joy or amazement.

Describe How You Reached This Point of Achievement

As you thank people, you can mention in a humble tone how you reached this point of recognition. If you are a gymnast, you can talk about your training and gymnastic meets. If you are a pianist, you can talk about practice and recitals. The audience wants to know that you worked for this award, that you deserve it, but that you are gracious and humble, too.

Use Anecdotes

As you express gratitude and explain how you have reached this point of achievement, select with care the events you want to mention in order to avoid an endless chronology of your life. Stories about your life, or personal anecdotes, give people a lasting impression of your achievements. Instead of simply telling your listeners "I am grateful to everyone who supported me in this project," provide your audience with a personal anecdote. For example, when Joanne received an award for being the Most Valuable Player on her soccer team, she provided this story as part of her acceptance speech:

> Three events contributed to my success on the soccer field. The first occurred on Christmas four years ago when I found a soccer ball under the tree and a completed registration form to a soccer camp held in my hometown.
>
> The second event was our final game during my senior year in high school when we won the city championship, and I was fortunate enough to score the winning goal. I cannot tell you the great sense of satisfaction and relief I felt when that kick took the ball past the goaltender and into the net.
>
> The third event was the call I received from our coach inviting me to be part of this great college team with its winning tradition and offering me an athletic scholarship. I hope I can live up to your expectations, coach.

Anecdotes engage the audience and help them understand more clearly why this person was a good choice for the award. Be careful not to be arrogant with the anecdotes you select, or you may leave the audience with regrets. If Joanne had, instead, talked about how she "single-handedly" pulled the team up from a losing record," or how her "teammates stood in awe" as she kicked the winning goal, the acceptance speech would be less effective.

Watch Colin Firth's 2011 Oscar acceptance speech for Best Actor. Do you think his speech is effective? Certainly, the bulk of the speech corresponds to the basic "thank you" theme. Does he meet all four guidelines? If yes, how? If no, does he compensate for any omissions in other ways?

> I have a feeling my career has just peaked. My deepest thanks to the Academy. I'm afraid I have to warn you that I'm experiencing stirrings. Somewhere in the upper abdominals which are threatening to form themselves into dance moves (www.nowpublic.com).

☛   Commemorative Speeches

When we commemorate an event, we mark it through observation and ceremony. Public or private, these ceremonies are often punctuated by speeches appropriate for the occasion. Commencement speeches at college graduation, eulogies at the funeral of a loved one, speeches to celebrate the spirit of a special event or a national holiday like the Fourth of July, toasts at a wedding or the birth of a baby or a business deal, inaugural speeches, and farewell addresses all fit into this category.

Although **commemorative speeches** may inform, their specific purpose is not informational. Although they may persuade, their primary purpose is not persuasive. They are inspirational messages designed to stir emotions. These speeches make listeners reflect on the message through the use of rich language that lifts them to a higher emotional plain. More than in any other special-occasion speech, your choice of words in the commemorative address will determine your success.

Many commemorative speeches express the speaker's most profound thoughts. As you talk about what it means to graduate from college, be inaugurated to office, or lose a family member, your goal is to leave a lasting impression on your audience. Although many commemorative speeches are short, they often contain memorable quotations that add strength and validity to the speaker's own emotion-filled message.

Commemorative speeches can vary significantly, but what they have in common is that they are inspirational. The next section covers three common forms of commemorative speeches: toasts, commencement speeches, and eulogies.

Toasts

Some credit the custom of toasting to the Norsemen, Vikings, and Greeks who lifted their glasses in honor of the gods. But the newer "toast" derives from the 17th-century British custom of placing toasted bits of bread in glasses to improve the taste of the drink. As the concept of the **toast** evolved, so did the customs surrounding it. In England, those proposing the toast knelt on "bended" knee. In France, elaborate bows were required. In Scotland, the toast maker stood with one foot on a chair, the other on a table. Today, Western tradition dictates the clinking of glasses while making strong eye contact (Bayless, 1988).

You are more likely to be asked to deliver a toast than any other form of commemorative speech. Toasts are given at engagements, weddings, graduations, quinceañeras, confirmations, births, the sealing of business deals, at dinner parties, and so on. They are brief messages of good will and congratulations.

Humor is a part of many occasions where toasts occur. However, it is imperative that boundaries on humor be observed. Tasteful humor is preferable to humor that can end up truly embarrassing or hurting individuals involved in the toast. We turn to the Irish for several examples of brief toasts; some which include humor.

> May those that love us, love us; and those that don't love us, may God turn their hearts; if he can't turn their hearts, then may he turn their ankles, so we'll know them by their limp.
> May the saddest day of your future be no worse than the happiest day of your past.
> May the roof above us never fall in, and may the friends gathered below it never fall out.
> May God be with you and bless you. May you see your children's children. May you be poor in misfortune, rich in blessings. May you know nothing but happiness from this day forward. (www.lollysmith.com)

Following are three guidelines to help you deliver a memorable toast:

1. **Prepare a short, inspirational message and memorize it.** If you are the best man at your brother's wedding, the mother of the new college graduate at his graduation dinner, a close associate of an executive just promoted to company president, you may be asked in advance to prepare a toast to celebrate the occasion. Even though most toasts are generally no more than a few sentences long, do not assume that you will be able to think of something appropriate to say when the glasses are raised. To avoid drawing a blank, write—and memorize—the toast in advance.

2. **Choose words with care that address the audience and occasion.** There is a time to be frivolous and a time to be serious. The audience and the occasion indicate whether it is appropriate to be humorous or serious, inspirational or practical. Here is an example of an appropriate toast to a new law partner:

   > Ken has been a portrait of strength for all of us. When four partners were sick with the flu at the same time last year, Ken worked tirelessly, seven days a week, to meet our deadlines. Here's to Ken—the best lawyer in town and the newest partner of our law firm.

3. **Be positive and avoid clichés.** A toast is upbeat. Look to the future with hope. It is inappropriate to toast a college graduate saying, "If John does as poorly at work as he did at college, we may all be asked to help pay his rent," or at a wedding to say, "After all those other women you brought home, your bride looks pretty good." Such comments will bring a big laugh, but will also wound, and therefore should not be used.

Remember that public speaking is a creative activity. Clichés such as "Down the hatch," "Here's mud in your eye," and "Cheers" waste an ideal creative moment. Instead, you can say something simple like, as is noted in the previous example, "Here's to Ken—the best lawyer in town and the newest partner of our law firm." If the tone is lighter, you might opt for something more creative.

Commencement Speeches

Most of us believe we will not be asked to give a commencement speech. However, colleges and universities have students and guests give commencement speeches every year. Either they are voted on by the student body or they are asked to speak because they were elected to a position, such as student senate president. A speaker may be a distinguished alumnus or may have achieved celebrity status.

No other speech offers greater potential to achieve the aims of a ceremonial speech than the commencement address delivered by an honored guest. Following are several guidelines for developing a commencement speech.

Author John Grisham began his May 9, 2010 commencement speech at the University of North Carolina, Chapel Hill with a brief *expression of honor*, giving thanks for the invitation to speak. Later in his speech, he makes tribute to the college as a place of excellence, saying how proud he is to be a Tar Heel.

Later in his speech, he makes *tribute to the college as a place of excellence.*

Traditional commencement speeches *offer counsel to the graduating members of the audience.*

All commencement speakers *should impart some memorable message.* Grisham moves on to the main point of his speech, which is the importance of finding and using one's "voice."

He concludes on a *congratulatory* note by telling the audience that their future has arrived and they should remember what they want to be right now, wishing them good luck.

Although Grisham's speech lasted only 17 minutes, the strength of its message endures, and it is a model commencement speech.

Eulogies

Eulogies are perhaps the most difficult commemorative speeches to make, since they involve paying tribute to a family member, friend, colleague, or community member who died. It is a difficult time for the speaker as well as the audience. A eulogy focuses on *universal themes* such as the preciousness and fragility of life, the importance of family and friends at times of great loss, and the continuity of life, while avoiding impersonal clichés. Here are five guidelines to help you develop and present a eulogy:

Acknowledge the loss and refer to the occasion Your first words should focus on the family and/or significant others of the deceased. Talk directly to them, taking care to acknowledge by name the spouse, children, parents, and special friends of the deceased. It is safe to assume that all members of the audience feel loss. People come together to mourn because they want to be part of a community; they want to share their grief with others. By using "we" statements of some kind, you acknowledge the community of mourners. For example, you might say, "We all know how much Andrew loved his family" or "I am sure we all agree that Andrew's determination and spirit left their mark."

Celebrate life rather than focusing on loss Some deaths are anticipated, such as dying from ailments related to old age or after a lengthy illness. Others are shocking and tragic, and those left behind may have unresolved issues. Although it is appropriate to acknowledge shared feelings of sadness and even anger, the eulogy should focus on the unique gifts and lasting legacy the person brought to their world.

Use quotes, anecdotes, and even humor Nothing is better than a good story to celebrate the spirit of the deceased. A well-chosen anecdote can comfort as it helps people focus on the memory of the person's life. Fitting anecdotes need not be humorless. Rather than using ambiguous phrases such as he was "a loving husband," "a loving father," or "a wonderful person," it would mean more to provide a brief story or a humorous account of some incident in the person's life. Saying something like "Getting an ice cream cone was a reward from Dad, even in my 30s" or "He was a great teacher who liked to experiment with new ideas, such as teaching class outdoors, until the day a bird pooped on his head." Stories and humor help mourners get through the experience of attending the memorial as they recall pleasant memories and laugh along with the speakers.

Quote others. You may choose to turn to the remarks of noted public figures such as Winston Churchill, John F. Kennedy, and Mark Twain, whose words are fitting for your speech. Know that you do not need to always rely on quotations from writers, poets, famous actors, or politicians. You may choose to include the words of friends and family members of the deceased. As part of her eulogy at her mother's funeral, a daughter said the following:

> After reading the cards sent by her many friends, it made sense to include some of what others thought of her. I'd like to share a few of these: "She was so full of enthusiasm and curiosity about everything. Whatever project she took on, she did it with a flair that no one else could match." "A gentle person who really did make a difference in each life she touched." "A warm, vibrant personality and so much courage." "I doubt that anyone has left more happy memories."

The person and occasion of the individual's death should provide guidance in terms of what qualities to highlight and stories to tell. Remember also, a eulogy can include input from others, so do not hesitate to seek advice from others close to the person being eulogized.

Control your emotions Composure is crucial. If you have any questions about your ability to control your grief, suggest that someone else be chosen. As you offer comfort to others, try not to call undue attention to your own grief. While an expression of loss and its attending emotions is appropriate, uncontrolled crying will prevent you from providing the needed healing your eulogy offers. If you do not think you can make it through without falling apart, have someone else do it or bring someone up to the podium with you who can take over, if necessary.

Be sincere and be brief Speak from the heart. Avoid "Words cannot express our sorrow," "The family's loss is too much to bear," and "She's in a far better place now." Rely instead on personal memories, anecdotes, and feelings. Eulogies need not be lengthy to be effective.

The following is an excerpt from a eulogy a woman gave for her father that indicates how she felt about him.

> Throughout the years, he has been there for my failures and successes, providing me with meaningful advice. His opinion has always been very important to me. My father was a warm and loving man, a man of integrity, a great teacher. I miss him and I love him.

Depending on the wishes of the family, several individuals may be called on to eulogize the deceased. A brief, sincere speech will be greatly appreciated by those attending the memorial service.

Keynote Speeches

A **keynote speaker** is the featured speaker at an event. There may be several people who speak briefly, but the keynote speaker has the top billing of the event. Whatever the setting, whether it is a gathering of members of the American Society of Journalists and Authors or the annual convention of the American Bar Association, the keynote address is usually anticipated as a highlight that has the potential to compel the audience to thought and action. Unlike many special-occasion speeches, the keynote speech is not brief. You may be called on to give a keynote speech at some point. We offer the following guidelines.

Remember That Your Speech Sets the Tone for the Event

Think of keynote speakers as cheerleaders and their speeches as the cheers that set the tone for an event. The purpose of the gathering may be to celebrate the group's achievements, to share information with each other, or to give individuals the opportunity to interact with people who are in similar positions or situations. The keynote speaker is there to excite people, and to stimulate thought and action.

Keynote addresses at political conventions are known for their hard-hitting approach and language. When he was a candidate for the U.S. Senate in Illinois, Barack Obama delivered the keynote address at the Democratic National Convention in Boston in July 2004. Following is an excerpt from that speech:

> Tonight, we gather to affirm the greatness of our nation not because of the height of our skyscrapers, or the power of our military, or the size of our economy; our pride is based on a very simple premise, summed up in a declaration made over two hundred years ago: "We hold these truths to be self-evident, that all men are created equal … that they are endowed by their Creator with certain inalienable rights, that among these are life, liberty, and the pursuit of happiness."

Obama's speech makes patriotic references that stirred many Americans' sense of pride in their country. But he also suggested that things could be better. His words clearly set the tone for Democrats at that convention.

Select Your Topic and Language *After* Analyzing the Audience and Occasion

There is a reason you were asked to be the keynote speaker. It may be fame, fortune, or simply achievement based on hard work. You may be provided with some basic guidelines for your speech, such as "motivate them," or "talk about success." How you develop the content of your speech and the words you choose to express yourself should be made after reflecting on the audience and occasion. As one of the keynote speakers at the Microsoft India, NGO (nongovernmental organization) Connection workshop in April 2010 in Jaipur, India, Rajendra Joshi, one of the organization's trustees, started her speech by making a specific connection between technology and governance.

> The most powerful weapon on the earth is public opinion [Paul Crouser]. *Governance* encompasses not just government, but also the civil society and the corporate sector.

Joshi asserts the importance of public opinion at the very beginning. Since her speech was presented to individuals connected with Microsoft and/or nongovernmental organizations, she tied technology together with governance to highlight an important aspect of nongovernmental organizations trying to improve the world.

Time Is Still a Factor

Yes, people are gathered to hear you. You are the focus of attention. Say what you need to say, but do not waste their time. Think about what has happened in the time before your speech, and what will happen after your speech. Even if you have what seems to be an unlimited amount of time, realize that your audience may have other things to do.

Consider the audience's attention span. Have they been in the same room for the last four hours? An audience can be enthralled for some period of time, but there is a limit as to how long they can pay attention. Time is a factor. You do not want to have your audience dreaming of an escape plan.

After-Dinner Speeches

If the keynote address is the meat-and-potatoes speech of a conference, the **after-dinner speech** is the dessert. It is a speech delivered, literally, after the meal is over and after all other substantive business is complete. Its purpose is to entertain, often with humor, although it may also convey a thoughtful message. Keep in mind, a more accurate description of this speech would be "after-meal" as an after-dinner speech can occur after any meal. Following are two suggestions for after-dinner speaking.

Focus on the Specific Purpose: To Entertain

Do not make the mistake of delivering a ponderous speech filled with statistics and complex data. Talking about the national debt would probably be inappropriate, as would a speech on what to do with the tons of garbage Americans produce each day. You can discuss these topics in a humorous way, however, relating, for example, how handling the national debt has become a growth industry for economists or how families are trying to cope with community rules to separate garbage into various recycling categories.

Use the Opportunity to Inspire

As is noted in the definition of the after-dinner speech, you do not have to rely solely on humor. You can also be inspirational, filling your speech with stories from personal experiences that have changed your life. This approach is especially effective if you are well known or if the events you relate have meaning to others.

Outlines for Other Special-Occasion Speeches

Following are 14 outlines for you to consider. Each commemorates an event you will probably encounter in the future. These outlines spell out both what is expected and the traditional order we expect to hear them in.

Speech of Introduction

1. Greeting and reference to the occasion
2. Statement of the name of the person to be introduced
3. Brief description of the person's speech topic/company position/role in the organization, etc.
4. Details about the person's qualifications
5. Enthusiastic closing statement
6. Inviting a warm reception for the next speaker

Speech of Welcome

1. Expression of honor this person's visit brings to the group
2. Description of the person's background and special achievements
3. Statement of the reason for the visit
4. Greeting and welcome to the person

Speech of Dedication

1. Statement of reason for assembling
2. Brief history of efforts that have led to this event
3. Prediction for the future success of the company, organization, group, or person

Anniversary Speech

1. Statement of reason for assembling
2. Sentimental significance of the event

3. Explanation of how this sentiment can be maintained
4. Appeal for encouraging the sentiment to continue in future years

Speech of Presentation

1. Greeting and reference to the occasion
2. History and importance of the award
3. Brief description of the qualifications for the award
4. Reasons for this person receiving the award
5. Announcement of the recipient's name
6. Presentation of the award

Speech of Acceptance

1. Expression of gratitude for the award
2. Brief praise of the appropriate people
3. Statement of appreciation to those giving the award
4. Closing of pleasure and thanks

Speech of Farewell

1. Expression of sorrow about the person's departure
2. Statement of enjoyment for the association with this person
3. Brief description of how the person will be missed
4. Announcement of friendship and best wishes for the future
5. Invitation to return again soon

Speech of Tribute (if honoree is alive) or the Eulogy (if deceased)

1. Expression of respect and love for the honoree
2. Reasons for paying tribute to this person
3. Review of the person's accomplishments and contributions
4. Clarification of how this person has touched the lives of others
5. Closing appeal to emulate the good qualities of this person

Speech of Installation

1. Orientation of the audience to the occasion and the theme of this installation
2. Introduction of the current officers
3. Praise of the current officers for the work they have accomplished
4. Announcement for the new officers to come forward
5. Explanation of the responsibilities for each office
6. Recitation of the organization's installation of officers pledge
7. Declaration of the installation of the new officers

Speech of Inauguration

1. Expression of appreciation for being elected or placed in office
2. Declaration of the theme or problem focus while in office
3. Explanation of policy intentions
4. Announcement of goals to achieve while in office
5. Closing appeal for confidence in a successful future

Keynote Address

1. Orientation of the audience to the mood and theme of the convention
2. Reference to the goals of the organization and their importance
3. Brief description of the convention's major events
4. Closing invitation for active participation in the convention

Commencement Address

1. Greeting to the graduates and the audience
2. Review of the graduates' successful accomplishments
3. Praise to the graduates for reflecting respected values
4. Prediction and discussion of future challenges
5. Closing inspiration for the graduates to meet these new challenges successfully

After-Dinner Speech

1. Statement of reference to the audience and the occasion
2. Humorous transition into the central idea or thesis
3. Presentation of major points developed with humorous supporting materials
4. Closing that is witty and memorable

Humorous Speech

1. Humorous attention-getter
2. Preview of the comic theme and intent of the speech
3. Presentation of humorous points and supporting materials that are typical of the audience in terms of events, feelings, experiences, or thoughts
4. Closing that presents a strong punch line (Harrell 1997)

👉 Summary

At some point in your life, chances are you will give a special-occasion speech. You may be called on to toast a member of your family, a colleague, or a good friend. Perhaps you will introduce a guest speaker, or your alma mater may invite you to address the graduating class.

All special-occasion speeches have certain characteristics in common. When delivering a speech for a special occasion, make sure it meets audience expectations. Tailor your speech to the honoree and the occasion, use personal anecdotes and appropriate humor, and avoid clichés. Be aware that you are speaking for others as well as yourself, be sincere, be humble, and be accurate.

The purpose of a speech of introduction is to introduce the person who will deliver an important address. Your role is to heighten audience anticipation of the speaker through a brief, personal description of why he or she has been chosen to speak. Speeches of presentation are delivered as part of special recognition ceremonies. These speeches tell the audience why the award is being given and state the importance of the award. Marked by grace and sincerity, speeches of acceptance express gratitude for an award. Commemorative speeches include toasts, commencement speeches, and eulogies. Commemorative speeches are inspirational messages designed to stir emotions and cause listeners to reflect. Keynote speeches often set the tone for an event through the use of direct language. After-dinner speeches are speeches of entertainment and inspiration, generally delivered at the conclusion of substantive business. Special occasion audiences have expectations concerning the ideas a speaker should address as well as the order in which they are presented. Guidelines for 14 special-occasions speeches will help you deliver what is expected in the many occasions you may face.

☞ References

Averbuch, Yael. *Speech*. Retrieved January 20, 2010 from potomacsoccerwire.com.

Bangs, M. (2010, December 13). *Avoid Clichés Like the Plague*. Retrieved June 19, 2011 from www.huffington post.com

Bayless, J. (1988). *Are You a Master of the Toast? The Toastmaster, November*, 11.

Dimon, Jamie. (2010, May 16). *Commencement Remarks*. Retrieved December 11, 2010 from syr.edu.

Firth, Colin. (2011). *Oscar Acceptance Speech*. Retrieved September 6, 2011 from www.nowpublic.com/culture/colin-firth-oscar-acceptance-speech-2011-video-transcript-2761763.html.

Grisham, John. (2010, May 9). *Commencement Speech*. Retrieved from Forbes.com.

Harrell, A. (1997). *Speaking Beyond the Podium: A Public Speaking Handbook*, 2nd Ed. Fort Worth: Harcourt Brace College Publishing.

Heller Anderson, S. (1990). Chronicle: Interview with Professor Melvin Helitzer. *New York Times*, (January 18), B6.

Henmueller, P. (1989, June 11). Diamonds of Hope: The Value of a Person (Speech). Reprinted in *Vital Speeches of the Day, September 1, 1989*, 680–681.

Irish Weddings Toasts, Blessings, Proverbs, Traditions. Retrieved September 6, 2011 from www.lollysmith.com/irwedtoasble.html.

Joshi, R. (2010, April 15–16). *Keynote Speech*. Retrieved from saath.wordpress.com.

Kudrow, Lisa. (2010, May 23). *Commencement Address*. Retrieved from commencement.vassar.edu/2010.

Nair, T. (2011). *Introduction Speech Examples*. Retrieved September 6, 2011 from www.buzzle.com/articles/introduction-speech-examples.html.

Obama, Barack. (2004). *Keynote Speech*. Retrieved September 6, 2011 from americanrhetoric.com/speeches/convention2004/barackobama2004dnc.htm.

Praetorius, D. (2011, May 23). *The Most Viewed Commencement Speeches in the History of YouTube* (VIDEOS). Retrieved June 19, 2011 from www.huffingtonpost.com.

Swanger, J. (2010, May 8). *The Tyranny of Certainty* (Baccalaureate Address).

Wells, J. (2009). *Word Choice*. Retrieved June 19, 2011 from www.owl.english.purdue/engagement.